1983

CRITICAL ESSAYS IN MODERN LITERATURE

CRITICAL ESSAYS IN MODERN LITERATURE

*The Plays and Novels
of Peter Handke*

The Plays and Novels
of
Peter Handke

June Schlueter

UNIVERSITY OF PITTSBURGH PRESS

Published by the University of Pittsburgh Press, Pittsburgh, Pa. 15260
Feffer and Simons, Inc., London
Manufactured in the United States of America

Library of Congress Cataloging in Publication Data

Schlueter, June.
  The plays and novels of Peter Handke.

  (Critical essays in modern literature)
  Bibliography: p. 195
  Includes index.
  1. Handke, Peter—Criticism and interpretation.
I. Title.   II. Series.
PT2668.A5A877   1981   838'.91409   81-50242
ISBN 0-8229-3443-4   AACR2
ISBN 0-8229-5330-7 (pbk.)

"Augmentations" and "Singular and Plural," from *The Innerworld of the Outerworld of the Innerworld* by Peter Handke, translation copyright © 1974 by Michael Roloff, are quoted by permission of The Continuum Publishing Corporation, New York.

Das Gewicht der Welt and *Wunschloses Unglück* are quoted by permission of Residenz Verlag, Salzburg. Quotations from all other works of Peter Handke in German are by permission of Suhrkamp Verlag, Frankfurt.

Permission to quote from the English language translations of the following works is granted by Farrar, Straus and Giroux, Inc., New York: from *Kaspar and Other Plays,* trans. Michael Roloff, copyright © 1969 by Farrar, Straus and Giroux, Inc.; from *The Ride Across Lake Constance and Other Plays,* trans. Michael Roloff in collaboration with Karl Weber, copyright © 1976 by Farrar, Straus and Giroux, Inc.; from *The Goalie's Anxiety at the Penalty Kick,* trans. Michael Roloff, copyright © 1972 by Farrar, Straus and Giroux, Inc.; from *Short Letter, Long Farewell,* trans. Ralph Manheim, copyright © 1974 by Farrar, Straus and Giroux, Inc.; from *A Sorrow Beyond Dreams,* trans. Ralph Manheim, copyright © 1974 by Farrar, Straus and Giroux, Inc.; from *A Moment of True Feeling,* trans. Ralph Manheim, copyright © 1977 by Farrar, Straus and Giroux, Inc.; from *The Left-Handed Woman,* trans. Ralph Manheim, copyright © 1977, 1978, by Farrar, Straus and Giroux, Inc.

Acknowledgment is also made to Eyre Methuen, Ltd., British publishers of *Offending the Audience and Self-Accusation* (1971), *Kaspar* (1972), *The Ride Across Lake Constance* (1973), *They Are Dying Out* (1975), *The Goalie's Anxiety at the Penalty Kick* (1977), *Short Letter, Long Farewell* (1977), and *The Left-Handed Woman* (1980); and to Souvenir Press, London, for permission to quote from *A Sorrow Beyond Dreams.*

For Paul

Contents

Preface

This study is intended primarily for an American audience that might not have access to the numerous critical books and essays published on Handke's work in German. Even for those familiar with the literature in German, however, this study offers a different approach. For while it acknowledges Handke as a German — more specifically, Austrian — writer, it focuses primarily on Handke's individual achievement, which, I believe, places him less securely in a German tradition than in an international postmodern one.

In preparing this study, I found it necessary to make certain decisions regarding operating principles. Keeping in mind that the main purpose of this book is to make Handke more accessible to Americans, I included existing English translations of German (and French) texts when they were available and my own when they were not. But because this study will also appeal to readers with fluency in German, who are, rightfully, more interested in reading the original than the translation, I have included the German as well. Throughout the book, I have referred to particular works by Handke and others by their English titles, giving the original title parenthetically the first time the work is mentioned. In all cases, the date given in parentheses refers to the earliest date of publication.

Because Handke's first two novels, *The Hornets* (*Die Hornissen,* 1966) and *The Peddler* (*Das Hausierer,* 1967) are unavailable in English, I have limited my discussion of them to a brief section in the introduction. Otherwise, all Handke's plays and novels published to date are covered, with references in the final chapter to the two works forthcoming in English translation.

The bibliography of secondary criticism appearing at the end of this study is necessarily selective. Readers interested in a more extensive, annotated list of secondary criticism should consult the bibliography Ellis Finger and I are compiling, forthcoming from Garland Publishing.

In the two years spent working on this book, I accumulated numerous debts of gratitude. For the help they have given me, in various ways, I thank:

Paul Schlueter, my husband, whose tenure as my resident advisor has helped make scholarship a joy;

Lafayette College, for its generous support, in the form of grants covering summer research, research in Europe, and photocopying costs;

Peter Handke, who graciously met with me in Berlin for an interview; Siegfried Unseld of Suhrkamp Verlag, Frankfurt, and Nancy Meiselas of Farrar, Straus & Giroux, New York, who helped arrange the interview; and Dietrich Büscher, of Hamburg, who offered considerable help in transcribing and translating it;

Ronald Robbins and Richard Everett, reference librarians at Lafayette College, whose readiness to help was constant;

Ellis Finger, of Lafayette College, who patiently read over all my translations;

Gabriele Spengemann and Clifford Johnson, of Gesamthochschule Kassel, and Edward McDonald and Maresa Fanelli, of Lafayette College, who offered advice regarding particular translating problems;

Marilyn Kastenhuber, Claudette Dahlinger, Arlene Ahles, and Hilda Cooper, all of Lafayette College, for help with typing the manuscript;

and Elaine Hallett, for whom I always have one more "thank you."

Three of the chapters in this book were published separately, in slightly different form, as follows: the chapter on *The Ride Across Lake Constance* appeared as "Peter Handke's *The Ride Across Lake Constance:* The Illusion of Self-Sufficiency," in *Comparative Drama* 11 (Summer 1977), and as the final chapter of my earlier book, *Metafictional Characters in Modern Drama* (New York: Columbia University Press, 1979); the chapter on *The Goalie's Anxiety at the Penalty Kick* appeared as "Handke's 'Kafkaesque' Novel: Semiotic

Processes in *Die Angst des Tormanns beim Elfmeter*" in *Studies in Twentieth Century Literature* 4 (Fall 1979), which also published the English translation of the interview in the same issue. The chapter on *They Are Dying Out* appeared as "Politics and Poetry: Peter Handke's *They Are Dying Out*" in *Modern Drama* 23 (January 1981). My thanks to the editors of these publications for permission to reprint and to Handke's publishers for permission to quote from his works.

*The Plays and Novels
of Peter Handke*

1
Introduction

When the twenty-three-year-old Peter Handke stood before the meeting of Group 47 at Princeton University in April 1966, boldly and injudiciously attacking the literary output of that prestigious gathering of writers, he was thought by many to be little more than an attention-getter, an aspiring, unknown writer eager to capitalize on such international exposure. At the time, Handke had only recently attached himself to this group of German writers, which, led by Hans Werner Richter, had been meeting for nearly twenty years, since Richter and others first gathered in 1947 at the Bavarian home of poet Ilse Schneider-Lengyel to read and discuss their writing. Virtually every German writer of reputation had participated in the gatherings, and when the angry young Handke spoke at Princeton, it was to an audience that included Günter Grass, Peter Weiss, Uwe Johnson, Siegfried Lenz, Hans Magnus Enzensberger, Ingeborg Bachmann, Jakov Lind, and Jürgen Becker, as well as over a hundred other writers, scholars, and reporters, including Americans Eric Bentley, Leslie Fiedler, and Susan Sontag.[1]

Even to those members accustomed to the verbal abuse that had for years characterized this group's self-criticism, Handke's speech in Princeton was intemperate, for he called not merely for a reform of literature but for a total revolution. Disgusted by the dull descriptive readings to which he had been listening for three days, Handke directed his acrimony at those members still committed to Richter's original purpose, which was to stimulate a cultural renaissance of an artistically depleted, war-torn Germany through a literature of engagement.[2] As one *Newsweek* reporter covering the Princeton meeting observed, quoting an unnamed participant, Group 47 members considered "concern with form at the expense of moral content . . . almost criminal."[3] Even as late as 1966, the older members of the group—Heinrich Böll and Günter Eich, for example—as well as many of the younger members were renewing their commitments to realistic writing which analyzed the horrors of the Hitler regime and its social, political, and moral aftermath.

It did not seem to matter to Handke that the group's members included such writers as Martin Walser—whose stream-of-consciousness technique bore little resemblance to Böll's near-journalistic prose—nor that the literary experiments of Helmut Heißenbüttel, Jürgen Becker, Peter O. Chotjewitz, and others had little to do with what Germany was then proclaiming the New Realism. Nor did it seem to matter that in removing—indeed, wrenching—himself from the mainstream of German literature, he was dissociating himself from a prestigious group of writers so heterogeneous it could hardly be considered a group on the strength of any criterion—ideology, style, national origin—other than its common language. In 1966 Handke seemed to feel there was a homogeneity to German writing, or, perhaps more accurately, that postwar German writing was uniformly deficient.

Shortly after the Princeton meeting, in an essay published in Hamburg's leftist literary magazine *konkret,* Handke explained and qualified his attack, though by no means mollified it. Although reports by others attending the meeting record Handke's outburst as having denounced description,[4] Handke clearly repeated here that he is not against description—indeed, he is for it—but that he is opposed to the art of description used by the New Realists. What Handke deplored as the impotence of contemporary German writing resulted from the failure of writers to realize that literature is made not of objects but of language, and that it is in the language itself, and not in what the words describe, that the reality of literature exists:

Es wird nämlich verkannt, daß die Literatur mit der Sprache gemacht wird, und nicht mit den Dingen, die mit der Sprache beschrieben werden. In dieser neu aufkommenden Art von Literatur werden die Dinge beschrieben, ohne daß man über die Sprache nachdenkt, es sei denn, in germanistischen Kategorien der Wortwahl usw. Und die Kritik mißt die Wahrheit der Literatur nicht daran, daß die Worte stimmen, mit denen man die Gegenstände beschreibt, sondern daran, ob die Gegenstände "der Wirklichkeit entsprechen". So werden die Worte für die Gegenstände als die Gegenstände selber genommen. Man denkt über die Gegenstände nach, die man "Wirklichkeit" nennt, aber nicht über die Worte, die doch eigentlich die Wirklichkeit der Literatur sind.[5]

People fail to recognize that literature is made with language and not with the things that are described with language. In this new, up-and-coming type of literature, things are described without one's thinking about language except in grammatical categories of word choice, etc. And criticism does not measure the truth of literature on the basis of whether the words by which the objects are described are correct but on whether the objects "correspond to reality." Thus the words for the objects are taken for the objects themselves. One ponders over the objects which one calls "reality," but not the words, which are in fact the reality of literature.

Critic Walter Höllerer was intrigued by the Beatle-haired rebel's remarks, feeling they raised questions that extended beyond Germany's New Realism, and Erich Kuby, correspondent for *Der Spiegel*, though calling Handke cunning, agreed he had spoken the truth.[6]

Few who heard Handke read from his own writing, however, could accept the tediously long and meticulous passages of nearly plotless prose as an alternative to the "empty" and "idiotic" description he attacked. In fact, Jakov Lind, himself thirty-nine at the time, dismissed Handke's first novel, *The Hornets* (*Die Hornissen*, 1966), as a "pedantisch aufdringlichen Beschreibung von Details" (a "pedantic, importunate description of details") and, with *Der Spiegel* as his forum, condemned the entire generation of young, experimental writers as "dry" and "lifeless":

Diese Überempfindlichkeit ist das Kennzeichen einer ganzen Generation junger Schriftsteller. Sie fühlen zart wie die sprichwörtlichen Mimosen und schreiben so trocken und leblos wie gestriges Laub. Ihre Überempfindlichkeit führt zu einem introvertierten Herumkramen. Der Mensch? Das sind nur noch Hand, Fuß und Kopfbewegungen. Seine Erlebnisse? Die Beobachtungen eines unbeteiligten Dritten. Seine Sprache? Entweder verklammert in indirekter Rede oder formal-banal.[7]

This hypersensitivity is the mark of a whole generation of young writers. They are as tender as the proverbial mimosa and write as dryly and lifelessly as yesterday's leaves. Their hypersensitivity leads to an introverted rummaging around. The human being? He is only hand, foot, and head movements. His experiences? The observations of a disinterested third party. His language? In parentheses, in either indirect speech or formal banality.

Handke's reply not only defended his own writing as being concerned only with language, but implicitly attacked, for the second time, his more traditional colleagues:

Wenn ich schreibe, interessiere ich mich nur für die Sprache; wenn ich nicht schreibe, ist das eine andere Sache. Beim Schreiben lenkt mich die Wirklichkeit nur ab und macht alles unrein. Ich interessiere mich auch nicht, während der literarischen Arbeit, für eine Kritik an der Gesellschaft. Es geht einfach nicht darum. Es wäre mir widerlich, meine Kritik an einer Gesellschaftsordnung in eine Geschichte zu verdrehen oder in ein Gedicht zu ästhetisieren. Das finde ich die scheußlichste Verlogenheit: sein Engagement zu einem Gedicht zu verarbeiten, Literatur draus zu machen, statt es gerade heraus zu sagen.[8]

When I write, I am interested only in language; when I am not writing, it is another matter. When I write, reality only diverts me and makes everything unclean. I am also not interested, during my literary work, in a critique of society. I am simply not concerned with this. It would be repulsive to me to twist my critique of the order of society into a story or to aestheticize it into a poem. I find it hideously untruthful for one to work one's "engagement" into a poem, to make literature out of it, instead of saying things right out.

As Lind's condemnation would suggest, however, Handke's repudiation of a literature with a social or political purpose in favor of a formalistic one was not a one-man crusade, and although Handke named no exceptions to his reproach, he was certainly not alone in a German avant-garde. From war-neutral Switzerland there were Margrit Baur, Werner Schmidli, and Rolf Geissbühler; from Germany there were Helmut Heißenbüttel, Jürgen Becker, Peter O. Chotjewitz, Hermann Peter Piwitt, and Ror Wolf; and from Handke's native Austria there was the distinguished Vienna Group, as well as its successor group in Graz, of which Handke was a member. Indeed, any national literary boundaries which might have been implicit in Handke's Princeton attack became virtually indistinguishable in the decade following the meeting, as the work of the German avant-garde became not merely individual upstart rebellions but an integral part of a developing alternative strain of European literature.

If Handke's persistent concern with literary form is not uniquely Austrian, however, it may be said to be distinctly so. During Handke's years at the University of Graz, he participated in a cultural group known as Forum Stadtpark and a literary group known as the Graz Group (Grazer Gruppe). Through his associations with these groups and with Alfred Kolleritsch, editor of *manuskripte,* a magazine for literature, art, and criticism,[9] Handke was able to write and publish several short stories, as were his colleagues Gert F. Jonke, Wolfgang Bauer, Barbara Frischmuth, and Michael Scharang.[10] Though receiving no official support, the Graz writers became unofficially recognized as the successors to the more famous Vienna Group (Wiener Gruppe), which had reigned for over a decade as Austria's underground literary elite.[11]

The older group, which was especially active in the 1950s, included among its members Hans Carl Artmann, Gerhard Rühm, Friedrich Achleitner, Konrad Bayer, and Oswald Wiener. As Austrians, these writers were officially excused from the obligation of artistically expiating a national sense of guilt, and they turned instead to what they saw as the group's primary commitment: the resuscitation of a language left breathless by its blatant propagandistic misuse. Often playing with the reader's presuppositions about literature, and always looking to expand the boundaries of art, these writers created scaffoldings of words, sentences, and sounds designed to parody, banalize, and deconstruct the foundations and edifices of language. Achleitner's "the good soup" ("die gute suppe," 1958), for example, is an unrelenting accretion of detail; Artmann's *the search for yesterday, or snow on a hot loaf of bread (das suchen nach dem gestrigen tag, oder schnee auf einen heißen brotwecken,* 1964) is a multilingual montage of art, dream, and reality; Bayer's *the sixth sense (der sechste sinn,* 1966) is a composite of seemingly endless, baroque sentences; and Rühm's

DA, a letter game for children (*DA, eine buchstabengeschichte für kinder,* 1970) is an elaborate picture pun which one critic has called "a sort of morphological fiction."[12] Even Wiener, who dissociated himself from the group in deference to literature that sought social reform, pursued that reform in his most ambitious work, *The Improvement of Central Europe* (*Die Verbesserung von Mitteleuropa,* 1969), through annihilation of language norms.

Handke's early work, including the short stories he wrote during his university days—"Greeting the Board of Directors" ("Begrüßung des Aufsichtstrats"), containing one 2,000-word paragraph, and "Eyewitness Report" ("Augenzeugenbericht"), containing one 350-word sentence, for example[13]—as well as his subsequent poetry, is especially reminiscent of the work of the Vienna Group, reflecting the young writer's willingness to take the risks involved in their brand of aesthetic anarchy. A few passages from Handke's poems might suffice to suggest the nature of these early language experiments. The first, from a poem entitled "Singular and Plural" ("Die Einzahl und die Mehrzahl") written in 1968, offers syntactical variations on an expositional situation:

> Auf einer Bank im Park sitzt ein Türke mit dick verbundenem
> Finger:
> ich sitze auf einer Bank im Park neben einem Türken mit dick
> verbundenem Finger:
> wir sitzen auf einer Bank im Park, ich und ein Türke mit dick
> verbundenem Finger:
> Ein Türke mit dick verbundenem Finger sitzt mit mir auf einer
> Bank im Park.

> On a bench in the park sits a Turk with a thickly bandaged finger:
> I am sitting on a bench in the park next to a Turk with a thickly
> bandaged finger:
> We are sitting on a bench in the park, I and a Turk with a thickly
> bandaged finger:
> A Turk with a thickly bandaged finger is sitting with me on a
> bench in a park.[14]

The poem builds gradually on this situation, adding first the fact that the two are gazing out at the pond, then the fact that the

narrator sees "von den schwimmenden Enten bewegt, ein Gras-
büschel schwimmen und auf das Ufer zu schwimmen" ("a tuft of
grass, propelled by swimming ducks, making its way to the
shore"), and so on, shifting the focus from the narrator to the
Turk to the object of perception. Following its longest central
paragraph, which still consists of only one sentence describing the
entire scene, the verses shorten until they return once again to the
opening situation, this time varied six times, with slight emenda-
tions. Another poem, "Augmentations" ("Steigerungen"), written
in 1968, is an exercise in logic which, in exposing an object (in this
example, a yellow mailbox) to the rigors of verbal analysis, succeeds only in deflating its own process:

> Und ebenso
> kann die Farbe des Briefkastens am Postamt gleich
> > gelb sein
> wie die Farbe des Briefkastens an der
> > Milchsammelstelle
> die Farbe des Briefkastens an der Landstraße am
> > Sonntagnachmittag
> und die Farbe des Briefkastens im Hitchcock film:
> aber
> in neunhundertneunundneunzig von tausend Fällen
> ist der Briefkasten an der Milchsammelstelle gelber
> > als der Briefkasten am Postamt
> und der Briefkasten an der Landstraße am Sonntag-
> nachmittag gelber als der Briefkasten an der Milch-
> > sammelstelle—
> und in tausend von tausend Fällen hat der Brief-
> kasten im Hitchcockfilm das schreiendste Gelb von
> > allen.

> And similarly
> the color of the mailbox at the post office can be just as
> yellow
> as the color of the mailbox at the milk-collecting station
> the color of the mailbox on the country road on a Sunday
> afternoon
> and the color of the mailbox in a Hitchcock film:
> but

in nine hundred and ninety-nine out of a thousand cases
the mailbox at the milk-collecting station will be yellower
than the mailbox at the post office
and the mailbox on the country road on a Sunday afternoon will be yellower than the mailbox at the milk-collecting station —
and in a thousand out of a thousand cases the mailbox in
the Hitchcock film will be the most excruciating yellow
of them all.[15]

"Unused Opportunities" ("Die unbenutzten Todesursachen"),
written in 1966, lists eight "when" clauses, each followed by a
result clause, then creates one sentence which sustains itself with
"while" clauses, the last of which contains seventeen adjective-
noun combinations, before it finally presents its main clause.[16]
"Comparisons for What's Incomparable" ("Vergleiche für nichts
Vergleichbares"), written in 1968, bombards the reader with
similes, introduced by twenty-nine "likes," but never offers its
final comparison.[17] "Breaking Off in Mid-Sentence" ("Abbrechen
mittem im Satz"), written in 1968, does just that; and "The
Japanese Hit Parade of May 25, 1968" ("Die japanische Hitparade
vom 25. Mai 1968"), also written in 1968, is just that.[18]

Handke's early dramas, and particularly the *Sprechstücke*, or
speech plays, of 1966–67, may well stand among the purest
examples in Austrian literature of language exercises, as concerned with acoustics as with words, and collectively committed to
disrupting the audience's complacent somnambulism. *Offending
the Audience* (*Publikumsbeschimpfung*, 1966) culminates in a stream
of invective directed at the carefully prepared theatergoers;
Prophecy (*Weissagung*, 1966) consists of 208 meaningless tautologi-
cal statements; *Self-Accusation* (*Selbstbezichtigung*, 1966) catalogues
the sins of an abstract "I," including his violation of language
conventions, castigating the cliché en route; and *Calling for Help*
(*Hilferufe*, 1967) searches through linguistic catacombs for the
word *help*. *Kaspar* (1967), Handke's best known and first full-
length play, traces the initiation of its central character into the
phenomenal and social worlds through language; *My Foot My
Tutor* (*Das Mündel will Vormund sein*, 1969), a play of gesture and
action, is a study in nonverbal language; and *Quodlibet* (1970), his

last short play, offers half-heard sentences which the audience must reconstitute.

But behind the seeming playfulness and technical precision of the work of Handke and the Graz and Vienna Groups stands Austria's rich tradition of linguistic-centered philosophy. Though impelled by the decayed condition of language following the war and influenced by literary movements originating outside Austria, including surrealism and concrete poetry, the Vienna Group —and, in turn, the Graz Group—was even more essentially the product of a sensitivity to language derived from such Austrian philosophers as Karl Kraus, Fritz Mauthner, Ludwig Wittgenstein, and the logical positivists of the Vienna Circle. Wittgenstein in particular, frequently mentioned in connection with Handke, was a pervasively strong presence, whose philosophical inquiry impressed upon both generations of writers the extraordinary significance of language in determining thought. Best known for the *Tractatus Logico-Philosophicus* (1921) and *Philosophical Investigations (Philosophische Untersuchungen,* 1953), Wittgenstein maintained that all philosophical problems are created by linguistic confusion. In the *Tractatus,* he suggests a direct correlation between the arrangement of words into a sentence and the elements of the reality that sentence represents. Since language shares the same form as reality—indeed, *contains* those forms—the learning of language is an initiation not only into grammar, syntax, and sound but into reality itself.

The possibilities and limitations about which Wittgenstein theorized found aesthetic form in the writing of Austria's avantgarde, in which sentences are dismantled, scrutinized, and reassembled in unexpected ways. Though Handke himself admits to having learned only one thing from Wittgenstein—that the meaning of a word is its use—the relationships among language, reality, and perception which Wittgenstein pursued are fundamental to all of Handke's work.[19] A familiarity with linguistic philosophy is manifest in the drama, and portions of *Kaspar* and *The Ride Across Lake Constance (Der Ritt über den Bodensee,* 1970) may well be read as dramatizations of Wittgensteinian ideas. In the first of these, Handke demonstrates the stages of perceptual development through a model character who progresses from one sentence bearing no conventional relationship to reality to a fluency that admits that character to the social world of his prompters but also creates in him a schizophrenic consciousness of self. In the second, Handke further analyzes the fragile foundation of language, and hence of reality, suggesting, through the image of somnambulism, the paradoxical necessity of consciousness and its maddening consequence.

Finally, however, Handke is neither a philosopher nor a linguist but an artist, whose rigorous investigation into language is firmly rooted in his search for literary form. In the essay entitled "I Am an Ivory Tower Dweller" ("Ich bin ein Bewohner des Elfenbeinturms"), which is still indicative of his aesthetics, Handke speaks of his expectations of literature, both as a reader and an author, explaining that he is not interested in having reality represented and criticized but in discovering new possibilities of reality. Referring specifically to the form of literature, he notes:

Ein Darstellungsmodell, beim ersten Mal auf die Wirklichkeit angewendet, kann realistisch sein, beim zweiten Mal schon ist es eine Manier, ist irreal, auch wenn es sich wieder als realistisch bezeichnen mag.[20]

A form of representation, the first time it is applied to reality, can be realistic; the second time it is already a mannerism, is unreal, even though it may again characterize itself as realistic.

Rejecting established forms of realism, Handke willingly retreats into his "ivory tower" formalism, implicitly joining with the Russian formalist who speaks of the possibility of language systems "in which the practical aim retreats to the background (it does not necessarily disappear altogether), and language resources acquire autonomous value."[21]

Handke's drama especially echoes the formalists' (and the futurists') campaign for the autonomy of language. In *Calling for Help,* for example, the word *help* is sought until found, at which point, no longer needed, it becomes autonomous. And in *The Ride Across Lake Constance,* Handke creates a "transrational language," an orchestration of words which, though appearing syntactically to have semantic significance, bears only a deceptive relationship to conventional meaning. Viktor Sklovskij's observations on the theory of prose describe the goal of art that Handke shares with Russian formalism: "Art exists to help us recover the sensation of life; it exists to make us feel things, to make the stone *stony*. The end of art is to give a sensation of the object as seen, not as recognized. The technique of art is to make things 'unfamiliar', to make forms obscure, so as to increase the difficulty and the duration of perception. The act of perception in art is an end in itself and must be prolonged."[22]

Throughout the canon, Handke's analyses of language are aimed at rendering the familiar unfamiliar so that we are forced to see rather than merely recognize. With the possible exception of his most recent drama, *They Are Dying Out* (*Die Unvernünftigen sterben aus,* 1973) Handke's plays are practical experiments in the act of perception. *Kaspar* and *The Ride Across Lake Constance* analyze the process onstage while provoking and inciting the audience, in the first play through having it witness the constructive and destructive powers of language, and in the second through isolating nearly recognizable poses which an audience *almost* understands. In the short pieces, Handke relies on an aesthetics of reception which functions through irritation. The *Sprechstücke* collectively attempt to exorcise the audience's complacency and to direct its attention to the reification and the power of language. *My Foot My Tutor* eliminates recognizable behavioral patterns in favor of ones demanding intense scrutiny yet still refusing to yield meaning. And *Quodlibet* teases the audience into distrusting its perceptions through partially articulated lines it can only imperfectly discern.

If Handke's investigation into the forms of literary discourse finds expression in the drama, so also does it constitute the mainstay of his fiction. Of the two novels that Handke published in the 1960s, the first, *The Hornets,* is an obscure, labyrinthine, piecemeal montage, recording a blind man's imperfect attempt to narrate the experiences of his life by relating them to those of the blind hero in a partially remembered novel. The man is not certain whether he read the novel before his blindness or whether he merely heard about it, and as he remembers events, he does not know whether those events happened to him or to the protagonist of the novel. His identity as narrator merges with that of the other fictive blind man as he repeatedly tries to distinguish among history, memory, imagination, and dream. The process of ordering through relationships is, in fact, precisely what the process of creating fiction rests in, and at the end of the novel Handke alludes to the presence of yet a third "blind man" who as author or reader is himself receiving these imperfect perceptions and attempting to order them into coherent experience: "In der fremden Mundart wird sowohl für einen, der blind ist, als auch für einen, der den andern nicht sichtbar ist, dasselbe Wort verwendet"[23] ("In the foreign idiom, the same word is used for one who is blind as for one who is not visible to others").

Handke's second novel, *The Peddler* (*Der Hausierer*, 1967), modeled after the murder mystery or *Krimi* so appealing to popular audiences in Germany, employs a related technique. Each of its customary twelve chapters follows the same substantive and stylistic pattern. The first part of the novel presents a scenario of what one might expect in terms of plot development; the second presents suggested possibilities of actions to support the scenario. The style of the first part is formal, detached, and legalistic, parodying not only typical narrators of the genre but also the style Handke himself learned as a law student in Graz. The second part, consisting of simply constructed declarative sentences, reads more like a catalogue of propositions than like anything conventionally associated with narrative prose. Objecting to Handke's deviation from conventional literary discourse, one reviewer acerbically observed: "For arcane reasons Handke actually covers most of the surface of his pages with words—words which are moreover grouped in sentences and arranged, declined, conjugated and inflected according to the most rigorous conventions of syntax and grammar. The sentences themselves form a verbal mosaic, linked as they are not by logic but purely geographical proximity."[24] Yet individually each sentence of Handke's text is suggestive of the kinds of situations and sentences one would normally find in a popular detective novel. Quoting Raymond Chandler as saying that nothing looks so empty as an empty swimming pool, Handke's epigraph suggests that this established form of fiction and, by implication, all established forms, when stripped and exposed, look equally empty. As Handke explains in an essay on this novel,

Ich wollte ein darstellungsschema aus der "trivialiteratur" wieder *wirklich* machen und neue möglichkeiten auch den lesenden zeigen: neue möglichkeiten zu lesen, zu spielen, zu überlegen: zu leben.[25]

I wanted to make a presentation scheme out of trivial literature *real* again and also to show the readers new possibilities: new possibilities to read, to play, to reflect on: to live.

Handke pursued these possibilities in various ways in his next five novels, all published in the 1970s. In *The Goalie's Anxiety at the Penalty Kick (Die Angst des Tormanns beim Elfmeter,* 1970), his central character, Joseph Bloch, is himself obsessed with the process of knowing, and particularly with the semiotics of experience. By the time he wrote this novel, Handke had lived in Paris for a year (he was later to return for an additional five years), where he was undoubtedly attracted to structuralism (the French version of formalism) and, more particularly, to semiotics. Like Roland Barthes, who sought to decode numerous aspects of culture, including literature, and who was an important figure for Handke early in his career (see Interview, pp. 166, 173–74), Handke attempts to decode experience through his protagonist, who sees everything—from a dishrag to an open drawer to cookies on a wooden plate—as a sign with particular significance for himself. Though appearing to be schizophrenic, Bloch's idiosyncratic behavior is the product of a heightened consciousness which insists on testing the various sign systems of life. In similar fashion, the unnamed protagonist of Handke's next novel, *Short Letter, Long Farewell (Der kurze Brief zum langen Abschied,* 1972), sees everything as a correlative for his own past and future experience. As he travels across America, Handke's hero notes the signs of America's rural beginnings and its development into an urbanized nation, deciphering its history as an analogue for his own failed relationships.

Handke's shortest novel, *A Sorrow Beyond Dreams (Wunschloses Unglück,* 1972), is among his most probing analyses of his own art. This deceptively simple piece of prose ostensibly explores Maria

Handke's reasons for deciding to end her life, but, more importantly, it examines the theories of realism professed by Georg Lukács and Roman Jakobson as it deals with the artist's problem of rendering reality in fiction. *A Moment of True Feeling (Die Stunde der wahren Empfindung,* 1975) is also overwhelmingly concerned with preformulated concepts of both literature and experience. It may be read as a pre-novel, a prelude examining the creative process itself and exorcising certain presuppositions about that genre. Even *The Left-Handed Woman (Die linkshändige Frau,* 1976), which appears not to be overtly concerned with literary form, suggests, through its refusal to intimate motivation, Handke's continuing rejection of established narrative technique.

Handke clearly does not see traditional fiction as the appropriate response to the current generation's need for "eine bestimmte erzählende Haltung" ("a definite narrative posture") (Interview, pp. 165, 173). Just as clearly, though, he sees literary discourse as the only means through which language and reality may be reclaimed.

2
The *Sprechstücke*

Offending the Audience

When Handke's first theater piece, *Offending the Audience* (*Publikumsbeschimpfung*, 1966), was produced in Germany in the late 1960s, it faced a public ill-prepared for its blatant unconventionality yet curiously receptive to its abuse. In Germany, where the modern theater enjoys a high standing among the arts, theatergoers of the sixties recalled two decades of postwar drama which might best be described as "comfortable." Disturbing, experimental plays such as Peter Weiss's *Marat/Sade* (1964)[1] were exceptional, and not the dominant fare. In the 1965–66 season during which *Offending the Audience* appeared, Shakespeare led the list of authors of plays most frequently performed, and he was followed, respectively, by Schiller, Brecht, Moliere, and Anouilh.[2] For this nation of state-subsidized theaters, theatergoing was still very much a social event; the participation of the well-dressed audience in the intellectual and emotional life of the drama was often subordinate to participation in the ritual of theater attendance. It was this complacency which appalled the young Handke and to which he addressed the abuse of *Offending the Audience*, cleverly inverting conventional expectations and turning the audience itself into the subject of, and the performers in, his play. As Handke remarks in a note concerning his first *Sprechstück*, or speech play, the piece was written "damit das übliche Publikum ein anderes Publikum wird"[3] ("in order that the usual audience becomes a different audience"). Apparently nothing short of a total revolution in drama, in both its rendering and its reception, would suffice.

Yet as is the case with all protests, Handke's revolution could be accomplished only within the context of the existing object of protest. Aware of using the theater to attack the theater, Handke qualifies his dissatisfaction, explaining that *Offending the Audience* is "kein Stück gegen das Theater. Es ist ein Stück gegen das Theater, wie es ist"[4] ("not a piece against the theater. It is a piece against the theater as it is"). He further describes the piece as a prologue, the aim of which is not "[zu] revolutionieren, sondern auf[zu]merksam machen"[5] ("to revolutionize, but to make aware"[6]). Handke's *Sprechstücke* may in general be viewed as prologues to a drama which was to offer full expression for the writer's rejection and reformation of the contemporary stage.

Shortly after Handke delivered a copy of the manuscript of *Offending the Audience* to Alfred Holzinger late in 1965, he received it back with a notation commenting on its ingenuity and linguistic excellence, but voicing reservations about its staging, which Holzinger could not imagine.[7] Indeed, it was no ordinary theater which undertook the production but rather Frankfurt's Theater am Turm, a pioneer in avant-garde drama. Under the direction of Claus Peymann, who accepted the piece after it was rejected by sixty other theaters,[8] the play was offered in June 1966 as part of *Experimenta 1,* signaling an audience that it should not expect a conventional play. On the one hand, the circumstances of its production may have lessened the impact of *Offending the Audience,* for the piece purports to depend completely upon an audience which does have conventional expectations. On the other hand, it is perhaps only the unconventional audience that can appreciate Handke's step-by-step negation of theatrical tradition and the intellectual response he demands of his spectators.

Upon entering Handke's theater, those attending the production encounter exactly what they expect: assiduous ushers, elegant programs, muffled sounds from behind the curtain, gradually dimming lights. As expected, latecomers are not admitted, there is no standing room, and anyone improperly dressed may not enter. Few, of course, would fall into this latter category, for a view of promenading German theatergoers invariably reveals men formally attired in dark suits and ties and women carefully clad in dresses designed and dyed so as not to offend standards of good taste. The members of this unsuspecting audience as yet have no idea that their promenading, their conversations, and their preparations for the play are part of the performance, and that they, not the speakers who will appear on stage, are the subject of the piece.

Through a carefully rendered orchestration of the rhythms of language and sound, the play appeals, on one level, to the emotional reaction of the audience. The four speakers, having prepared for this event by listening to the litany of Roman Catholic churches, the cries of a crowd watching a football game, the rhythmic chanting at demonstrations, the simultaneous arrival and departure of trains, the simultaneous interpreters at the United Nations, the screaming of a bullet-wounded mute, the Beatles' movies, manipulate their "mob" through rhythm, harmony, dissonance, crescendos of sound, confusion, and the sheer excitement created by the rapid delivery of their lines.

When they first appear on stage, the speakers abuse one another simultaneously, their words unintelligible to the audience until, like an orchestra tuning up, they produce one word (or note) in unison. Like the prompters in *Kaspar*, the speakers deliver their lines in quick succession, frequently repeating, always accusing, curiously combining the hypnotic effects of rock music, propaganda, and audio-lingual pedagogy:

Sie sehen uns sprechen und Sie hören uns sprechen. Ihre Atemzüge werden einander ähnlich. Ihre Atemzüge passen sich den Atemzügen an, mit denen wir sprechen. Sie atmen, wie wir sprechen. Wir und Sie bilden allmählich eine Einheit.[9]

You see us speaking and you hear us speaking. You are beginning to breathe in one and the same rhythm. You are beinning to breathe in one and the same rhythm in which we are speaking. You are breathing the way we are speaking. We and you gradually form a unit.[10]

Such persuasion, however, is not limited to the emotional, for if Handke is to achieve his goal of awareness, he must appeal to the intellect as well. Beneath its hypnotic mesmerism, the above passage achieves the breakdown of one of the mainstays of illusionist drama: the division between actors and audience. In order for the transposition of audience and actor to occur, the playwright must first dispose of the presupposition that an audience peers across a gap of space and time, through the fourth wall of a stage set, into another reality. Handke's speakers repeatedly make clear that no such division exists in his theater. The actors are not actors but merely speakers; they assume no roles, reenact no actions, create no alternate reality. Their time is the present, the same time the audience is experiencing. Nothing on the bare stage signifies anything; the lighting is now the same both onstage and off; the speakers do not pretend the audience does not exist:

Das ist kein Spiel. Wir treten aus keinem Spiel heraus, um uns an Sie zu wenden. Wir haben keine Illusionen nötig, um Sie desillusionieren zu können. Wir zeigen Ihnen nichts. Wir spielen keine Schicksale. Wir spielen keine Träume. Das ist kein Tatsachenbericht. Das ist keine Dokumentation. Das ist kein Ausschnitt der Wirklichkeit. Wir erzählen Ihnen nichts. Wir handeln nicht. Wir spielen Ihnen keine Handlung vor. Wir stellen nichts dar. Wir machen Ihnen nichts vor. Wir sprechen nur. (Pp. 20–21)

This is no play. We don't step out of the play to address you. We have no need of illusions to disillusion you. We show you nothing. We are playing no destinies. We are playing no dreams. This is not a factual report. This is no documentary play. This is no slice of life. We don't tell you a story. We don't perform any actions. We don't simulate any actions. We don't represent anything. We don't put anything on for you. We only speak. (P. 9)

Having negated, in several dozen lines more, every expectation of drama except speech, and repeated and rephrased each negation, the speakers credit their audience with having reached the level of awareness to which it has been manipulated, and announce:

Sie haben sich bereits Ihre eigenen Gedanken gemacht. Sie haben erkannt, daß wir etwas verneinen. . . . Sie haben erkannt, daß dieses Stück eine Auseinandersetzung mit dem Theater ist. (P. 27)

You have made up your mind now. You recognized that we negate something. . . . You recognized that this piece is conducting an argument with the theater. (P. 14)

This argument with the theater, which continues through all Handke's plays, destroys in order to reconstruct. Unlike the "happening," which merges the two traditionally separate constituents of theater, Handke's play transposes stage and audience. The speakers may have no representational value, but the audience is a society, representing an order:

Sie stellen etwas dar. Sie sind jemand. Hier sind Sie etwas. Hier sind Sie nicht jemand, sondern etwas. Sie sind eine Gesellschaft, die eine Ordnung bildet. Sie sind eine Theatergesellschaft. Sie sind eine Ordnung durch die Beschaffenheit Ihrer Kleidung, durch die Haltung Ihrer Körper, durch die Richtung Ihrer Blicke. . . . Sie verkleiden sich. Indem Sie sich verkleiden, zeigen Sie, daß Sie etwas tun, was nicht alltäglich ist. Sie betreiben einen Mummenschanz, um einem Mummenschanz beizuwohnen. Sie wohnen bei. Sie schauen. Sie starren. Indem Sie schauen, erstarren Sie. Die Sitzgelegenheiten begünstigen diesen Vorgang. Sie sind etwas, das schaut. (P. 30)

You represent something. You are someone. You are something. You are not someone here but something. You are a society that represents an order. You are a theater society of sorts. You are an order because of your kind of dress, the position of your bodies, the direction of your glances. . . . You dress up. By dressing up, you demonstrate that you are doing something that you don't do every day. You are putting on a masquerade so as to partake of a masquerade. You partake. You watch. You stare. By watching, you become rigid. The seating arrangement favors this development. You are something that watches. (P. 17)

Once the role reversal has been achieved, the speakers can concentrate on their ultimate goal, which is to make the audience aware of the fact that it *is* an audience and as such has the primary obligation of consciousness. The play offends, insults, and abuses the spectators on the assumption that no new theory of drama can be assimilated by them unless they first come to life. The image of somnambulism which later appears in *The Ride Across Lake Constance* and reappears in the novels originates here, where the audience is, by degrees, awakened from its sleep:

Dadurch, daß wir zu Ihnen sprechen, können Sie sich Ihrer bewußt werden. Weil wir Sie ansprechen, gewinnen Sie an Selbstbewußtsein. Sie werden sich bewußt, daß Sie sitzen. Sie werden sich bewußt, daß Sie in einem Theater sitzen. Sie werden sich Ihrer Gliedmaßen bewußt. Sie werden sich der Lage Ihrer Gliedmaßen bewußt. Sie werden sich Ihrer Finger bewußt. Sie werden sich Ihrer Zungen bewußt. Sie werden sich Ihres Rachens bewußt. Sie werden sich der Schwere Ihres Kopfes bewußt. Sie werden sich Ihrer Geschlechtsorgane bewußt. Sie werden sich des Zuckens Ihrer Augenlider bewußt. (P. 34)

Because we speak to you, you can become conscious of yourself. Because we speak to you, your self-awareness increases. You become aware that you are sitting. You become aware that you are sitting in a theater. You become aware of the size of your limbs. You become aware of how your limbs are situated. You become aware of your fingers. You become aware of your tongue. You become aware of your throat. You become aware how heavy your head is. You become aware of your sex organs. You become aware of batting your eyelids. (P. 20)

When the speakers then direct the members of the audience to try not to blink their eyelids, or swallow, or move their tongues, or breathe, their prohibitions are greeted with the very responses they sought to forbid. The piece becomes a masterful exercise in manipulation, in submission and resistance, and, above all, in consciousness-raising.

When the speakers first appear onstage, they greet the audience and say, "Dieses Stück ist eine Vorrede" (p. 19) ("This piece is a prologue," p. 7). The statement reappears just before the stream of abuse at the end of the play, creating a frame for the argument of that portion of the piece and marking it not as the play's central concern but as a prologue:

Es ist nicht die Vorrede zu einem andern Stück, sondern die Vorrede zu dem, was Sie getan haben, was Sie tun und was Sie tun werden. Sie sind das Thema. Dieses Stück ist die Vorrede zum Thema. Es ist die Vorrede zu Ihren Sitten und Gebräuchen. Es ist die Vorrede zu Ihren Handlungen. Es ist die Vorrede zu Ihrer Tatenlosigkeit. Es ist die Vorrede zu Ihrem Liegen, zu Ihrem Sitzen, zu Ihrem Stehen, zu Ihrem Gehen. Es ist die Vorrede zu den Spielen und zum Ernst Ihres Lebens. Es ist auch die Vorrede zu Ihren künftigen Theaterbesuchen. Es ist auch die Vorrede zu allen anderen Vorreden. Dieses Stück ist Welttheater. (P. 42)

This piece is a prologue. It is not the prologue to another piece but the prologue to what you did, what you are doing, and what you will do. You are the topic. This piece is the prologue to the topic. It is the prologue to your practices and customs. It is the prologue to your actions. It is the prologue to your inactivity. It is the prologue to your lying down, to your sitting, to your standing, to your walking. It is the prologue to the plays and to the seriousness of your life. It is also the prologue to your future visits to the theater. It is also the prologue to all other prologues. This piece is world theater. (P. 28)

Following the prologue, which has prepared the audience for the abuse promised by the play's title, four or five pages of criticism and invective recall the scene that was shown when the curtain rose: the unintelligible abuse, like an orchestra tuning up, was indeed a rehearsal, a rehearsal for a play that does not begin until now. Nicholas Hern, in his fine study of Handke's drama, views this final section as a coda, maintaining that the play climaxes at the point where the speakers talk of past drama, explaining what it was and rejecting all its tenets.[11] Yet this is precisely what the speakers have been doing throughout the play, and this particular restatement seems hardly to warrant any more importance than any of the other repetitions of Handke's argument. Rather, the section that Hern sees as the climax falls within the prologue, leaving the final passages of abuse standing not only as the climax but as the play itself.

This is not to say that the prologue is an inessential part of the play, for the abuse in the final passages could only be productive if the audience is prepared. The prologue brings the audience to the point of emotional and intellectual readiness at which it can be called vile names and be jeered at as the speakers observe its reaction and applaud its performance. Following the prologue, the audience is sufficiently self-aware to be amused by the application of drama critics' clichés to their own performance: "Ihr habt unvergeßliche Szenen geliefert," "Ihr wart lebensecht," "Ihr zeugtet von hoher Spielkultur," "Ihr wart atemberaubend" (pp. 44, 45, 45, 46) ("Your scenes were unforgettable," "You were true to life," "You reached Shakespearean heights," "You did not disappoint our wildest hopes," pp. 29, 30, 30, 31). Once guided through the prologue, the audience can listen to the cry of outrage of the angry young playwright and recognize itself as the "jerks," the "rednecks," the "subhumans," the "fuck-offs," the "farts" of the theatergoing world.[12] That any audience would take such epithets personally is, of course, an egotistical impossibility, but this audience is in a curious way theatrically mature enough to recognize the validity of the outcry.

At least two members of Handke's audience, however, saw the playwright and not themselves as the subject of the piece. Joachim Neugroschel, for example, in an essay entitled "The Theater as Insult," comments unfavorably on *Offending the Audience*, calling the play "narcissistic, because rather than wanting to correct the world by inciting action on the part of others, it tries to arouse audience attention to the author. . . . This small-scale nihilism abolishes theater tradition for the sake of absolute, gratuitous rebellion."[13] Helmut Heißenbüttel, though himself prone to experiment, feels the negative approach of Handke's *Sprechstücke* accomplishes little more than to give voice to the naiveté of a young man whose rejection of traditional forms amounts only to a narcissistic insistence upon uniqueness. He reproaches Handke as a writer who is simply unwilling to be measured by standards other than his own.[14]

But Handke, in an interview with Artur Joseph, defends his approach, explaining, "Das sollte den Leuten unter die Haut gehen. Diese Verkünstlichung durch Rhythmen sollte eine Art von Transportmittel für die Wörter darstellen. Sie sollte die Wörter an den Zuschauer heranbringen"[15] ("I wanted to get under people's skins. The rhythmic artificiality was meant as a kind of vehicle to transport the words. It was to bring the words closer to the audience").[16] At least, the play succeeded in attracting attention to this unconventional playwright; at most, it began to awaken theatergoers from their sleepwalk, which is as much as Handke had hoped to achieve.

Prophecy

Prophecy (*Weissagung*, 1966), was written a year ealier than *Offending the Audience* but produced some four months later, at a time when the success of *Offending the Audience* meant that a Handke play was bound to draw a considerable crowd.[17] In October 1966, *Prophecy* and *Self-Accusation* appeared in a double bill at the Städtische Bühne in Oberhausen, under the direction of Günther Büch. Like *Offending the Audience*, both pieces left their audiences pensive, puzzled, dazzled, and sufficiently persuaded that the young playwright who toyed with their traditions was more than merely a charlatan. Apparently satisfied that his earlier piece had succeeded in embuing theatergoers—or at least those theater-goers who would see a Handke play—with a degree of self-awareness, Handke continued his argument for a nonrepresentational theater, presenting that argument in an especially specific and forceful fashion in *Prophecy*.

On its face, *Prophecy* appears to have been written for the author's own self-indulgence or, at best, for the amusement of the private reader; it surely does not appear to have been intended for the theater. Nicholas Hern expresses a typical attitude toward this piece, feeling that *Prophecy* probably would not have found public exposure had it not been for Handke's earlier theatrical success: "Indeed, it is problematical whether it was first conceived for performance at all. Unlike *Offending the Audience,* it can gain no genuine extra dimension in the theater. For although a director might trick out a production with movement, effects, and rhythmic delivery, he would be unlikely to add anything to the meaning of the piece."[18]

Prophecy consists of 208 statements, each to be recited by one or more of four speakers, and each a tautology. Like the statement which defines certified mail as mail which is certified, each of these statements likens its subject to itself: "Die Fliegen werden sterben wie die Fliegen," "Die Berserker werden kämpfen wie die Berserker," "Die Rose wird duften wie die Rose"[19] ("The flies will die like flies," "The maniac will fight like a maniac," "The rose will smell like a rose"[20]). More than circular definitions, however, these statements are aphorisms, each making a comparison. The apparently unassailable truth of these comparisons—who can deny that "Donald Duck wird gehen wie Donald Duck" (p. 55) ("Donald Duck will walk like Donald Duck," p. 6)?—accounts for their amusing effect, but the very fact that they are comparisons is what turns *Prophecy* into a piece very much for and about the theater.

In an essay written in 1968, Handke points to the nearly automatic need we have to compare:

Während ich das schreibe, sehe ich draußen auf der Straße zwei Straßenkehrer mit großen Besen den Gehsteig kehren. Beide haben einen orange-weiß gestreiften Dress *wie Radrennfahren,* beide haben weite, verknüllte Hosen *wie Landstreicher* oder *wie Figuren in einem Beckett-Stück,* beide haben Gesichter *wie Südländer,* beide tragen Mützen *wie auf Kriegsgefangenenbildern aus dem ersten Weltkrieg,* beide gehen mit steifen Knien und platten Füßen *wie Tippelbrüder,* alle drei—jetzt kommt ein dritter, ein vierter dazu—tragen schwarze Fäustlinge *wie die Schneeräumtrupps im Winter,* alle fünf gleichen mit ihren riesigen Besen und Schaufeln, die sie recht klein aussehen lassen, *Figuren auf einem Bild von Breughel.*

Aber: der eine Straßenkehrer hat *schneller* gekehrt *als* der andre, und der andre Straßenkehrer hatte die Mütze *tiefer* im Gesicht *als* der eine, und der andre andre Straßenkehrer hatte gar ein *deutscheres* Gesicht *als* der andre Straßenkehrer, und der andre andre andre Straßenkehrer schien seine Arbeit *unwilliger* zu verrichten *als* der andre andre Straßenkehrer, und schließlich—inzwischen sind die Männer aus meinem Blick—kam mir der letzte Straßenkehrer, weil er den Besen schon geschultert hatte, *mächtiger* vor *als* die andern.[21]

As I write this, I see, outside in the street, two streetsweepers cleaning the sidewalk with huge brooms. Both have orange and white striped uniforms *like bicycle racers,* both have white, crumpled stockings *like tramps* or *like characters in a Beckett play,* both have faces *like Southerners,* both wear caps *like those in photographs of prisoners of war from the First World War,* both walk stiffed-kneed *like bums,* all three—now a third joins them, and a fourth—wear black mittens *like the snow removal crew in the winter,* all five are alike with their gigantic brooms and shovels, which make them appear quite small, *like figures in a painting by Breughel.*

But—one of the streetsweepers swept *faster than* the other, and the other streetsweeper wore his cap *lower* on his face *than* the one, and the other other streetsweeper had a much *more German* face *than* the other streetsweeper, and the other other other streetsweeper seemed to perform his work *more unwillingly than* the other other streetsweeper, and finally—meanwhile the men have moved from my view—the last streetsweeper came to mind because he had, it seemed, shoved the broom forward *more powerfully than* the others.[22]

This need to compare finds tangible form in the theater, which has for centuries been *like* life, its main task being to represent. Obviously, Handke's emerging dramatic theory does not support such representational drama but seeks to eliminate the mimetic relationship between these separate realities. For Handke, drama is not like life, drama is like drama. As such it is intensely artificial, "endlich wieder ungewohnt, unvertraut" (p. 325) ("endlessly *un-usual,* unfamiliar," p. 175), with the result that:

Eine unerhörte Gleichzeitigkeit entsteht, des Sehens, des Atmens, des Unterscheidens. Der Raum bildet eine theatralische Einheit, in der man immer aufmerksamer, immer gespannter wird, bis etwa das Reißen eines Klebebandes, mit dem sich eine Person die Kleider über-spannt, nicht mehr nur sichtbar außen, sondern mitten *im* Bewußtsein des Zuschauers vor sich geht. (P. 325)

An unheard-of simultaneity of sight, breath, and discrimination is created. The space forms a theatrical unity, in which one becomes increasingly self-conscious and tense, almost to the point that the socially protective adhesive tape with which everyone wraps himself is ripped, is no longer visible, not only without, but also within, in the consciousness of the viewer. (Pp. 174–75)

Clearly *Prophecy* is another statement of Handke's persistent argument for nonrepresentational drama, and clearly it has a place in the theater. For only in performance does the piece achieve its full effect.

Some time after the production of his speech plays, Handke appended a note to *Prophecy:*

Die *Weissagung* ist von den drei Sprechstücken das rein formalistische. Nicht *ein* Satz gibt, wie in der *Selbstbezichtigung,* einen Sinn vor, dem der Sinn eines anderen Satzes dann widerspricht. In der *Weissagung* ist schon jeder Satz für sich sinnlos; der Sinn braucht nicht erst durch einen anderen Satz aufgehoben zu werden. Die *Weissagung* hat keinen Sinn, weder einen tieferen noch einen anderen. Sie hat keinen Sinn, weil ihr Sinn nicht bestimmbar ist. Es wird mit ihr nichts ausgesagt, auch nicht etwa, wie absurd Weissagungen in Wirklichkeit seien. Es steckt nichts dahinter, auch nichts zwischen den Worten und Zeilen. Die *Weissagung* ist kein Sinnspiel, sondern ein Sprachspiel. Was erreicht werden soll, ist eine größtmögliche akustische Dichte, die einen größmöglichen akustischen Reiz erzeugt. Die Erde soll dröhnen von Metaphern.[23]

Of the three speech plays, *Prophecy* is the purely formalistic one. Not one sentence presents, as in *Self-Accusation,* a meaning which the meaning of another sentence then contradicts. In *Prophecy* every sentence is already meaningless in itself; the meaning need not first be contradicted by another sentence. *Prophecy* has no meaning, neither a deeper meaning not another meaning. It has no meaning, because its meaning is not definable. Nothing is expressed by it, not even how absurd prophecies are in reality. Nothing hides behind it, not even between the words and lines. *Prophecy* is no play on meaning, but a play on language. What is to be achieved is the greatest possible acoustic density, which produces the greatest possible acoustic stimulus. The world is to resound with metaphors.

As in *Offending the Audience,* Handke seeks an acoustic effect that will irritate his audience into self-awareness. But more important than this effect or the play's implicit argument for nonrepresentational theater, though closely related to both, is Handke's preoccupation with metaphor. The last sentence of the note echoes the lines by the Russian poet Osip Mandelstam, which serve as epigraph to *Prophecy:*

> Wo beginnen?
> Alles kracht in den Fugen und schwankt.
> Die Luft erzittert vor Vergleichen.
> Kein Wort ist besser als das andre,
> die Erde dröhnt von Metaphern . . .
>
> (P.51)

> Where to begin?
> Everything is out of joint and totters.
> The air quivers with comparisons.
> No word is better than the other,
> the earth booms with metaphors . . .
>
> (P. 3)[24]

The senselessness of every sentence in *Prophecy* suggests that describing an object in terms of another might be as meaningless as describing an object in terms of itself. "Men will die like flies" would appear to be more significant than "Flies will die like flies," and the first time the comparison was made, it was. Thereafter, however, it became meaningless. Speaking in "The Misery of Comparison" ("Das Elend des Vergleichens") of a statement he has personally made several times—"Ich gehe lieber ins Kino als in Theater" (p. 316) ("I like going to the movies more than to the theatre," p. 167)—Handke tells of his refusal to make this statement another time, for now it embarrasses and bores him:

Mir scheint, so wie man nur einmal durch denselben Fluß gehen kann, so kann man nur einmal denselben Satz verwenden, beim zweitenmal ist es schon ein Irrtum, beim nächsten Mal schon eine Schande, schließlich nur noch Idiotie. (P. 316)

It seems to me that as you can go through the same stream only once, so can you use the same sentence only once. The second time it is already a mistake; by the next time it is a disgrace; and finally it is only an idiocy. (P. 167)

Handke refers to "the idiocy of language" again a few years later in the interview with Artur Joseph concerning his short dramatic pieces and *Kaspar:*

Das einzige, was mich, als Schriftsteller, . . . angeht, ist der Ekel vor der stumpfsinnigen Versprachlichung und damit Verrohung der Leute. . . . Höchstens sollte man, wie der Held in Sartres *Der Ekel* vor den Dingen, sich auch ekeln lernen vor der Sprache. Das ist schon ein Anfang des Bewußtseins.[25]

The only thing that preoccupies me as a writer. . . is nausea at stupid speechification and the resulting brutalization of people. . . . One should learn to be nauseated by language, as the hero of Sartre's *Nausea* is by things. At least that would be a beginning of consciousness.[26]

Handke's note to *Prophecy,* which focuses on the relationship among sentences and on the meaninglessness of every proposition, echoes Wittgenstein's *Tractatus,* and particularly the linguistic and philosophical question, "Can whether one proposition makes sense depend on the truth of another?" As though testing the possibilities of this query, Handke creates a series of aphorisms (the form, as well, of the *Tractatus*), each of which bears no relationship to any other except in form, with the determination of the truth or falsity of each to be a self-contained matter. Wittgenstein's philosophical concern with the fact that the sense of every sentence or proposition lies in its containing the possibility of being either true or false finds its reflection in *Prophecy* in Handke's positing of sentences which are logically irrefutable and, therefore, senseless. In *Prophecy,* despite the meaninglessness of every sentence in relation to reality, the significance of each proposition as a linguistic model is not only preserved but emphasized. And it is only the blatant use of clichés and tautologies which causes the meaning to fail, obviating the relationship the sentence, by virtue of its recognizable structure, should have had to reality.

Prophecy, like *Offending the Audience* before it, is far from mere self-indulgence. The ending of the first piece, which amuses the audience with stock phrases of theatrical criticism just before abusing it, and *Prophecy*, which assaults the audience with tautologies, are both serious and sophisticated pleas for an awareness of the way in which language affects, even determines, our perceptions. *Prophecy*, written in the future tense and itself a prophecy, is, like all Handke's speech plays, an apocalyptic vision of a world in which language, though still existent, is dead.

Self-Accusation

It hardly seems surprising that Handke should create the form of the *Sprechstücke* for the early dramatic pieces, for just as he considered the theater an appropriate forum for an attack on theater, so also would he consider a piece consisting solely of language an appropriate means of attacking language. By the time he wrote his third speech play, however, he was planning a play with a plot. Speaking of how *Self-Accusation* (*Selbstbezichtigung*, 1966) became finally another piece consisting solely of language, Handke explains:

Ich hatte zunächst ein Stück mit einer echten Handlung geplant, mit einer Geschichte. . . . Nun reduzierte sich diesen Plan des Stücks immer mehr auf Wörter, weil sie keine Gegenstände auf der Bühne, weil sie keine Probleme auf der Bühne meinen, sondern nur zitieren und am wenigsten den Anschein einer anderen Wirklichkeit haben— sie stellen eine eigene Wirklichkeit der Wörter her. Es war also ein Reduktionsvorgang, der nicht willkürlich war, sondern einfach sich ergeben hat.[27]

I had been planning a play with a genuine plot, with a story. . . . Then this plan was gradually reduced to words, which don't refer to any objects or problems onstage; they merely quote, and what they do least is give the appearance of another reality—rather, they create their own reality of words. It was a reductive process which wasn't arbitrary: it simply came about.[28]

Although *Self-Accusation* remains a *Sprachspiel,* or language game, it looks forward to the full-length drama, and, specifically, to *Kaspar.* And even though the form is strictly presentational, with speakers who attempt acoustic effects as in the earlier pieces, Handke's approach in *Self-Accusation* is once again both disturbing and new.

Although Handke claims to have abandoned the story, the remnants of plot remain. The "you" of *Offending the Audience* has been transformed now into an "I" who narrates personal events:

> Ich bin auf die Welt gekommen. . . .
> Ich habe mich bewegt. . . .
> Ich habe gesprochen. . . .
> Ich habe wahrgenommen. . . .
> Ich habe meinen Namen gesagt. . . .
> Ich habe zu Können gelernt. . . .
> Ich habe nicht mehr nur der Natur folgen müssen. . . .
> Ich habe Regeln gelernt. . . .
> Ich bin gesellschaftsfähig geworden.
> Ich bin geworden: ich habe sollen. . . .
> Ich bin von allen Regeln erfaßt worden. . . .[29]

> I came into the world. . . .
> I moved. . . .
> I spoke. . . .
> I perceived. . . .
> I said my name. . . .
> I learned to be able. . . .
> I no longer had to obey only nature. . . .
> I learned rules. . . .
> I became fit for society.
> I became: I was supposed to. . . .
> I was included in all the rules. . . .[30]

Unlike the narrator of *A Sorrow Beyond Dreams* or *The Weight of the World,* however, the "I" of *Self-Accusation* is not intended to be autobiographical or even personal (despite the similarities between the concerns of this protagonist and those of the young

Handke in the essay "1957").[31] The "I" is rather the voice of a generalized human being; the progression from innocence to experience, from the undifferentiated world of childhood to the adult world of restraints, suggests the universal experience of everyone. Handke's instructions to have the piece presented by one male and one female speaker, alternately or in unison, support his intention that the protagonist be more than a specific individual:

Selbstbezichtigung ist ein Stück ohne Fabel. In ihr geht keine Geschichte vor sich, jedenfalls nicht die besondere Geschichte eines besonderen Menschen. Das "Ich" der *Selbstbezichtigung* ist nicht das "Ich" einer Erzählung, sondern nur das "Ich" der Grammatik. Es ist kein persönliches Ich, sondern ein unpersönliches. Die Geschichte der *Selbstbezichtigung* zeigt nicht eine besondere Geschichte.[32]

Self-Accusation is a piece without a plot. In it no story occurs, in any case not the particular story of a particular person. The "I" of *Self-Accusation* is not the "I" of a narrative, but only the "I" of grammar. It is no personal I, but an impersonal one. The story of *Self-Accusation* does not show a particular story.

The protagonist of *Self-Accusation,* having reached maturity and become socialized, becomes aware of the countless restrictions in life; with every new capability surfaces a limitation imposed by society:

Ich bin geworden: ich habe sollen. . . . Ich bin fähig geworden, heiß und kalt zu unterscheiden: ich habe das Spiel mit dem Feuer vermeiden sollen. Ich bin fähig geworden, Gutes und Böses zu trennen: ich habe das Böse vermeiden sollen. Ich bin fähig geworden, nach Spielregeln zu spielen: ich habe einen Verstoß gegen die Spielregeln vermeiden sollen. (P. 52)

I became: I was supposed to. . . . I became capable of distinguishing between hot and cold: I was supposed to avoid playing with fire. I became capable of separating good and evil: I was supposed to eschew evil. I became capable of playing according to the rules: I was supposed to avoid an infraction of the rules of the game. (P. 39)

In one central paragraph, which changes from the indicative to the interrogative, the speaker asks the climactic question: "Habe ich mich gegen die Regeln, Pläne, Ideen, Postulate, Grundsätze, Etiketten, Satzungen, allgemeinen Meinungen und Formeln der ganzen Welt vergangen?" (p. 74) ("Did I violate the rules, plans, ideas, postulates, basic principles, etiquettes, general propositions, opinions, and formulas of the whole world?", p. 41). The answer is, "Ich habe getan" ("I did"). The guilty narrator is now obsessed with the need to atone, and the rest of the piece is a confession.

Apparently the greatest sin of the protagonist has been self-expression, which has invariably conflicted with society's rules. The seemingly inexhaustible catalogue of violations reminds the audience that this is the confession of a multitude of people, including the audience itself, individual members of which have undoubtedly committed some of these same sins. For surely at least one person in the audience has touched objects labeled "do not touch," failed to throw litter in the litter basket, or opened the door of a train before it stopped. The more the list grows, the greater the chances of recognition, of silent confessions on the part of audience members as they communally affirm their individual guilt. Like *Offending the Audience*, *Self-Accusation* transforms the audience into the subject of the piece, making each individual member the narrative "I."

Yet to purge his audience of its individual or collective sins through confession seems hardly to be the purpose of the writer who had long ago given up aspirations to the priesthood. If the purpose of the speech plays is to encourage audience awareness, what are the benefits of the kind of awareness fostered by *Self-Accusation?* Obviously, Handke's inversion of speaker and audience is part of his argument for a more meaningful drama, but his attainment of the audience's awareness of itself as a participant in the drama is also essential to his continuing concern with language. Perhaps even more than the previous speech plays, *Self-Accusation* invites the linguistic nausea of which Handke later speaks. For in this piece he combines a negative attitude toward society's restrictions with his opposition to the deadening effects that language, and particularly public language, can have.

One of the confessed sins, in fact, is specifically that of having violated the rules of language:

Ich habe die Regeln der Sprache nicht beachtet. Ich habe Sprachver-
stöße begangen. Ich habe die Worte ohne Gedanken gebraucht. Ich
habe den Gegenständen der Welt blindlings Eigenschaften gegeben.
Ich habe den Worten für die Gegenstände blindlings Worte für die
Eigenschaften der Gegenstände gegeben. Ich habe mit den Worten für
die Eigenschafte der Gegenstände blindlings die Welt angeschaut. Ich
habe die Gegenstände tot genannt. Ich habe die Mannigfaltigkeit bunt
genannt. Ich habe die Traurigkeit dunkel genannt. Ich habe den
Wahnsinn hell genannt. Ich habe die Leidenschaft heiß genannt. Ich
habe den Zorn rot genannt. (P. 78)

I failed to observe the rules of the language. I committed linguistic
blunders. I used words thoughtlessly. I blindly attributed qualities to
the objects in the world. I blindly attributed to the words for the objects
words for the qualities of the objects. I regarded the world blindly with
the words for the qualities of the objects. I called objects dead. I called
complexity lively. I called melancholy black. I called madness bright. I
called passion hot. I called anger red. (P. 44)

The speaker's confession of thoughtless, blind use of language is a
general complaint of which every member of the audience is
surely guilty. The more specific complaint of rhetorically mistak-
ing the part for the whole once again recalls Wittgenstein. In the
Philosophical Investigations, Wittgenstein objects to the proposition
that "mein Besen steht in der Ecke" ("my broom is in the corner"),
explaining that this actually means "der Stiel sei dort und die
Bürste, und der Stiel stecke in der Bürste" ("the broomstick is
there, and so is the brush, and the broomstick is fixed in the
brush").[33] He concludes that it is illogical to designate a complex
object by a simple sign, for this causes the proposition to have an
indeterminate sense.

The catalogue that completes the paragraph of language violations and recalls the arguments of both *Offending the Audience* and
Prophecy is also significant:

> Ich habe die letzten Dinge unsagbar genannt. . . .
> Ich habe die Freiheit unabdingbar genannt. . . .
> Ich habe die Finsternis undurchdringlich genannt. . . .
> Ich habe das Vertrauen blind genannt. . . .
> Ich habe die Kritik konstruktiv genannt. . . .
> Ich habe die Wahrheit tief genannt. . . . (Pp. 78–79)

I called the ultimate questions unanswerable. . . .
I called freedom inalienable. . . .
I called darkness impenetrable. . . .
I called trust blind. . . .
I called criticism constructive. . . .
I called truth profound. . . . (Pp. 44–45)

Handke reveals the cliché not only as a deadener of language but also as an agent capable of unyielding control over human action. For the others in Handke's confessional booth, that is, the audience, the passage is filled with echoes of mothers' voices, teachers' voices, priests' voices, and visions of the countless signs of civilized society—"Eintritt Verboten," "Bitte Ruhig," "Vorsicht!" ("Entrance Forbidden," "Please Be Quiet," "Handle With Care")—all of which engender automatic, thoughtless responses on the part of an obedient public. In the face of such codes of behavior, which have all been frozen into linguistic phrases, self-expression is discouraged, and the person who enters through a forbidden door is subject to punitive redress.

This is, of course, a picture of contemporary drama, held hostage by the conventions of theater. But it is also a picture of contemporary society, which, though not limited to Germany, may have special significance for a people whose recent history includes the mindless reception of propaganda and unquestioning commitment to fascism, as well as an enduring propensity for following rules.

Yet Handke is reluctant to call any of his plays political or social indictments. Speaking of *Offending the Audience* with Artur Joseph, he remarks:

Es wäre zu hoch oder zu niedrig gegriffen, wenn man behaupten wollte, ich hätte damit eine neue Gesellschaftsordnung interpretieren wollen. Ich dachte nur an die formal-dramaturgischen Ausdrucks- und Denkformen.[34]

To say that I was trying to interpret a new social order with this play would be reaching too high, or too low. I was thinking only of the formal, dramaturgical side, of the forms of thought and expression.[35]

Elsewhere in the same interview, Joseph comments:

Im *Kaspar* kritisieren Sie weniger das Theater—wie in der *Publikumsbe-schimpfung*—als die Gesellschaft, die schöne Ordnung, die Vergesell-schaftung überhaupt. . . .[36]

In *Kaspar* your criticism was aimed less at the theatre—as in *Offending the Audience*—than at society, at the beauties of order, at social organiza-tion in general. . . .[37]

Handke replies:

Es ist schwierig zu sagen, ob und daß dieses Stück die Gesellschaft oder überhaupt jede universalistische Gesellschaft kritisiert, weil es vor allem aus Satzspielen und Satzmodellen besteht, die von der Unmög-lichkeit handeln, mit der Sprache etwas *auszusagen*. . . . Im *Kaspar* wird die Idiotie der Sprache gezeigt, die, indem sie vorgibt, dauernd etwas *auszusagen*, nur ihre eigene Stumpfsinnigkeit aussagt.[38]

It's hard to say whether, or that, this play criticizes universal society or any society at all, because it consists primarily of sentence games and sentence models dealing with the impossibility of *expressing* anything in language. . . . What is shown in *Kaspar* is the idiocy of language. In constantly pretending to express something, it expresses nothing but its own stupidity.[39]

When in 1967 Handke accepted the Gerhart Hauptmann Prize from Berlin's Freie Volksbühne, he chose to discuss a current political situation rather than his craft or his literary achievement. Yet in his critical writing he has attacked the blatantly political Brecht as a trivializer and denied the possibility of a "literature of engagement."[40] Just as Wittgenstein attributes all philosophical problems to language, so Handke considers language to be at the heart of society's most serious problems:

Was mich beunruhigt, ist die Entfremdung vom eigenen Sprechen der Leute. Das ist auch etwa das Grundübel der jungen Revolutionäre in Deutschland: Sie sind ihrer Sprache entfremdet, die nicht mehr *ihre* Sprache ist—so können sie sich auch nicht verständigen.[41]

What bothers me is people's alienation from their own speech. In a way, this is the basic trouble with the young revolutionaries in Ger-many: they're alienated from their language. It isn't *their* language anymore, so they can't even communicate.[42]

Handke returns repeatedly to the fact that language is his central concern. The rules he attacks are not those of society but those of language, which threaten to turn reality into "a tale told by an idiot . . . signifying nothing."

Calling for Help

In his review of the 1971–72 production at Lincoln Center of Handke's second full-length play, *The Ride Across Lake Constance*, John Simon asks, with obvious disapproval, "When is a play not a play but a fraud? When, in fact, is any so-called work of art not a work of art but a piece of trickery, a hoax, a nonsensical game, a fraud?"[43] With characteristic perspicacity (though somewhat hasty displeasure), Simon has posed the single most important question concerning our attitude toward Handke's drama. For it is only when we decide Handke is *not* a charlatan that we can begin to discover the underpinnings — and hence the substance — of his artistic tricks.

It is difficult to imagine a play more worthy of Simon's question than Handke's fourth speech play, *Calling for Help* (*Hilferufe*, 1967), which was first produced in Stockholm in 1967 by actors from the Oberhausen Städtische Bühne, under the direction of Günther Büch. This piece, shorter even than the others (only twelve minutes in production), is literally described by its title, for it consists simply of the search for the word *help* in order that the speakers may make use of it.

The piece (which uses lowercase letters) begins with an ending, the pro forma conclusion to a public speech of undesignated content:

zum abschluß indem wir noch einmal an euch alle denken rufen wir euch auf und laden euch ein mit uns gemeinsam die wege zu gegenseitigem verstehen zu vertieftem wissen zu einem weiten herzen zu einem brüderlichen leben in der einen wahrhaft weltumspannenden gemeinschaft der menschen zu suchen.[44]

and in conclusion, while we think of all of you once more, we call on you and invite you to search with us for ways to mutual understanding, to deepened knowledge, to an open heart, to a fraternal life in the one truly world-embracing community of men.[45]

It continues with a series of statements, both indicative and imperative—"unmittelbar nach dem mordanschlag haben die behörden alle zur verfügung stehenden mittel aufgeboten um klarheit über die mordtat zu gewinnen," "folgen sie mir unauffällig," "türen schließen" (pp. 93, 94, 95) ("immediately after the assassination the authorities employed all available means to obtain a clear picture of the murder," "follow me unobtrusively please," "close the doors," pp. 23, 24, 25)—which gradually become interspersed with fragments of sentences—"in namen der republik," "auf vielfachen wunsch," "nur an werktagen" (pp. 95, 96) ("in the name of the republic," "because of unprecedented demand," "only on weekdays," p. 25)—and, finally, become single words—"niemals!" "ja!" "heilig!" "heiß!" (p. 96) ("never!" "yes!" "holy!" "hot!" p. 26). As the length of the statements diminishes, the intensity of sound increases, reaching a climax with the word "help." To each of the proferred statements or words the speakers respond "NO," for these are not the word they seek. They cry "YES!" only when "help" is offered. But the sense of relief and joy experienced by both speakers and audience turns to amusement when one realizes that, paradoxically, the word is no longer needed, for the speakers sought assistance only in finding it.

The piece, however, is not merely a joke, but an ingenious demonstration of a fundamental truth about language: it has a reality of its own. In the interview with Artur Joseph, Handke comments on the autonomous quality of language: "Ich meine, jeder Satz bedeutet nicht etwas (andres), sondern bedeutet sich selber"[46] ("I think a sentence doesn't mean something else: it means itself"[47]). He makes the same point in *Prophecy* through the use of tautologies, which, as Anthony Kenny notes in the following passage, Wittgenstein describes as statements saying nothing about the world.

The only propositions which really belong in logic books are the tautologies whose nature is shown by the truth-tables. Being tautologies, they say nothing about the world, because they are true in every possible state of affairs and consequently cannot pick out one state of affairs rather than another. They are propositions of a unique sort, because their truth can be discovered by a mere study of the symbols which express them. They say nothing about the world, but they reveal the structure of the symbols which make them up.[48]

Taking the demonstration of *Prophecy* one step further, Handke now presents statements and words which are not intrinsically insignificant but which in the context of the speech play become "pure" language, with no relationship to phenomenal reality. Every statement is offered only as another guess in the language game the speakers are playing, and once the audience realizes the speakers are in search of a particular word, they, like the speakers, cease to consider the usual significance of the statements but view them simply as words to be rejected as unsatisfactory.

In the foreword to the piece, Handke explains: "die sätze und wörten werden dabei nicht in ihrer üblichen bedeutung gesprochen, sondern mit der bedeutung des suchens nach hilfe" (p. 91) ("while the way to the word help is being demonstrated, the sentences and words are not uttered with their usual meaning, but only to signify that help is being sought," p. 21). But the most effective example of language divested of its usual meaning resides in the word *help* itself, for, as Handke points out:

während die sprecher nach dem wort hilfe suchen, brauchen sie hilfe; wenn sie dann aber endlich das wort hilfe gefunden haben, haben sie keine hilfe mehr nötig. bevor sie das wort hilfe finden, sprechen sie *um* hilfe, während sie dann, wenn sie das wort hilfe gefunden haben, nur noch *hilfe* sprechen, ohne es mehr nötig zu haben, *um* hilfe zu sprechen. . . . das wort HILFE hat seine bedeutung verloren. (P. 91)

while the speakers are seeking the *word* help they are in need of *help;* once having found the *word* help they no longer need any help. before they find the word they ask *for* help, whereas once they have found the word help they only speak *help* without needing to ask *for* help any longer. . . . the word HELP has lost its meaning. (P. 21)

Yet *Calling for Help* does not only demonstrate a linguistic principle, which might adequately have been done through a dictionary recitation. *Calling for Help,* like the other speech plays, protests the reified condition of a language that thrives—or at least exists—on staleness. Every statement or phrase in *Calling for*

Help is recognizable as one of the many signs of society one repeatedly sees, accepts, and obeys without thought. The piece is a collage of advertising slogans, clichéd orders and responses, announcements, prohibitions, newspaper headlines, and moral maxims which reduce language to a weather-worn bumper sticker.

In the context of this piece, the audience does precisely what Handke hopes it will do outside the theater: it rejects as meaningless the ready-mades of mass and private communication. Only in retrospect does an audience realize the didactic intention of the piece and consider its effectiveness in dramatizing the need for new forms. The opening appeal for "mutual understanding," "deeper knowledge," and "an open heart" ironically applies to Handke's plea as readily as it does to any other: Handke is calling for a "community of men" who will reject inherited rhetoric and revitalize language and perception. He is, finally, calling for help.

3

Kaspar

Kaspar (1967), Handke's first full-length play, premiered simultaneously at the Theater am Turm in Frankfurt (under the direction of Claus Peymann) and the Oberhausen Städtische Bühne (under the direction of Günther Büch) and became the most frequently performed modern play in Germany, Austria, and Switzerland during the 1968–69 season.[1] The same audiences who had smiled wryly at the abuse they endured from Handke's first *Sprechstück*, along with thousands of others, flocked to the theaters to see the producton which *Theater heute* was to declare "Play of the Year" in 1968, which Peter Brook was later to direct in Paris prisons, and which theaters in New York, London, Paris, and numerous other major cities were to perform in subsequent years. Enthusiastic reviewers praised the play as a major theatrical event, suggesting a greatness akin to that of *Waiting for Godot* (*En Attendant Godot*, 1952) and predicting a permanent place for *Kaspar* in literary history. Jack Kroll called Handke "the hottest young playwright in Europe" and Clive Barnes referred to him as "one of the most important young playwrights of our time."[2]

The historical Kaspar Hauser, well known in German literature and alluded to in Ernst Jandl's prefatory poem (chosen by Handke), was an autistic young man who appeared in Nuremberg in 1828, after some sixteen years of presumably solitary existence, in possession of only one sentence: "A söchener Reiter möcht i wärn, wie mei Voter aner gween is" ("I want to become a horseman like my father once was").[3] Recognizing in the Kaspar Hauser story what he calls "das modell einer Art von sprachlichem Mythos"[4] ("the model of a sort of linguistic myth"[5]), Handke alters the sentence but not the situation of his protagonist and turns Kaspar into a universalized character who shows not "wie ES WIRKLICH IST oder WIRKLICH WAR mit Kaspar Hauser. Es zeigt, was

41

MÖGLICH IST mit jemandem"[6] ("how IT REALLY IS or REALLY WAS with Kaspar Hauser. It shows what IS POSSIBLE with someone"[7]). Since the play does not pretend to be retelling Kaspar Hauser's story, nor even telling Kaspar's, but offering instead a model of possibility, Handke's preface correctly suggests that what the audience experiences is not a story but a theatrical event.

The sixteen stages of Kaspar's development, delineated by Handke at the beginning of the play, take the representative protagonist from birth to death, from innocence to experience, and from unity to schizophrenia, through speech. Barely able to walk, apparently incapable of reasoning, and obviously in possession of only one sentence, the uninitiated Kaspar stumbles across the boards like an oversized infant wandering in the undifferentiated world of childhood. He appears to learn little from his contacts with objects onstage yet displays a constant need to describe and evaluate those experiences through the statement and restatement of his one sentence. He sticks his hands in the crevice between two sofa cushions, with difficulty removes them, and remarks: "Ich möcht ein solcher werden wie einmal ein andrer gewesen ist" ("I want to be a person like somebody else was once"). He pulls out a table drawer, watches as the objects contained in it fall to the floor, and remarks: "Ich möcht ein solcher werden wie einmal ein andrer gewesen ist." He battles with a chair in his path, kicks it, and remarks: "Ich möcht ein solcher werden wie einmal ein andrer gewesen ist."

For an audience that cannot function without language, Kaspar's single sentence is woefully incapable of describing or evaluating even those few experiences he encounters. As far as the audience can see, only when one possesses a multitude of sentences can all things be possible, for only when a person can differentiate among objects and experiences can there be a meaningful relationship between that person and the world.

The *Einsager*, or prompters, who are disembodied loudspeaker voices, support the audience's concern and take it upon themselves to educate Kaspar. Listening intently to the *Einsager*'s paradigms, Kaspar proves to be a model student: he learns to use their grammatical constructions;[8] he learns to generalize, then discovers the faults of his generalizations and begins to particularize. He not only learns everything the *Einsager* teach him about language, he also develops a surprisingly wide-ranging vocabulary, until, finally, he is ready to be weaned. Convinced that their job is complete, the *Einsager* pronounce Kaspar prepared to function in life:

Du hast Modellsätze, mit denen du dich durchschlagen kannst: indem du diese Modelle auf deine Sätze anwendest, kannst du alles, was scheinbar in Unordnung ist, in Ordnung setzen: du kannst es für geordnet erklären: jeder Gegenstand kann der sein, als den du ihn bezeichnest. (P. 57)

You have model sentences with which you can get through life: by applying these models to your sentences, you can impose order on everything that appears chaotic: you can declare it ordered: every object can be what you designate it to be. (P. 102)

Such faith in the omnipotence of language has been apparent throughout the *Einsager*'s teaching, suggested especially when they ceased adjusting their sentences to Kaspar's movements and watched him begin to adjust his movements to their sentences. For the *Einsager*, experience is the product of language, which has the unquestionable power of controlling reality. This is precisely what they, who are nothing themselves *but* language, have done with Kaspar.

By this time, however, the audience, who at first applauded the progress of Kaspar's education, recognizes that his enlightenment may perhaps not be so positive an achievement after all. Kaspar's first learned sentence is a lament: "Damals, als ich noch weg war, habe ich niemals so viele Schmerzen im Kopf gehabt, und man hat mich nicht so gequält wie jetzt, seit ich hier bin" (p. 29) ("At that time, while I was still away, my head never ached as much, and I was not tortured the way I am now that I am here," p. 77), suggesting the pain his emergence into a language-centered world has created. In moving from his world of innocence into the socialized world of the *Einsager*, Kaspar has acquired a consciousness that demands expression and differentiation. He now knows not only that pain is distinct from other feelings but that his present pain is more intense than the pain he had previously felt.

He is tortured by his compulsion to name the pain while at the same time aware that such naming is, under his new circumstances, less adequate than his earlier means of naming the pain, through his sentence. With that sentence, he could perfectly express the sensation, at least for himself. As soon as he subscribes to the convention of language which names this sensation as "pain," he is aware that the relationship has changed, for the word "pain" is not his word, but others'. It is invested with meaning and a range of connotations, none of which offers him the possibility the uneducated Kaspar had.

Kaspar discovers that through following the *Einsager*'s models he can incorporate names into sentences, ostensibly ordering his world. But he also realizes that the necessity of interpretation, to which everyone who has access to language must defer, makes every perception impure. Despite Wittgenstein's picture theory, which attempts to correlate language and phenomenal reality, individual perceptions remain unique, creating an infinite number of linguistic expressions for any object. Any sentence, then, because it is filtered through the individual's interpretive process, is both an expression and a distortion of the object it seeks to describe. The *Einsager* tell Kaspar that he must be mistaken if he sees an object differently from the way he speaks it, yet within a language system, the two can never coincide.

The problem becomes even more complex when language attempts to describe abstract concepts and when Kaspar considers whether anything can be perceived independently of words. The security of order which Kaspar first feels upon discovering he can name the objects of his world deteriorates into confusion as he contemplates the endless ways of representing phenomenal and experiential reality. He realizes that despite the apparent limitations of his original sentence, it enabled him to contain the diversity of the world. The *Einsager* themselves point out that with his one sentence Kaspar could do anything: make himself noticeable, explain things to himself, name everything that comes in his way and move it out of his way, familiarize himself with all objects, bring order into every disorder.

As soon as Kaspar develops a consciousness of himself as distinct from his environment, however, his sentence fails. This crucial moment, precipitated by the *Einsager*'s steady stream of language, is punctuated by Kaspar's sudden interruption of his sentence; he sits in silence as the voices continue to offer him the last hope of hiding behind it. But the hope is already dead, for Kaspar has experienced the beginnings of self-consciousness. The brightly lit stage falls into darkness, signaling the end, and the irretrievability, of Kaspar's primeval world.

As his education into language progresses, Kaspar becomes increasingly conscious of his estrangement from the very world into which he is being initiated. In torment and despair, he asks, "warum man mich denn von allem, was zu mir gehörte, abgetrennt habe?" (p. 93) ("why have I been cut off from everything that belongs to me?" p. 133). By this time, Kaspar—and the audience as well—realizes that in permitting his one sentence to be exorcised and replaced by the established patterns of language and hence of society, he has sacrificed his individuality. Metaphorically expressing this by populating the stage with duplicates of Kaspar, Handke directs that five other clownlike figures roam about, playing a symphony of cacophonous sounds, reflecting Kaspar's internal confusion. Handke's hero, ironically, has had his wish fulfilled, for now he is, visibly, someone like others. In a moment that combines triumph and defeat, Kaspar's voice rises out of the chaos to pronounce final judgment on his learning experience: "Jeder Satz ist für die Katz" (p. 92 ("Every sentence is for the birds," p. 132) and "Ziegen und Affen" (pp. 101–02) ("Goats and monkeys," p. 140), the cry of Othello, similarly victimized by the power of words.[9]

In one version of the play, Kaspar's final cry, punctuated by the staccato pulls of the closing curtain, is "Ich/bin/nur/zufällig/ich" ("I/am/only/accidentally/I"),[10] a statement which contrasts starkly with his earlier, defensive assertion "Ich bin, der ich bin" (p. 56) ("I am the one I am," p. 102), spoken in affirmation of his individuality when he first begins to realize it is endangered. Kaspar's final lament perfectly embodies his plight: the sentences he uses are not his sentences, the morality he supports is not his morality, yet they are the tools and guidelines with and within which he must function. Kaspar realizes that he has achieved expression, but because it is simply a borrowed mode, his identity, like reality itself, is arbitrary.

As he approaches the microphone to deliver his "good citizen" speech, Kaspar appears to be the ideal social creature. He is honest, frugal, conscientious, industrious, reticent, modest, friendly, dutiful, receptive. He loves order, does perfectly everything he is asked to do, has an untarnished record, would like to be a member, would like to cooperate, is proud of what has been achieved so far. Poetically relating the story of his life, Kaspar reaches the epitome of articulateness. But then his monologue deteriorates into didactics. In a voice much like that of the prompters, he begins to speak of conforming actions, of what everyone must do and must not do in relation to others, reciting the same kinds of moral maxims that were fundamental to the *Einsager*'s training: "Jeder muß sich vor dem Essen die Hände waschen / jeder muß im Gefängnis die Taschen leeren" (p. 86) ("Everyone must wash his hands before eating / everyone must empty his pockets before a beating," p. 127). The *Einsager*'s—and society's—insistence upon order has given Kaspar not only a language but, along with it, an established moral pattern; while seeming to open up possibilities to him, it has instead imposed limitations of both language and living.

The *Einsager* have proved to be no different from the societal order attacked in more abstract terms in the *Sprechstücke* and no less destructive than Nazi propagandists. Insisting as they do on the necessity of order, they have bombarded their victim with the negative commands of society, the prefabricated patterns of language and behavior which are intended to be assimilated but not understood. But where the abstract "I" of *Self-Accusation* defers to social order, confessing a myriad of sins, Kaspar rebels against the prescriptiveness of the order preached by the *Einsager*, defending, even in defeat, not only his individuality but the basic right of, and need for, self-expression.

Just before the play's chaotic ending, the desperate Kaspar cries, "Was habe ich doch gerade gesagt? Wenn ich nur wüßte, was es ist, was ich gerade gesagt habe!" (p. 90) ("What was it that I said

just now? If I only knew what it is that I said just now!" p. 131).
Painfully conscious of the arbitrary connection between language
and reality, he now sees the loss in his gain. His lesson has been
that without language, phenomenal reality can only be sensed;
with language it can be named, which, in turn, permits differ-
entiating, valuing, and, ultimately, constructing. But language
brings with it a history of predetermined meanings against which
Kaspar has no immunity. As Handke's protagonist acknowledges,
"Schon mit meinem ersten Satz bin ich in die Falle gegangen" (p.
98) ("Already with my first sentence I was trapped," p. 137)—
trapped by the repressiveness of a system that makes puppets of
men. Individually, as one who has become one of many, Kaspar
serves as a forceful indictment of society; but on a higher and, for
Handke, more significant level, that is, as a model of what is
possible, he serves to dramatize the very process of knowing, to
which verbal capability is central.

Dramaturgically, *Kaspar* may appear more traditional than the
purely presentational *Sprechstücke*, but, as Handke remarks in the
interview with Joseph, the full-length play is no more concerned
with characterization or plot than the shorter pieces were:

Das [*Kaspar*] ist nichts Neues. Das ist eine Entwicklung, zu der ich
einmal kam, weil ich mich da wieder in ein automatisches Produzieren
von Stücken aus purer Sprache einlasses mußte, wo die Wörter nur sich
selbst beleuchten. Die Wörter, die puren Wörter, die vorher in der
Publikumsbeschimpfung auf der Bühne vor sich gehen, verdichteten sich
nun zu einer Figur.[11]

It [*Kaspar*] was nothing new, it only evolved because I was again forced
to produce plays automatically from pure language, in which the words
only illuminate themselves. The words, the pure words which first
occur onstage in *Offending the Audience,* are condensed into a character.[12]

Over the years, a number of productions of *Kaspar* have emphasized the clown characterization implicit in the name (*Kasper*
in German means clown) or the characterization suggested by the
similarity of the name to the *Kasperle* of the traditional Viennese
puppet show. Handke himself mentions the clown reference in

his preface, but maintains that there is no resemblance, that his Kaspar is, rather, like Frankenstein's monster: a newborn adult whose discovery of the world leads to his victimization.

In The Living Theatre's production of *Frankenstein* (which was touring Europe while Handke was writing *Kaspar*), Julian Beck and Judith Malina emphasized the anarchistic portions of Mary Shelley's novel as they brought the monster from creation through the stages of discovery to the destruction of its ego. Working from the company's sketchbooks and staging directions, Pierre Biner, in his book on The Living Theatre, re-creates the European production, quoting the monster's description of his preverbal experience of the world, which is strikingly similar to Kaspar's:

"It is with a considerable difficulty that I remember the original era of my being: all the events of that period appear confused and indistinct. I saw, felt, heard, and smelt, at the same time. By degrees, I remember, a stronger light pressed upon my nerves, so that I was obliged to shut my eyes. Darkness then came over me, and troubled me; but hardly had I felt this, when, by opening my eyes, the light poured in upon me again. I walked. Before, dark and opaque bodies had surrounded me, impervious to my touch or sight; but I now found that I could wander on at liberty, with no obstacles which I could not either surmount or avoid. The light became more and more oppressive to me; and, the heat wearying me as I walked, I sought a place where I could receive shade. It was dark when I awoke; I felt cold also and half-frightened. I was a poor, helpless, miserable wretch; I knew, and could distinguish, nothing; but feeling pain invade me on all sides, I sat down and wept."[13]

The monster goes on to speak of his development:

"I obtained a knowledge of the manners, governments, and religions of the different nations of the earth. Was man, at once so powerful, so virtuous and magnificent, yet so vicious and base? To be a great and virtuous man appeared the highest honor that can befall a sensitive being; to be base and vicious appeared the lowest degradation. I could not conceive how one man could go forth to murder his fellow, or even why there were laws and governments; but when I heard details of vice and bloodshed, my wonder ceased, and I turned away with disgust and loathing. The strange system of human society was explained to me. I heard of the division of property, of immense wealth and squalid poverty; of rank, descent, and noble blood. And what was I? Of my creation and creator I was absolutely ignorant; but I knew that I possessed no money, no friends, no kind of property. I was, besides, endued with a figure hideously deformed and loathsome. Was I then a monster, a blot upon the earth, from which all men fled, and whom all men disowned?"[14]

In describing the monster's passage from innocence to experience, Biner refers to an "April countryside" passing into "the desolation of winter": "Innocence turns into crime and repression by the police, harmony among the faculties of the mind into cacophony and strife, transforming the faculties into victims and executioners."[15] If, as Christopher Innes suggests, *Kaspar* may be read as an "interior, psychological drama," in which "the table, chair and cupboard are the furniture of Kaspar's mind, the prompters are the stream of sense data that impinges on the consciousness, and the verbal forms represent mental states," then the "projection of complete schizophrenia" in the second act may well parallel the monster's experience, and the multiple Kaspars may be the "victims and executioners" of Kaspar's mind.[16]

Undoubtedly the parallels between the two plays can be pursued further, but not without implying a stronger influence than was probably present. Handke's first full-length play clearly evolved from the *Sprechstücke*, and particularly from *Self-Accusation*, but just as Handke saw in Kaspar Hauser a model for his character, so also did he recognize the affinities between the Frankenstein monster and the dramatic model he himself was creating. If he indeed did see The Living Theatre's production, this may have been responsible for his making the comparison between the monster and Kaspar in his preface.

In addition to the abstract Everyman entrapped by language, the figure of Kaspar may suggest, more specifically, the poet, who, in sacrificing his unique language to one of everyday formulations, relinquishes his distinctive voice and permanently ensures the distance between man and his world. The seeds of this idea will flourish in Handke's later work, beginning with *Short Letter,*

Long Farewell, in which he thinks in terms of two languages—
everyday and poetic—and mourns the loss of the latter. Even in
1967, though, when Handke was still an angry young man, his
work was beginning to look to language as not only the source of
chaos but its solution as well.

4

My Foot My Tutor

It may seem surprising that after the speech plays and *Kaspar*, which were so relentlessly concerned with language, Handke's next play should contain no language at all. *My Foot My Tutor (Das Mündel will Vormund sein*, 1969), however, which premiered at Frankfurt's Theater am Turm in January 1969, eight months after *Kaspar*, is entirely consistent with the earlier work in both philosophy and dramaturgy. Handke himself remarked, in an interview for the Munich *Abendzeitung*, that this "contemplative" piece is "another version of *Kaspar*."[1]

Das Mündel will Vormund sein, literally translated, is "The Ward Wants to Be Guardian." *My Foot My Tutor* is the quotation from Shakespeare's *The Tempest* that Handke uses as an epigraph and that is usually rendered in German as "Was, das Mündel will Vormund sein?" With either title, the suggestion of a master-slave relationship is clear, and the actions and images of dominance and servility make this silent piece most immediately reminiscent of *Kaspar*. Consisting of a similar educational experience, the movement of *My Foot My Tutor* passes from the "tiefer Frieden"[2] ("profound peacefulness"[3]) of the opening scene to the dissection and destruction in the beet-chopping sequence, and, finally, to the Ward's closing activity of pouring sand into a basin of water. Though the destruction of the subservient protagonist does not materialize here, as it does in *Kaspar*, the Warden, like the *Einsager*, controls the protagonist's every move.

In the play's opening scene, the Ward, disturbed by the Warden's sudden presence, is cowed into leaving his apple half eaten; the intrusion proves to be one of several assaults that reduce the Ward to meekness. When the two men sit at opposite ends of the table, a position which is to begin each new sequence of action, the Warden extends his legs and the Ward does likewise, only to draw

51

them back under his chair when they interfere with the Warden's. His repeated backing off, however, is only one sign of the Ward's subservience. He also imitates the Warden, placing his hands on the table when the Warden does so, lowering his head when the Warden lowers his, and climbing atop the table, yet remaining below the height of the Warden, who himself has climbed atop a chair atop the table. And the Ward waits on the Warden: he fetches the Warden's newspaper, arranges his boots and socks, and picks up his nail clippings. The relationship remains an indefinite one, however—are they father and son, employer and employee, prison warden and prisoner?—permitting the significance of the play to extend beyond a specific relationship to a more general situation in which someone, or something, is subservient.

As in *Kaspar,* the master-slave relationship in *My Foot My Tutor* is both destructive and inescapable. In *Kaspar,* learning language accounts for Kaspar's loss of self-expression and individuality, a fact dramatized by the presence of the other Kaspars and the schizophrenic behavior of the protagonist just before his destruction. In *My Foot My Tutor,* Handke suggests the negative quality of the relationship more subtly, yet it surfaces as an equally frightening phenomenon. The opening scene, for example, is intended to be idyllic: the Ward, in a bucolic setting, unselfconsciously munches on an apple, anticipating the enjoyment of a second, until the appearance and uncompromising stares of the Warden disturb him. The Ward may leave the fruit unfinished because he has become conscience-stricken over the violation of some rule (he perhaps should be working) or simply because he has become self-conscious (Sartre's "ocular assault"). In either case his enjoyment ceases, and the idyllic world disappears as he and the Warden reappear inside the more confined atmosphere of the house, where the Ward continues to cease certain activities—such as drawing on his arm or gazing around the room—as he realizes he has been noticed.

Yet one is never quite certain whether the Ward is emotionally capable of securing his freedom. One thinks of similar parasitic relationships in the plays of Beckett, most notably those of Hamm and Clov in *Endgame* (*Fin de partie,* 1957) and Pozzo and Lucky in

Waiting for Godot. In these dependencies the pair is inseparable in spite of the blatant maltreatment of one. Though perfectly mobile, Clov confines himself to a boxlike structure and suffers the abuse of his blind, wheelchair-ridden master, unable to leave. Lucky, once capable of reciting eloquent poetry and thinking original thought, will carry his master's picnic basket, crawl on all fours, and beg before he will sever the rope that binds him to Pozzo. Kaspar, though physically unbound, is, like Clov, bound by "the dialogue" and reduced to a subservient position through language. In the case of the Ward and Warden, Handke permits us only speculation as to what binds the two, but dramatically emphasizes their inseparability in a scene in which the Warden, after abusing the Ward, walks out the door, only to have the Ward cling to the door handle and then scamper after him through a hole in the wall.

The title of the play reflects the Ward's dissatisfaction with his lot in life; the Shakespearean allusion, ending as it does with a question mark, further suggests amazement over the possibility that someone who is in a subservient position could hope to be master not merely of his own fate but of another human being. When the Warden arbitrarily decides to assault the Ward physically with a barrage of bottles, plates, and glasses, the audience silently defends the underdog and is rather pleased at the Ward's success, though accidental, in catching one of the objects, interpreting this as a minor victory in a game of one-upmanship. Similarly, when the Ward throws burrs at the Warden's back, the audience silently applauds this act of aggression as an attempt at rebellion.

In the presence of the potentially destructive beet-cutting machine, that mysterious object concealed beneath a black raincoat since the beginning of the play, the audience's imagination awakens to the possibility that the Ward will achieve his dream through this newly learned art of beet-chopping. Indeed, Handke suggested just such an uprising on the part of a ward once before, in "Eyewitness Report." In that short story, a subservient idiot, having learned to operate such a machine, inserts his master's head in it and with great difficulty keeps chopping away until the head is severed from the neck. Though the play only suggests such violence, just before writing *My Foot My Tutor* Handke was working on a play, subsequently scrapped, with a title similar to that of the story: *Eyewitness (Der Augenzeuge).*[4]

We never know precisely what happens to the Warden. Are the beets a symbol of the relationship? In severing their heads, has the Ward severed his ties as well? Does the recurring sound of labored breathing, perhaps of one in his death throes, suggest the Warden has been killed? The final scene returns to the outdoors and to the bizarre behavior of the Ward, who, having filled a basin with water in much the same manner as his master had earlier filled the tea kettle, slowly allows sand to run through his fingers into the water. One thinks of the metaphorical sands of time, recalling the earlier scene where pages are torn from a calendar, and also of Beckett's repeated symbolic use of sand. Yet one comes to no conclusions, precisely because Handke intended none. In fact, despite obvious allusions, Handke specifically denies that any Beckett-like situation exists or that *My Foot My Tutor* has any symbolic meaning.[5]

One may be tempted to read meaning into the boiling of water, the grinding of coffee, the chopping of beets, or the pouring of sand, but any attempt to do so would be a strain. Those actions which do contribute to the dominance-subservience motif are abundant enough to convey this theme. But not all actions are so readily explainable, and one must finally look to what Handke was attempting with the play dramaturgically in order to understand them.

Following a production in Paris by the Bread and Puppet Theatre from New York, Handke spoke of his conviction that direct presentation of actions and words should replace the traditional dramaturgy which uses only those actions and words that *serve* the story. In "The Misery of Comparison," Handke writes that he would hope to create a theater in which actions, words, and sounds

werden Vorgänge, die nichts andres zeigen, sondern sich selber vorzeigen als theatralische Vorgänge: Handlungen handeln von sich selber und Wörter reden von sich selber: der Zuschauer, der im Theater die *Finalität* jedes Wortes und jeder Handlung auf einen thematischen Sinn, auf eine Geschichte *zu* erwartet, wird mit der Handlung alleingelassen. Das Heben der Hand ist eine Geschichte. Das Summen ist eine Geschichte. Sitzen, Liegen, Stehen sind Geschichten. Eine sehr spannende Geschichte ist das Schlagen eines Hammers auf Eisen. Jedes Wort, jeder Laut, jede Bewegung ist eine Geschichte: sie führen zu nichts, sie bleiben für sich allein sichtbar. So wird jede Natur auf der Bühne aufgehoben: jede Äußerung wird gerade *gemacht*, keine Handlung ergibt sich natürlich aus der vorhergehenden Handlung, keine Äußerung bedeutet etwas anderes außer sich selber, sie *deutet sich selber*.[6]

become incidents which show nothing else, but present themselves as theatrical events. Actions act themselves and words talk themselves. The viewer, who awaits in the theatre the resolution of every word and every action, the thematic sense, the story, will be left with the action alone. The raising of a hand is a story. Buzzing is a story. Sitting, lying, and standing are stories. A very exciting story is the striking of a hammer against iron. Every word, every sound, every movement is a story: they lead to nothing, they remain visible for themselves alone. Every utterance is *made;* no action results naturally from the preceding action; no utterance means anything other than itself—it signifies itself.[7]

Handke attempted to create a semiotics of theater in all his early plays, and in *My Foot My Tutor* in particular. How otherwise can one respond to the Warden's boiling of water and the Ward's subsequent grinding of coffee, for surely these actions make no contribution to either "story" or theme. In that sequence of action the Warden, who tends to the mundane chore himself, is no more dominant than the Ward, whose task of grinding coffee neither imitates the Warden's action nor differs qualitatively from it. How also can one otherwise respond to the insertion of prerecorded breathing sounds into the action? One may speculatively impose a symbolic meaning upon the laborious breathing that follows the beet-chopping, but how does one interpret the breathing that follows the apple-eating scene? Without context in the play's "story," how does one attribute symbolic value to the Ward's nosebleed, which he experiences without reaction just prior to being assaulted with objects? Clearly no cause-and-effect relationship exists between several of the play's scenes, and not all the play's actions contribute to the idea of dominance and servility.

Yet one is exceedingly reluctant to attach the label of "absurd" to any of these actions. Handke's play world has no discernible metaphysical dimension nor any references to the absence of it, making it inappropriate to respond to this piece as one would to a Beckett play. In fact, the unrelated and unexplainable actions of *My Foot My Tutor* are purely theatrical events. Commenting on *My Foot My Tutor*, Handke refers to the objects and actions on stage: "Sie seien, was sie darstellten, theatralische Szenen eben, und sonst gar nichts"[8] ("They were what they represented, just theatrical scenes and nothing more").

In the preface to *Kaspar*, Handke expressed his intention that the audience "erkennen sofort, daß sie einem Vorgang zusehen werden, der nicht in irgendeiner Wirklichkeit, sondern auf der Bühne spielt. Sie werden keine Geschichte miterleben, sondern einen theatralischen Vorgang sehen"[9] ("should recognize at once that they will witness an event that plays only on stage and not in some other reality. . . . They will not experience a story but watch a theatrical event"[10]). Since that play consists of carefully integrated sequential scenes reflecting the development of Kaspar's situation, however, the play's social significance, which Handke intended to be only secondary, surfaces as prominently as the dramaturgy. Through a continual flow of events which all serve the story, *Kaspar* effectively reflects Handke's vision of the relationship between language and behavior, yet the play argues less convincingly for the autonomy of the theatrical event. *My Foot My Tutor*, like *Kaspar*, also has social significance. In fact, for a 1969 article in *Theater heute* concerning the play, Handke helped create a collage which includes a newspaper clipping and several posters regarding "Mitbestimmung," the cry of the German Trade Unions Congress, echoed by university student groups, actors, and others, for a voice in their own government.[11] But in *My Foot My Tutor*, Handke succeeds in subordinating the social dimension to the theatrical event. It may be that he created this "other version of *Kaspar*" precisely because he sensed the dramaturgical shortcoming, in terms of his own philosophy, of his first full-length play. Or it may be that *Kaspar*, having demonstrated the "idiocy of language," could only be followed by silence.

The most notable difference between *Kaspar* and *My Foot My*

Tutor is, of course, that the first relies almost solely on language, whereas the second contains no spoken words. Explaining that he was fascinated by the idea of bringing optical and acoustical processes onto the stage without language,[12] Handke created a play whose sparseness and precision awaken the audience to the theatrical process itself. The play, which could be performed in fifteen minutes or two and a half hours,[13] but which usually lasts an hour, engages the audience's visual and auditory senses throughout, to a degree not usually expected in the theater, making it hyper-aware of every movement and sound. Like a silent movie (music is played throughout and the play is rich with other such associations), because it is without explanatory text, the play forces the audience to pay particularly close attention or be in danger of missing something which will not later be explained.[14] As a result, nothing onstage goes unobserved, no sound unheard. The exceedingly self-conscious nature of the play creates the simultaneity of sight and sound of which Handke speaks in "The Misery of Comparison," making each member of the audience aware of his or her own sensual reception and thoughts.

In the interview for the *Abendzeitung,* Handke says that in *My Foot My Tutor* he hoped to isolate processes, like sitting, walking, or eating, from the plot.[15] This goal of liberation is curiously consistent with the dominance-servility theme, for the play frees the elements of drama from their traditional status.

My Foot My Tutor, however, seems only to have been an experiment, and perhaps a corrective to *Kaspar*. Handke himself refers to it as an étude in preparation for his next major play,[16] and in *The Ride Across Lake Constance,* which once again resumes the use of language, he finally achieves what he considers his best piece of drama, one which may truly be called "pure" theater. Before creating the full-length play, however, which Handke himself suggested might still be years in the future,[17] he tested his ideas further in another short piece, *Quodlibet.*

5
Quodlibet

Although *Quodlibet* (1969) was written shortly after *My Foot My Tutor*, it was not staged until January 24, 1970, when the Baseler Theater, under the direction of Hans Hollmann, undertook the production of this fragile piece of drama. Handke was present on opening night, and afterward joined in a discussion of the piece in which he referred to the members of the audience as Pavlovian dogs, reacting in predictable ways based on previously established stimulus-response patterns.[1] Some in the audience objected to the association, protesting they had not responded in the way Handke described, but were only perplexed at not having been able to hear the whole of the conversations on stage nor decipher those words and sentence fragments which had been spoken in a slightly louder tone. Others undoubtedly were drawn into the theatrical experience sufficiently to react in the way Handke had anticipated they would; they, in retrospect, would probably most clearly understand Handke's intent in this peculiar theater piece.

Quodlibet, which may be translated from the Latin as "What You Will" or "As You Like It," is the most loosely structured of all Handke's plays, permitting a director almost total freedom in orchestrating the piece and the actors free license to create virtually all their own dialogue. In a note to the play, Handke cautions against having the few prescribed words and sentences follow one another too regularly, suggesting such articulations might even present themselves simultaneously at times. Yet he sees the play as "eine organische, verschlungene, trotzdem ganz klar strukturierte Abfolge von Sprache und Bewegungen"[2] ("an organic, intertwined, nevertheless very clearly structured succession of language and movement").

It was not surprising that some members of the discussion group in Basel complained of hearing problems, for Handke did

not intend that the audience hear everything that is spoken on
stage. In fact, the play specifically functions on that assumption,
creating its meaning not out of its dialogue but out of its misunderstandings. What is *not* said—or, what the audience *thinks* is
said—is far more significant than what *is* said. For example, at one
point the word "ausschwitzen" (to sweat) is mentioned, a word
which could readily be mistaken for "Auschwitz." Continuing the
violence motif, the words "no palms" (in Roloff's English adaptation)[3] may be heard as "napalm," "hero sandwich" as
"Hiroshima," "bicycle path" as "psychopath," "dirty knickers" as
"dirty niggers," "Sisyphus" as "syphilis." Or the audience may
hear only certain words of a sentence, such as "bomb" in "what a
bomb this play was," or "shot through his head" in "thoughts shot
through his head," or "clap" in "thunderclap." In fact, the entire
play consists of the overlapping conversations of eleven characters who spend most of their time speaking inaudibly, but whose
individual voices occasionally rise to mislead the audience into
thinking it has finally deciphered a portion of the dialogue.

Speaking in an interview with Rainer Litten about his purpose,
Handke explains:

Ich wollte mit dem *Quodlibet* eben zeigen, wie die Leute reagieren, auf
einzelne Wörter und Sätze. . . . Und darüber wollte ich eigentlich ein
Stück schreiben: Wie man hört und wie man schaut, ein Stück über die
Wahrnehmungsästhetik, und wie komplex das ist und wie subtil, und
wie man im Theater sofort inhaltlich reagiert auf Formen.[4]

With *Quodlibet,* I wanted to show how people react to single words and
sentences. . . . And I wanted to write a piece about that: how one hears
and sees, a piece about the aesthetics of perception, and how complex
that is and how subtle, and how in the theater one reacts to forms with
immediate concern for content.

No less so than in his earlier work, Handke is still exploring the
theatrical experience. Populating his stage with what he calls "the
figures of world theater"—general, bishop, dean, Maltese knight,
German student, Chicago gangster, politician, two bodyguards,
dance contest couple, "grand dame," and pants-suit-clad woman
with poodle—Handke not only recalls theatrical clichés through
these figures' identities, all readily recognizable by their uniforms,

but, in the note to the play, further insists on the theatricality of the cast:

Die Figuren treffen sich nicht auf einer PARTY, bilden keine PARTY-Sprechfiguren, begrüßen sich nicht, WIE auf einer Party, treffen sich nicht IRGENDWO oder IM IRGENDWO, sondern auf der Bühne.[5]

The figures do not meet at a PARTY, form no PARTY-conversation figures, do not greet each other AS at a party, do not meet SOME-WHERE or IN SOME PLACE, but on the stage.

Among the characters onstage, only the two bodyguards do not speak; they spend the entire forty minutes or so of playtime (the piece may be stretched out to any length) looking around. The members of the audience not only notice their glances, but as they follow the glances around the theater, they become more conscious of the fact that they are in a theater. The searching looks of the bodyguards, however, conspicuously avoid the audience itself, suggesting what the other characters demonstrate: an ostensibly complete indifference to its presence. Though the traditional stance of drama is to pretend the audience does not exist, Handke's play goes beyond such realism, ostensibly ignoring his audience to the point of not even having the dialogue spoken loudly enough to be understood.

The acoustic irritation toward which Handke had been working in the *Sprechstücke* seems to be clearly realized here in a piece dominated at times by the confusion of overlapping conversations, at times by silence, and at times by the mere rustling of the actors' clothes. The overall effect is one in which the audience, unable to distinguish clearly the dialogue it feels it should be hearing, is understandably frustrated. The emotional effect Handke wants to achieve is no small order:

Furcht und Mitleid, Zärtlichkeit und Wut. Furcht vor der Unabänderlichkeit, die die Figuren darstellen, Mitleid für ihre träumerische Abgeschlossenheit, Zärtlichkeit für ihre Schönheit, Wut über ihr Selbstbewußtsein und ihre Ruhe.[6]

Fear and pity, tenderness and rage. Fear of the immutability which the figures represent, pity for their dreamy seclusion, tenderness for their beauty, rage over their self-consciousness and their silence.

Though surely Handke is reaching too high when he foresees this curiously Aristotelian reaction to his play, *Quodlibet* does indeed stimulate through emotional and intellectual irritation and cannot help succeeding in "getting under the skin" of the audience.

In *Quodlibet*, Handke is also continuing his exploration into the nature of language. The comment about the Pavlovian dog, inspired perhaps by Beckett's play *Act Without Words* (*Acte sans paroles*, 1957), performed at the same *Experimenta* as *Offending the Audience*, neatly distills Handke's resentment toward a public which responds without thought to an established lexicon. Transferring the comparison to the Pavlovian dog from the character, as in Beckett's play, to the audience itself, Handke creates an ingenious construct of words and phrases that suggests the rhetoric of sex, politics, and violence, areas in which emotions are likely to be volatile. The success of the play depends on the audience's predictable associations and responses. Though the dialogue that the audience strains to hear contains nothing sexual, when so many words and phrases *sound* like sexual references, the sheer accumulation of such a seeming vocabulary will begin to dominate response, and the audience will almost automatically hear "ramrods have passed" as "rammed a rod up his ass" or "forgot the cows" as "fucked the cows." Handke expects that the audience will be annoyed by the preponderance of such indecorous utterings and will respond to the associations they themselves supply. The play not only protests the predictable correspondences implicit in an emotionally prescriptive language, so also does it point to the equivocal nature of a language that can distort reality as well as control it. The characters, after all, never say such things in the first place.

But as with *My Foot My Tutor*, *Quodlibet* is only a *Vorspiel*, a prologue to *The Ride Across Lake Constance*. Although not used as a curtain raiser for the longer work, it would have appropriately served as one. While still working on his second full-length play, Handke was asked some questions concerning *Quodlibet* and remarked:

Quodlibet ist eigentlich nur das Vorspiel zu einem längeren Stück, das ich schreibe. Es heißt *Der Ritt über den Bodensee*. Da kommen die gleichen Welttheaterfiguren vor: der General, der Bischof, der Rektor der Universität usw. Aber sie treten in ganz anderen, deutlicheren Beziehungen zueinander auf. Es findet eine Geschichte statt zwischen diesen Figuren. . . . Das Klima dieser Figuren, ihre Bewußtseinshaltung wird in *Quodlibet* analysiert, und im *Ritt über den Bodensee* wird dann in Einzelheiten gezeigt, wohin die Bewußtseinhaltung dieser Figuren führt in den alltäglichen Beziehungen der Menschen.[7]

Quodlibet is really only the prologue to a longer piece that I am writing. It is called *The Ride Across Lake Constance*. There the same figures of world theater appear: the general, the bishop, the dean of the university, etc. But they appear in other, clearer relationships to one another. A story takes place among these figures. . . . The climate of these figures, their self-conscious behavior, is in *Quodlibet* analyzed and then in *The Ride Across Lake Constance* it will be shown in detail what the self-conscious behavior of these figures leads to in the daily relationships of men.

6

The Ride Across Lake Constance

If theatergoers expected to find in *The Ride Across Lake Constance* (*Der Ritt über den Bodensee,* 1970) the clarity of relationships missing from *Quodlibet,* they could only have experienced one hour and forty minutes of frustration. Instead of relationships measurable in familiar terms, the language and gestures of the play's five main characters (who, though not the same figures of world theater Handke had promised, are nonetheless stock theatrical characters) are strung together in a seemingly nonsensical order, with no apparent deference to traditional patterns of behavior. As William L. Lederer points out in an essay in the *Chicago Review,* "Language is a convention arrived at by consensus, but in Handke's *Ride* there is no consensus. . . . all that is predictable in life is undermined on the stage."[1] Yet in an interview for the Munich *Abendzeitung,* Handke defends his play as realistic, as

einfach ein Stück über Gefühle, über die Liebe und wie man die zueinander äußert, über tägliche Verhaltensweisen, wenn man was einkauft, wenn man über das Sterben was erzählen will, das ist einfach ein ziemlich realistisches Stück.[2]

simply a play about feelings, about love and how people express these to each other, about daily behavioral modes, when one shops for something, when one wants to tell something about dying, it is simply a rather realistic play.

The premiere of *The Ride Across Lake Constance* took place on January 23, 1971, at the Berlin Schaubühne am Halleschen Ufer, under the direction of Claus Peymann and Wolfgang Wiens.[3] One year later, it was staged by Joseph Papp at Lincoln Center in New York, where it was received with more hisses than applause. Stanley Kauffmann commented on the irritation of an audience accustomed to a reasonably consistent vocabulary of the stage,

which *The Ride Across Lake Constance* does not offer: "It *is* disturbing and, for many, must be enraging. Not sexually: the sex content is very mild. Not politically or religiously: no overt mention of
these matters. The rage doesn't even come from direct affront, as
in Handke's earlier play *Offending the Audience*. It comes simply
from his utter contravention of what an audience expects from a
play."[4] In the *New York Times*, Clive Barnes remarked frankly: "To
say I didn't understand Peter Handke's play *The Ride Across Lake
Constance* . . . would be to underestimate shamefully the cavern-
ous profundity of my ignorance. The play had only been going
for two minutes when I realized that I did not know what was
going on."[5] The clarity and realism to which Handke had alluded
were apparently not visible. Yet Barnes and most of the other
reviewers were not simply perplexed, they were also intrigued,
and their fascination with this play expressed itself in judgments
which, though perhaps relying more on theatrical instinct than
critical insight, declared the piece an important one, even a
"landmark" of modern drama.[6]

The program issued by Schaubühne am Halleschen Ufer contained several pages of notes by Handke from which he constructed the play; it also contained an explanatory essay which, if
not especially helpful in interpreting the characters' individual
actions, does offer some insight into his intent. Referring to *My
Foot My Tutor* and *Quodlibet* as forerunners of this play, Handke
explains that in *The Ride Across Lake Constance* he wanted to demonstrate the modes of human interchange in our society through
precise observation:

Erste Versuche, diese Beobachtungen festzuhalten, waren dann die
Stücke *Das Mündel will Vormund sein* und *Quodlibet,* in denen Theater-
formen so von den sie sonst unkenntlich machenden Geschichten
isoliert erschienen, daß die Formen zu POSEN wurden und identisch
werden konnten mit Posen im täglichen Leben: die Darstellung der
Theaterposen war unter anderm ein Versuch, auch die täglichen Um-
gangsformen als Posen vorzuführen.[7]

The first attempts to define these observations were the plays *My Foot
My Tutor* and *Quodlibet,* in which theater forms appeared isolated from
the stories which otherwise make them unrecognizable, so that the
forms became POSES and could become identical with poses in daily

life: the presentation of theater poses was, among other things, also an attempt to present the modes of everyday behavior as poses.

Though more fully developed than his earlier studies in perception, *The Ride Across Lake Constance* functions in much the same way as the shorter pieces in attempting to achieve audience awareness. In *My Foot My Tutor,* actions were wrenched from their normal relationships to language and microscopically examined by an audience whose visual and auditory senses were magnified by the isolation of these events. Similarly, in *Quodlibet,* the audience was forced to strain its auditory capacity to its limits in order to discern the words and sentence fragments spoken onstage. Now, in *The Ride Across Lake Constance,* the audience, disoriented by its inability to perceive any correlation among the language, events, and objects onstage, pays particular attention to every word and gesture in an effort to find the familiar in the strange. Whatever the final effect, the audience is inescapably aware that Handke has annihilated the axiomatic structures of both the theater and reality.

In apparent contrast to the dialogue, the set of *The Ride Across Lake Constance* is arranged in a manner which evokes instant recognition for the theater audience; the furnishings are those typical of a nineteenth-century drawing room, characteristically arranged. The stage directions, however, reflect a self-consciousness which suggests Handke is not simply creating a Chekhovian set:

Alle Gegenstände stehen so sehr auf ihrem Platz, daß es schwer vorstellbar ist, sie woanders stehen zu sehen; sie könnten es nicht einmal ertragen, auch nur ein bißchen verrückt zu werden. Alles ist wie eingerastet, nicht nur die Gegenstände, sondern auch die Abstände und Zwischernräume.[8]

All objects are in such a position that it would be difficult to imagine them standing elsewhere; it is as though they could not bear being moved ever so slightly. Everything appears as though rooted to the spot, not only the objects themselves but also the distances and empty spaces between them.[9]

Within moments, it becomes clear that the carefully arranged furniture is before us not because Handke wishes to create an impression of realism, but rather because he wants to undercut that impression, for in the context of this unrealistic drama, the realistic drawing room quickly becomes precisely what it is: an obviously artificial stage set.

Two men, arbitrarily given the names of actors Emil Jannings and Heinrich George, begin the play with a conversation which might more accurately be called a linguistic game than communication. What would constitute the exposition in traditional dramaturgy becomes an introduction to the language games that will be played and the questions regarding the relationship between language and reality that will be raised. The first scene ends with George's declaration, "Das Leben ist ein Spiel" (p. 87) ("Life is a game," p. 87), a comment intended not as an epiphany but as a reference to just another clichéd expression which has lost its meaning and, by implication, to the relationship of the theater, which has also become stale from habit, to reality. Earlier in their exchange Jannings had pointed to the blue sky on the label of a cigar box and proclaimed with profundity, "Diesen blauen Himmel, den Sie da auf dem Etikett sehen, mein Lieber, den gibt es dort wirklich!" (p. 66) ("That blue sky you see on the label, my dear fellow, it really exists there," p. 74). The sky is not a representation, just as the play is not a representation; both possess an autonomous reality. Jannings and George discuss an incident of the past, now reduced to a story, and question its present reality. And they name things, considering what each name designates. They find it ridiculous to speak of kidneys flambé, something that is not present, but quite satisfactory to talk of Jannings's rings, which have physical presence and correspond to and confirm the mental image of them. Jannings and George look around the room and pronounce names: "Auto!" "Affenschaukel!" "Bluthende!" "Hungerödeme!" "Ausklinkknopf!" (p. 71) ("Car." "Cattle prod." "Bloodhounds." "Swollen bellies." "Trigger button," p. 81). But, of course, these names bear no relationship to what is onstage.

Moments after the beginning of the play, the audience (with Barnes) is not only asking what is going on, but, with Jannings and George, it is asking what constitutes reality. Are the rings which are present in the phenomenal world and which can be identified by language the only true reality? Or are the kidneys flambé, which can be recalled and named but are not now visible, just as real? And what of objects that have physical presence but are either referred to by names which traditionally designate certain objects now without physical presence, or those which do not have the equivalent in an acceptable language pattern, such as "feurigen Eskimo" (p. 75) ("fiery Eskimo," p. 85)? Are these real? Is the world the totality of things; or is it, as Wittgenstein's *Tractatus* suggests, the totality of facts; or is it the totality of possibilities? What then are the responsibilities and the limitations of language? The play continues to assault linguistic conventions through repeated use of non sequiturs, examinations of the logical possibilities of a premise, alogical progression, and confusions with respect to the designations of language—all in an attempt to disturb our comfortable sense of the way language corresponds to our perceptions of reality.

In one instance, we see how language can be prescriptive. As Porten descends the stairs, George and Jannings count: "One, two, three, four, five, and seven!" When she hears "seven," she is just about to place her foot on the sixth step, becomes greatly disturbed, and retreats to the top of the stairs. She resumes her descent. "One, two, three, four, five, six, and seven!" But there is an eighth step, over which Porten stumbles; she is again upset, and rushes back to the top. On her third descent, George and Jannings count again: "one, two, three, four, five, six, seven, eight, nine!" But there are only eight steps, and at the count of "nine," she bounces on the floor, her knees buckle, and she staggers. It is a fine example of the lesson taught by the *Einsager* in *Kaspar:* "wenn du den Gegenstand anders siehst als du von ihm sprichst, mußt du dich irren" ("if you *see* the object differently from the way you *speak* it, you must be mistaken").[10]

Jannings and George engage in a game of commands, each in turn demanding an object: "Die Zeitung!" "Meine Brille!" "Den Senf!" "Die Haarbürste!" "Das Fotoalbum!" Die Pinzette!" "Das Skalpell!" "Die Schere!" "Die Kombizange!" "Den Schraubenschlüssel!" "Den Lötkolben!" "Die Sonne!" (pp. 85–86) ("The newspaper!" "My glasses!" "The mustard!" "The hairbrush!" "The photo album!" "The pincers!" "The scalpel!" "The scissors!"

"The pliers!" "The monkey wrench!" "The soldering iron!" "The sun!" p. 94). When questioned, "Warum die Sonne?" ("Why the sun?"), Jannings defends his command: "Das sind *meine Worte!* Ich weiß es nicht" ("Those are *my words.* I don't know why.") And George insists, "Es ändert doch nichts, daß Sie es sagen" ("Your saying so doesn't change anything"). He has suggested the other side of the coin: where Porten's descent suggested the power of language to control reality, we now have the suggestion of a reality that exists independently of language, which may be designated by, but not altered by, language. Von Stroheim strongly objects, "Falsch! Ganz falsch!" (p. 86) ("Wrong! Entirely wrong!" p. 95).

Other examples of the relationship or nonrelationship of language to reality occur. Porten asks, "Welche Schneestürme?" (p. 84) ("What snowstorms?" p. 92), long after snowstorms are mentioned. George asks for the first time, "Noch einmal: ich biete Ihnen meinen Fauteuil an! . . . Darf ich Ihnen meinen Fauteuil anbieten?" (p. 83) ("Once more: I offer you my fauteuil. . . . May I offer you my fauteuil?" p. 91). Bergner cries, "Passen Sie auf, der Kerzenhalter fällt um!" (p. 83) ("Watch out! the candlestick is falling!" p. 92). The candlestick remains motionless on the table.

Von Stroheim and Porten have each experienced moments in which they fully understood language as a correlative of reality. Von Stroheim tells his story: "Ich saß am Morgen am Ufer eines Sees, und der See glitzerte. Plötzlich fiel mir auf: der See *glitzert.* Er glitzert ja wirklich" (p. 108) ("I was sitting by a lakeshore in the morning and the lake was sparkling. Suddenly I noticed: the lake is *sparkling.* It is really sparkling," p. 114). And Porten tells hers: "Mir erging es einmal ähnlich, als mir jemand sagte, daß seine Taschen leer seien. 'Meine Taschen sind leer!' Ich glaubte ihm nicht, und er stülpte seine Taschen nach außen: sie waren wirklich leer! Unglaublich!" (p. 108) ("Something similar happened to me one time when someone told me that his pockets were empty. 'My pockets are empty!' I didn't believe him and he turned his pockets inside out. They really were empty. Incredible!" p. 114).

The action sequences in *The Ride Across Lake Constance* do not conform to any recognizable real action; they consist of unmotivated acts and alogical responses, yet the pattern these actions form appears somehow vaguely familiar. Jannings and George, for example, engage in a series of gestures which are observed by Bergner, apparently without judgment: the two slap each other's thighs, pull each other's ears, and pat each other's cheeks; then Jannings shows George the back of his hand, George makes a circle with his forefinger and thumb and holds his hand in front of his face; Jannings raises his hands above his head, clasps one wrist with the thumb and forefinger of the other hand, and lets the clasped hand circle about. Each gesture bears no apparent causal relationship to the next, but the series is smoothly enacted and is followed by an outburst of laughter by the two men and exclamations of "Genau!" "Erraten!" (p. 78) ("Exactly!" "You guessed it!" p. 88). There has apparently been some form of communication, some understanding involved in the silent gestures, but it is alien to the audience's preconceived notions of logically motivated and interpreted action.

In another sequence involving von Stroheim and Porten, gestures that begin as apparent signs of affection end in apparent violence, and the final act is palpably alogical. Von Stroheim first places his finger under Porten's chin, lifting her face, then strokes the back of her head and pats her fondly on the shoulder. These actions are followed by his drumming two fingers on her cheek, snapping his fingers against her teeth, lowering her eyelid with his finger, and patting her rather hard on the buttocks. At the end of the sequence, Porten is positioned with her back to von Stroheim, who stands with his left knee raised, apparently ready to kick her.

Not all the action sequences appear absurd because they do not conform to our traditional patterns. Some are poses that have usual associations but here are stripped bare, revealing simple, dissociated actions:

HENNY PORTEN: Jemand schaut sich öfter um, während er geht: hat er ein schlechtes Gewissen?

ELIZABETH BERGNER: Nein, er schaut sich nur einfach öfter um?

HENNY PORTEN: Jemand sitzt mit gesenkten Kopf da: er ist traurig?

ELIZABETH BERGNER: . . . Nein, er sitzt einfach nur mit gesenktem Kopf da!

HENNY PORTEN: Jemand zuckt zusammen: schuldbewußt?

ELIZABETH BERGNER: . . . Nein, er zuckt nur einfach zusammen!

HENNY PORTEN: Zwei sitzen da, schauen einander nicht an und schweigen: sind sie böse aufeinander?
ELIZABETH BERGNER: . . . Nein, sie sitzen nur einfach da, schauen einander nicht an und schweigen!
HENNY PORTEN: Jemand schlägt auf den Tisch: um seinen willen durchzusetzen?
ELIZABETH BERGNER: . . . Darf er nicht einmal nur einfach auf den Tisch schlagen? (Pp. 100–01)

PORTEN: Someone keeps looking over his shoulder while he's walking. Does he have a guilty conscience?
BERGNER: No, he simply looks over his shoulder from time to time.
PORTEN: Someone is sitting there with lowered head. Is he sad?
BERGNER: . . . No, he simply sits there with lowered head.
PORTEN: Someone is flinching. Conscience-stricken?
BERGNER: . . . No, he's simply flinching.
PORTEN: Two people sit there, don't look at each other, and are silent. Are they angry with one another?
BERGNER: . . . No, they simply sit there, don't look at each other, and are silent.
PORTEN: Someone bangs on the table. To get his way?
BERGNER: . . . Couldn't he for once simply bang on the table? (Pp. 107–08)

In Handke's theater, every act and every word finds significance in itself; it does not represent. In traditional drama and in life, no action or word is free from the previous one, and no action or word exists for its own sake—action and language are arranged in patterns that have set interpretations. In Handke's drama, language and action still constitute the play and they still fall into patterns, but the patterns are not familiar ones. They are fresh combinations which have been freed to create new meanings. *The Ride Across Lake Constance* rejects clichés, presenting instead that intensely artificial event of which Handke speaks and creating a self-conscious theater which exists not mimetically, but as its own spontaneous, self-defining reality.

Handke has said that he was attempting, through the creation of theatrical poses, to present the modes of daily behavior as poses as well. His designation of the dramatis personae of *The Ride Across Lake Constance*—"die Personen sind zugleich ihre Darsteller" (p. 56) ("The actors are and play themselves at one and the same time," p. 69)—suggests an identity closer to that of a real-life individual than that of a traditional dramatic character. Handke does not even give his players fictive names, using, in the German text, the names of famous movie stars (Jannings, George, Bergner, von Stroheim, Porten, Kessler) simply to avoid the designations "Actor A" and "Actor B." But in performance, all the actors are called by their own names, minimizing the usual consciousness on the part of an audience that an actor is assuming the part of a character for the sake of performance. Here we are viewing a role-playing individual possessing no reality beyond his role. We are actually witnessing character-in-the-making. As the play progresses, the actors "discover who they are onstage in terms of each other, give each other identities, play identities, are captured by their identities—their identities become their roles or vice versa; are held together by the relationships they establish with each other—which at first are only a playing, but into which they get locked."[11]

Handke is obviously aware of how a character can become stagnant, not only in drama but in life. In his explanatory essay on *The Ride Across Lake Constance,* he comments that "Der letzte Gedanke an *Kaspar* wurde der erste Gedanke zu *Der Ritt über den Bodensee*"[12] ("The last idea in *Kaspar* became the first idea in *The Ride Across Lake Constance*"). As in *Kaspar,* where the central character is "normalized" to the point of metaphorical multiplication, *The Ride Across Lake Constance* dramatizes the fact that identity is no longer an individual's essence, but the product of prescribed responses. Because Bergner has been tender previously, she is expected to be tender now; her past action has determined her present action. Von Stroheim and George demonstrate how one of them can identify a person on the strength of predetermined associations:

STROHEIM: . . . Jemand täschelt einen Gegenstand oder lehnt sich an ihn?

GEORGE: Der Eigentümer!

STROHEIM: Jemand bewegt sich mit eingezogenen Schultern zwischen Sachen, macht einen Bogen um sie?

GEORGE: Der Gast!
STROHEIM: Jemand, der schielt, hält einen Gegenstand in der Hand?
GEORGE: Der Dieb! (Pp. 110–11)

VON STROHEIM: . . . Someone fondles an object or leans against it?
GEORGE: The proprietor.
VON STROHEIM: Someone moves with hunched shoulders among objects, makes a curve around them?
GEORGE: The guest.
VON STROHEIM: Someone who is squinting holds an object in his hand?
GEORGE: The thief. (P. 116)

Von Stroheim abhors how readily actions are translated into patterned meanings. He insists it is as ridiculous to interpret someone's feelings or thoughts by his actions as it is to call an easy chair a life preserver. And he demonstrates how he can predict responses: by asking Jannings what he has in his mouth he can make Jannings remove his cigar; by asking Jannings why his collar button is open he can make Jannings close his collar button; by drawing attention to Jannings's seriousness he can make Jannings laugh. Handke shows that character in life has become the fixed entity it has been in drama. Not only do we learn to interpret a person's character by his actions, we also learn to expect certain actions of him. And, even more importantly, the person begins to respond in accordance with our expectations. Bergner asks:

Spreche ich dir zuviel? Habe ich dir zu spitze Knie? Bin ich dir zu schwer? Ist dir meine Nase zu groß? Bin ich dir zu vernünftig? Bin ich dir zu laut? Sind die Brüste zu klein? Bin ich dir zu fett? Bin ich dir zu schnell? Bin ich dir zu mager? War ich gut? (P. 119)

Do I talk too much for you? Are my knees too bony? Am I too heavy for you? Is my nose too big? Am I too sensible for you? Do you find me too loud? Are my breasts too small? Do you think I'm too fat? Am I too fast for you? Am I too skinny for you? Was I good? (P. 124)

And Jannings assesses her remarks: "Du siehst, sie selber sorgt für die Kategorien, in denen man von ihr denkt" (p. 119) ("You see, she herself uses the categories in which one thinks of her," p. 124). When this line of characterization is carried to the extreme, the terrifying result is an unthinking automaton, completely submissive to control:

JANNINGS: . . . Sie haben es einmal getan, ohne daß ich etwas gesagt habe, im Halbschlaf oder weil es sich so ergab. Dann sagte ich es, und sie taten es wieder. Dann fragten sie mich: 'Darf ich das für Sie tun?', und ich sagte: 'Du sollst!' Und von da an taten sie es, ohne daß ich etwas sagen mußte. Es hatte sich eingebürgert. Ich könnte mit dem Fuß auf etwas zeigen, und sie würden springen und es holen! . . . eine Ordnung ergab sich, und um weiter miteinander verkehren zu können, machte man diese Ordnung ausdrücklich: man formulierte sie. Und als man sie formuliert hatte, mußte man sich daran halten, weil man sie schließlich formuliert hatte! (P. 116)

JANNINGS: . . . They did it once without my saying anything while they were half asleep, or because it just happened like that. Then I said it and they did it again. Then they asked me: 'May I do that for you?' and I said: 'You shall!' And from then on they did it without my having to say anything. It had become the custom. I could point my *foot* at something and they would jump and get it. . . . An order resulted; and for people to continue to socialize with one another, this order was made explicit: it was formulated. And once it had been formulated, people had to stick to it because, after all, they had formulated it. (P. 122)

This vision of absolute power, of dominance and submission, which Handke explored in *My Foot My Tutor* and so closely related to language in *Kaspar,* pervasively informs *The Ride Across Lake Constance* as well. One reviewer, who could otherwise see no meaning or value in the play, acknowledges "the exercise of power and authority" as the one coherent theme, suggesting that the relationship between Jannings and George "may represent the eerie bond between Germany and Hitler."[13] Those two characters do, in fact, have what could be called a master-slave relationship, very much akin to that of the Warden and Ward in the earlier play.

The tone of this relationship is set by the early conversation concerning kidneys flambé, in which Jannings intimidates George into admitting that because he has no knowledge of kidneys flambé, he should not talk of them. The domination becomes an overt issue when Bergner, trying to understand why Jannings has answered the question posed to George, asks, "Sind Sie denn mächtiger als er?" (p. 84) ("Are you more powerful than he is?" p.

93). As though newly struck with the idea, Jannings replies, "Mächtiger? Ja. . . . Ja, warum nicht?" (p. 85) ("More powerful? Yes. . . . Yes, why not?" p. 93). And, in affirmation of this power, he begins to issue commands, which George immediately obeys. The extent of Jannings's control over George becomes disturbingly obvious when at a point later in the play George questions one of Jannings's commands, asking, "Wenn ich aber nicht will?" (p. 115) ("But what if I don't want to?" p. 121), and Jannings, addressing George now in the familiar "du" form, replies:

Jetzt ist es zu spät. Die ganze Zeit hast du getan, was ich dir gesagt habe, und nie etwas gesagt. Du warst bis jetzt zufrieden, sonst hättest du etwas gesagt—warum solltest du also jetzt unzufrieden sein? Du hast die ganze Zeit nicht widersprochen—wie solltest du also jetzt widersprechen dürfen? Nein, was du jetzt sagst, gilt nicht mehr! Tu, was ich dir sage! (P. 115)

Now it's too late for that. All the time you did as I asked you to and never said anything. You were content until now or you would have said something. So why should you be dissatisfied now? You didn't contradict me at any time. Why should you be allowed to contradict me now? No, what you utter now doesn't count any more. Do as I say! (P. 121)

The idea of the destructive consequences of conformity, the ultimate result of such power, may be suggested by the appearance near the play's end of identical twins, who wander onstage as if by mistake. The Kessler sisters, who, with their predictable dialogue, intrude upon the unusual world of the other five, suggest the same "normal," nondescript nonindividual that Kaspar's doubles do, a kinship which is further implied by the deterioration of their behavior into frenetic activity.

If the foregoing discussion suggests a Brechtian didacticism surfacing in a Handke play, then it must quickly be qualified by noting that any such attack on established patterns of language and behavior or attempt at reform reveal themselves only in analysis. In performance, the play sustains itself primarily through the dominance of its unusual atmosphere, created by its surreal sequences of language and action and by frequently recurring images of sleep. The play opens with Jannings seated in an armchair, his eyes closed; George enters and stumbles because his foot has fallen asleep, and Jannings admits that his hand has also. George asks Jannings, "Sie haben geträumt?" ("You were dreaming?"), to which Jannings replies, "Als die Nächte besonders lang waren" ("When the nights were especially long"), to which George retorts, "Sie müssen träumen" (p. 66) ("You must be dreaming," p. 75). Throughout the play, various characters fall asleep, and Handke's remarks direct that a particular character respond as though he were asleep. Bergner (as if asleep) comments on "der unüberwindliche Dreck, die Fröste, Schneesturme, die große Entfernungen" ("the insurmountable filth, the frost, the snowstorms, the immense distances"); and when Jannings asks, "Was hat sie gesagt?" ("What did she say?"), George replies, "Nichts. Sie träumt" (p. 83) ("Nothing. She is dreaming," p. 91). Similarly, because Jannings's story of his restaurant experiences has lost its sense of reality, the two men decide that it, like all the past, is only a dream or, even more insubstantially, only a dream that might occur. Quoting two characters from Shakespeare's *The Comedy of Errors,* Jannings asks:

> Ist dies die Erd? Ist's Himmel oder Hölle!
> Schlaf oder wach ich? Bin ich bei Verstand?
> Mir selbst ein Rästel, bin ich hier bekannt?
> Sagt mir, bin ich vertauscht, bin ich noch ich? (P. 144)

> Am I in earth, in heaven, or in hell?
> Sleeping or waking, mad or well-advised?
> Known unto these, and to myself disguised:
> Am I transformed, master, am not I? (P. 149)[14]

The screaming doll at the end of the play is, according to Handke's notes, tired, or longing for sleep.[15] And perhaps most significantly, George's and Jannings's dialogue links dream and language:

JANNINGS: Sie reden?
GEORGE: Träumen Sie? (P. 144)

JANNINGS: You're talking?
GEORGE: Are you dreaming? (P. 148)

expressing the connection suggested by the play's epigraph: "Träumt Ihr oder redet Ihr?" ("Are You Dreaming or Are You Speaking?").

In one of the more perceptive analyses of *Quodlibet*, Rainer Nägele and Renate Voris note that that play functions in a manner analogous to French psychoanalyst Jacques Lacan's description of the unconscious. Working from Freud's investigations into the dream state as one which simultaneously conceals and reveals, Lacan suggests linguistic equivalents of metaphor (which displaces something with something else, e.g., rose equals love) and metonymy (which substitutes a part for the whole, e.g., sail equals ship).[16] In *Quodlibet*, one word is substituted for another not for its metaphorical value but because of the associative mental process inherent in the closeness of sound. Similarly, the part is substituted for the whole not for the poetic effect but because the audience hears only portions of what is being said and, on the basis of its preconceptions, comes to mistaken conclusions.

On a more readily recognizable level, the somnambulistic state of the characters in *The Ride Across Lake Constance* may be seen as a correlative for the anesthetized state of unawareness which Handke sees as characterizing our daily lives, and particularly our use of language. The title of the play refers to "The Rider and Lake Constance" ("Der Reiter und der Bodensee"), a ballad by Gustav Schwab (reproduced in the Schaubühne program), which tells of a horseman who rode fearlessly across a frozen lake only to die when he reached the other side and was told how thin the ice he had traversed was. Nicholas Hern suggests that the thin ice is a metaphor for the state of somnambulism we and the characters of Handke's play are in and of which we must remain unaware if we are not finally to "disintegrate with shock."[17] Botho Strauss, pointing to the analogy between language and Handke's play, similarly suggests the peril of awareness:

Diesem Ritt gleicht das Funktionieren unserer sprachlichen und sinnlichen Vernunft, der Grammatik und des Zuordnungssystems von Wahrnehmungen und Bedeutungen; es ist nur eine provisorische, durchlässige Ordnung die, zumal da, wo sie sich selber zu Bewußtsein kommt, wie in Handkes Stück, von . . . Schizophrenie, [und] Wahnsinn . . . bedrängt wird.[18]

The ride parallels the functioning of our grammar, of our system of coordinating perception and meaning, and of our linguistic and sentient powers of reason; it is only a provisional, permeable order, which, particularly when, as in Handke's play, it becomes conscious of its own existence, is threatened by . . . schizophrenia, and madness.[19]

This paradox of consciousness—that it is prerequisite to our perception yet destructive of our unity with the world—has its counterpart in language, which, as *Kaspar* has shown, is a necessary part of knowing (indeed, it is synonomous with it) but alienates man through the knowledge of his separateness. Ira Hauptman perhaps describes this paradox best in his essay on the play in *Partisan Review:* "The predicament is our reliance on the mind's interpretations of experience, and even more on arbitrary communal assignments of meanings to actions so that minds can work together. This insistence on the meaning of events gives our perceptions a function, gives ourselves a function of interpretation—something to do while existing—and of course makes communication possible. But it destroys our own relation to the world and to our own experiences. This self-estrangement is our dreamlike state. When the play's characters wake themselves into an authenticity where interpretation of experience is no longer unconsciously compulsive, they experience great joy, but find it no longer possible to live."[20]

At one point, Bergner excitedly exclaims, "Ich sah mich! Ich bemerkte mich! Ich hörte mich!" (p. 100) ("I saw myself! I noticed myself! I heard myself!" p. 107). Her epiphany, which is only temporary, comes after a dramatic confrontation with the thin line between sanity and madness. Trying to cut her hair while looking in a mirror, she keeps missing the strands; applying makeup, she confuses her directions. Finally, pleading for help, she negotiates inappropriate gestures and clumsily bumps into the objects onstage. The extreme self-consciousness she experiences when she confronts her own image draws her suddenly into a schizophrenic state from which Porten can retrieve her only through offering her the security of sentence models which help her affirm her existence.

The play, while probing into the paradox of consciousness, offers language as our only defense against the madness language itself fosters. Recognition of the fragile relationship between the world and the self, possible only through language, is prerequisite to a perception that transcends the somnambulism of habit. If at the end of *The Ride Across Lake Constance* the audience can say with Bergner, "I saw myself! I noticed myself! I heard myself!" then language, reality, and self can all begin, in Richard Gilman's words, "to take on, like the color returning to the cheeks of a nearly hanged man, the signs of a strange and unexpected resurrection."[21]

7

The Goalie's Anxiety at the Penalty Kick

When *Die Angst des Tormanns beim Elfmeter* appeared in German in 1970 and in English translation as *The Goalie's Anxiety at the Penalty Kick* in 1972, reviewers quickly dubbed it "Kafkaesque." Some invoked the name of Kafka without pointing to specific parallels—other than to note the Kafka-sounding name of the protagonist, Joseph Bloch—but simply as a shortcut to accounting for what could not be understood; others pointed to the unexplained behavior of the protagonist, the anxiety-inducing events, and the sustained quality of fuzzy suggestiveness which inform both writers' fictive worlds.[1] Just as the reader of Kafka's *The Trial* (*Der Prozeß*, 1925), for example, is left with speculative, unverifiable explanations for K's guilt, so also is the reader of Handke's novel left with the feeling that he never knows why Bloch is fired from his job as a construction worker (if indeed he is), why he strangles the woman with whom he spent the night, nor why he acts as he does in the days following these events. In both novels, a guilty, isolated hero attempts to understand the nature of his relationships, K through probing into his sins of commission and omission and Bloch through analyzing the terms of reality. And though the prose in both is distinguished by its clarity, both Kafka's and Handke's narratives create a surreal atmosphere seemingly resistant to interpretation.

Despite their long critical history as unsolvable metaphysical enquiries, the questions in Kafka may be at their core no more (and no less) than questions of language. Anthony Thorlby, defending such a thesis in his fine essay, "Anti-Mimesis: Kafka and Wittgenstein," suggests that with Kafka, "the more intelligently we think about the situation, the less we experience its essential reality. Criticism becomes a way of missing the point."[2] With Susan Sontag, he would agree that to interpret Kafka's work mimetically or allegorically is to impoverish the text, wherein Kafka's significance lies.[3] Kafka's purpose "could have been to illumine the character of meaning rather than to illumine the character of the world."[4] The application of this central premise to *The Goalie's Anxiety at the Penalty Kick* yields considerable insight into the enigmatic texture of Handke's novel and the strange behavior of Joseph Bloch.

The Goalie's Anxiety at the Penalty Kick sketches a series of events in the life of a former soccer goalkeeper, beginning in Vienna, where he leaves his job and murders a woman he barely knows, and following the occurrences of his daily life thereafter as he seeks refuge in a small southern border town. Though much of what constitutes Bloch's daily experience following the murder is patently unnoteworthy, the reader wants to understand what Bloch does and says in even the seemingly insignificant moments of his life and is never relieved from the sustained perplexity of experience the novel creates. As in a Kafka novel, the question of meaning in *The Goalie's Anxiety at the Penalty Kick* is pervasive, but in the Handke novel there is less of a temptation to impute mimetic or allegorical significance, for here there is no doubt that the inscrutable actions of Joseph Bloch are inextricably related to Handke's own investigation into the nature of language and his hero's obvious preoccupation with words.

In this respect, Bloch is strongly reminiscent of Roquentin, the hero of Sartre's *Nausea* (*La Nausée*, 1938), a man who is driven to nausea by the presence of things and who comes to confront the insubstantiality of a reality of which his very body is a part. Realizing the fragile nature of the phenomenal world in the climactic scene beneath a chestnut tree, Roquentin discovers:

Je ne me rappelais plus que c'était une racine. Les mots s'étaient évanouis et, avec eux, la signification des choses, leurs modes d'emploi, les faibles repères que les hommes ont tracés a leur surface.[5]

I couldn't remember it was a root any more. The words had vanished and with them the significance of things, their methods of use, and the feeble points of reference which men have traced on their surface.[6]

The recognition that reality must be actualized through language becomes even more maddening for Roquentin when he considers that there is no innate correspondence between words and the objects they denote, rendering phenomenal reality—and existence itself—logically unintelligible.

One passage in Handke's *The Goalie's Anxiety at the Penalty Kick* particularly recalls the experience of Sartre's hero; it is a point at which Bloch himself experiences nausea over his unbearable alienation from the objects surrounding him and his incessant need to name:

In seinem Zimmer im Gasthof wachte er kurz vor dem Morgengrauen auf. Unvermittelt war ihm alles ringsherum unerträglich. . . . Ein heftiger Ekel packte ihn. Er erbrach sofort in das Waschbecken. Er erbrach einige Zeit, ohne Erleichterung. Er legte sich wieder aufs Bett. Er war nicht schwindlig sah im Gegenteil alles in einem unerträglichen Gleichgewicht. . . . Drinnen im Zimmer erblickte er an der Wand die Zwei Wasserrohre; sie liefen parallel, wurden begrenzt oben von der Decke, unten vom Fußboden. Alles, was er sah, war auf die unerträglichste Weise abgegrenzt. Der Brechreiz hob ihn nicht etwa auf, sondern drückte ihn noch zusammen. Es kam ihm vor, als hätte ihn ein Stemmeisen von dem, was er sah, abgestemmt, oder als seien vielmehr die Gegenstände ringsherum von ihm abgehoben worden. Der Schrank, das Waschbecken, die Reisetasche, die Tür: erst jetzt fiel ihm auf, daß er, wie in einem Zwang, zu jedem Gegenstand das Wort dazudachte. Jedem Ansichtigwerden eines Gegenstands folgte sofort das Wort nach. Der Stuhl, die Kleiderbügel, der Schlüssel.[7]

In his room at the inn he woke up just before dawn. All at once, everything around him was unbearable. . . . A fierce nausea gripped him. He immediately vomited into the sink. He vomited for a while, with no relief. He lay back down on the bed. He was not dizzy; on the contrary, he saw everything with excruciating stability. . . . Inside the room he noticed the two water pipes along the wall; they ran parallel to each other, cut off above by the ceiling and below by the floor. Everything he saw was cut off in the most unbearable way. The nausea did not so much elate him as depress him even more. It seemed as though a crowbar had pried him away from what he saw—or, rather, as though the things around him had all been pulled away from him. The wardrobe, the sink, the suitcase, the door: only now did he realize that he, as if compelled, was thinking of the word for each thing. Each glimpse of a thing was immediately followed by its word. The chair, the clothes hangers, the key.[8]

Like Roquentin, Bloch is experiencing the basic existential problem of the disconnection between one's own consciousness and the external world and the painful awareness that the only link between them is language.

But Handke is only a limited disciple of Sartre. In the interview with Artur Joseph, Handke sees Roquentin's nausea as a healthy alternative to the numbed consciousness which neither considers nor is disturbed by "the idiocy of language."[9] But in "Literature Is Romantic" ("Die Literatur ist Romantisch"),[10] written in 1966, he takes issue with Sartre's ideas about a literature of engagement, suggesting that the one truly "engaged" literature is that which is concerned only with itself, that is, only with language. While Sartre the novelist defines the existential-linguistic problem with which Handke too is concerned, Sartre the philosopher finds a solution for Roquentin's alienation in a Hegelian rationalism, a solution which Handke cannot concede.

The Goalie's Anxiety at the Penalty Kick may have kinships with both Kafka and Sartre, but, more strongly than either, the novel reflects Handke's exploration into the science of signs.[11] For it is Bloch's extreme awareness of the semiotic processes of everyday life that gives the novel its Kafkaesque quality and accounts for the strange isolation of its hero. If the horror of consciousness is suggested in *The Ride Across Lake Constance* through Bergner's schizophrenic response to her own image, through the wailing doll, and through the metaphor of the horseman riding across thin ice, it is *lived* in *The Goalie's Anxiety at the Penalty Kick* in the character of Bloch, who is aware that it is only arbitrary interpretation which creates the tenuous bond between man and the world.

The metaphor of the soccer goalkeeper anticipating the ball's coming into the cage he protects reflects the instability of this relationship. Shifting his weight from one foot to the other, the goalie is aware that his interpretation of the penalty kicker's movements can determine whether the kicker scores, but he is also aware that while he is assessing the kicker, the kicker is assessing him, and even the slightest hint of movement by either of them becomes critical. Bloch's former position as a goalie gives the title a practical relevance, for as a man whose job it once was to interpret gesture, Bloch is now hypersensitive to the signs of human life.

Bloch leaves his job as a construction worker because he interprets a gesture—no one but the foreman looked up at him as he reported to work—as meaning he is fired. On the street a taxi stops for him because the driver interprets Bloch's raising of his arm as a signal for a cab. A movie cashier hands Bloch a ticket when he wordlessly lays his money on the turntable before her. A hotel clerk refuses Bloch a room because he has only a briefcase with him. The first several pages of the novel create the terms of the world through which Bloch moves, a world which must constantly be interpreted but which, with each successive decoding, seems more and more a dishonest joke.

Only after Bloch murders the young movie clerk does his awareness of semiotic processes and the role that language plays in them become excruciatingly intense. Explaining the principle behind the novel, Handke singles out that event, which occurs very early in the novel, as the point at which Bloch begins to realize that perceptions must have verbal form, a recognition which leads Bloch to see everything as an insinuation or command. Writing in a letter published in part in *Text und Kritik*, Handke explains:

Das Prinzip war, zu zeigen, wie sich jemandem die Gegenstände, die er wahrnimmt, infolge eines Ereignisses (eines Mordes) immer mehr versprachlichen und, indem die Bilder versprachlicht werden, auch zu Geboten und Verboten werden. Beispiel aus einer Abhandlung über *Die beginnende Schizophrenie:* ein "Schizophrener" sieht ein Stücke Käse unter einer Käseglocke liegen (ein Bild), und aus diesem Käse treten Tropfen hervor (ein Bild): statt nun aber es beim Sehen der Bilder zu lassen, sieht der Schizophrene gar nicht die Bilder allein, sondern nimmt sofort auch deren Übersetzungen in Sprache wahr: "Der Käse schwitzt"; d.h. er, der etwas sieht, s o l l schwitzen, das wird ihm dadurch angedeutet (Norm), d.h. er soll sich mehr anstrengen, mehr konzentrieren, mehr arbeiten. Der Schizophrene nimmt also die Gegenstände als Anspielung auf sich, als "Wortspiele" wahr, metaphorisch.[12]

The principle was to show how the objects which someone perceives are transformed into language [*versprachlichen*] more and more following an event (a murder) and how, as the images are given linguistic form, they also become commands and prohibitions. An example from a treatise on *Beginning Schizophrenia:* a "schizophrenic" sees a piece of cheese lying under a cheesebell (an image) and out of this cheese appear drops (an image): henceforth, instead of seeing only the image, the schizophrenic sees not the images alone, but also immediately notes their translation into language: "the cheese is sweating!"; i.e., he who is looking at it should sweat; this is what is suggested to him (model), i.e., he should strain himself more, concentrate more, work more. The schizophrenic perceives objects as correspondences to himself, as "word games," metaphorically.

Transformed into narrative, Bloch's view of objects as regulations containing the imperative of a programmed response appears in a passage such as this:

Der Abwaschfetzen, der über dem Wasserhahn lag, befahl ihm etwas. Auch der Verschluß der Bierflasche auf dem inzwischen sonst leergeräumten Tisch forderte ihn zu irgend etwas auf. Es spielte sich ein: überall sah er eine Aufforderung: das eine zu tun, das andere nicht zu tun. Alles war ihm vorformuliert, das Regal mit den Gewürztiegeln, ein Regal mit Gläsern frisch eingekochter Marmelade. (Pp. 98–99)

The dish rag hanging over the faucet told him to do something. Even the cap of the bottle left on the table, which by now had been cleared, summoned him to do something. Everything fell into place: everywhere he saw a summons: to do one thing, not to do another. Everything was spelled out for him, the shelf where the spice boxes were, a shelf with jars of freshly made jam. (Pp. 116–17)

And his insistence on finding symbolic meaning in every object is reflected in these questions:

Sagt Ihnen dieses Stempelkissen etwas? Was denken Sie, wenn Sie diesen ausgefüllten Scheck sehen? Was verbinden Sie mit dem Herausziehen der Schublade? (P. 83)

Und warum hatten die Kekse dort auf dem Holzteller die Form von Fischen? Auf was spielten sie an? Sollte er 'stumm wie ein Fisch' sein? Durfte er nicht weiterreden? Sollten ihm die Kekse auf dem Holzteller das andeuten? (P. 98)

Does this ink pad mean anything to you? What do you think of when you see this filled-out check? What do you associate with that drawer's being open? (Pp. 96–97)

And why were the cookies on the wooden plate fish-shaped? What did they suggest? Should he be "mute as a fish"? Was he not permitted to talk? Was that what the cookies on the wooden plate were trying to tell him? (P. 116)

As Bloch's idiosyncrasies reveal themselves, it becomes increasingly clear that although his world is made up of everyday objects and events, he is no ordinary participant in the quotidian world. Yet Handke contends that Bloch is "normal." In the letter describing the principle behind the narrative, he writes that although he used the schizophrenic state of mind as a model for the behavior of his protagonist, he nonetheless created Bloch as a "normal" hero:

Das ist das Prinzip der Erzählung, nur daß eben dieses Verfahren nicht auf einen Schizophrenen angewendet wird (sofern es überhaupt Schizophrene gibt), sondern auf einen "normalen" Helden.[13]

That is the principle of the narrative, only because this behavior is not applied to a schizophrenic (to the extent that there are in general schizophrenics), but to a "normal" hero.

Though it is difficult to see the seemingly unmotivated murder that Bloch commits as the act of a "normal" man, when one reads the novel as the working out of the principle Handke describes it becomes clear that the strange behavior of the protagonist following that act is simply the ongoing consequence of one man's rethinking of the relationships of reality. Bloch's exceptional consciousness of himself and the world and his urgent questioning of correspondences following the deed dictate his every move, precluding our judgment of him in traditional terms. For with one who is trying as hard as Bloch to understand existence itself, psychological and moral concerns would seem to belong to an order of criticism that can only be considered once the primary level is clear.

Bloch is exceedingly aware of the fact that if man is to come to any understanding of his relationship to the phenomenal and experiential world, he must do this through the one system which informs his every contact with it, and that is language. As Roland Barthes suggests in his introduction to *Elements of Semiology* (*Éléments de Sémiologie*, 1964), it is doubtful whether any extensive system of signs can exist independently of language:

Certes, objects, images, comportements peuvent signifier, et ils le font abondamment, mais ce n'est jamais d'une façon autonome; tout système sémiologique se mêle de langage. . . . il paraît de plus en plus difficile de concevoir un système d'images ou d'objets dont les *signifiés* puissent exister en dehors du langage: percevoir ce qu'une substance signifie, c'est fatalement recourir au découpage de la langue: il n'y a de sens que nommé, et le monde des signifiés n'est autre que celui du langage.[14]

It is true that objects, images and patterns of behaviour can signify, and do so on a large scale, but never autonomously; every semiological system has its linguistic admixture. . . . it appears increasingly more difficult to conceive a system of images and objects whose *signifieds* can exist independently of language: to perceive what a substance signifies is inevitably to fall back on the individuation of a language: there is no meaning which is not designated, and the world of signifieds is none other than that of language.[15]

Barthes suggests here what Bloch obviously senses: that without language (in the ordinary sense of the term), reality would have no meaning. Indeed, the governing principle of semiotics is that significance lies in neither the plane of content (the signified, the object) nor the plane of expression (the signifier, the word) but in the relation of the two planes. It is clear that this novel is the recording of one man's attempt to undertake what Barthes designates as the future task of semiotics: "retrouver les articulations que les hommes font subir au réel"[16] ("to rediscover the articulations which men impose on reality"[17]).

But Bloch's awareness of the role language plays in creating reality is not equivalent to his coming to terms with this fact, and he spends the days following his murder of Gerda T. thinking of nothing but the way in which language as part of a system of signification works. At one point he finds it impossible to visualize anything with his eyes closed; he attempts to restore his sense of reality through first naming objects and then creating sentences about them. Failing, he opens his eyes and immediately becomes aware of the pressure of objects, which, though great, is not so intense for him as the pressure of words for those objects. In a general store he notices that the clerk seems uncomprehending when he speaks to her in sentences, but reacts immediately to the naming of items: a handkerchief, a tie, a wool sweater. When viewing a gatekeeper's butterfly collection, he notices that the insects have deteriorated to the point of being indistinguishable as individual specimens, but that each is recognizable by the description attached to it. At times Bloch feels as though every word is a joke or requires an explanation, or that the names of objects are call letters for those objects, which are advertisements for themselves. Aware that he must order his world through language, Bloch seeks security in reconstructing events of the recent past through sentences and retracing how one sentence leads to the next. When successful, the sense of artificiality fades and all goes well for him, yet the process itself still strikes Bloch as artificial: *"Wenn er aufpaßte und sich vorstellte,* gab noch immer ein Wort schön das andre" (p. 71) (*"When he put on an act,* one word still nicely yielded the next," p. 82) (emphasis added).

Bloch simply cannot sustain participation in the systems of significance to which others respond without thought. When he cannot comprehend why a policeman would tell him a story about a goat which soils the walls of the swimming pool area, he decides that the story did not say what he thought but was simply a series of mispronounced words. Dissatisfied with the way in which names designate people, he thinks of calling the waitress with the pierced ear "a hole through the ear lobe" and the woman with a purse, "You Purse." Aware that the sign yielded by the relationship of the signified and the signifier itself becomes a signified through connotation, Bloch's probing mind follows the complicated process of interpretation further, seeing a gatekeeper with a key as though he should be seeing him in a figurative sense and a policeman as though he is a simile for something else. In other words, he is not concerned simply with the identification of the fish-shaped cookies but with their symbolic value as well, and much of Bloch's experience of the world hinges on his awareness of this secondary order of significance. Overwhelmed by the feeling that everything suggests and insinuates, Bloch cannot maintain the pretense and instead falls prey to moments of intense irritation.

It may well be Bloch's developing consciousness of the persistence of language that provokes his murder of Gerda T., for while Handke offers nothing by way of explanation of Bloch's motive, he vividly describes the scene preceding the murder, which consists simply of an ostensibly "normal" conversation. Bloch, however, only occasionally feels natural about talking; more often he notices the peculiarities of his conversation with Gerda T. He, for example, is unable to speak of *her* experiences or friends in familiar terms, always referring to them by quoting her or preceding new names with "this" or "that" in order to distance them. Yet she freely speaks of Bloch's acquaintances as if she knew them personally. Gradually, Bloch finds himself unable to complete his sentences, feeling that the woman already knows what he is going to say. Bloch is mystified by these phenomena, and the unexpected strangling seems clearly to be the necessary act of release for a feeling of intense irritation which finally overwhelms him.

Bloch responds in a similar fashion in another situation when his irritation reaches a level of intolerability, this time because a tavern patron cautions him against leaving a folded bill on the table in payment for drinks, for another might be tucked inside. "So what?" responds Bloch and begins a punching session which he continues despite repeated defeats. Finally too weak even to lift a beer bottle, Bloch stops, and for several moments experiences a relationship with reality which makes it seem like "peacetime":

Er sah und hörte alles unvermittelt, ohne es erst, wie früher, in Worte übersetzen zu müssen oder es überhaupt nur als Worte und Wortspiele zu erfassen. Er war in einem Zustand, in dem ihm alles natürlich vorkam. (P. 94)

He saw and heard everything with total immediacy, without first having to translate it into words, as before, or comprehending it only in terms of words or word games. He was in a state where everything seemed natural to him. (P. 111)

Only when Bloch feels he has escaped the tyranny of words does he become comfortable with existence. He constantly struggles to achieve this state of feeling natural, for conscious as he is of the necessity of "languagizing" everything, Bloch is obsessed with the awareness and wants desperately to lose it. At one point he sits in his room naming objects; then, moments before he falls asleep, the words on the novel's printed page give way to outlines of the objects Bloch perceives, indicating that he has once again reached a state of "total immediacy." But both such experiences, and one or two others, take place when Bloch is in a state of physical and mental exhaustion, suggesting not the possibility of perception without language but simply that Bloch has lost consciousness of semiotic processes to the extent that he momentarily believes it is possible.

Bloch's intense awareness of the way in which objects become language and his simultaneous need to escape this awareness can be explained not only in terms of the unsettling quality of such heightened perceptivity but also in terms of the murder mystery. Throughout the novel Bloch is the object of a countrywide manhunt which will eventually culminate in his capture. Despite appearances to the contrary, he responds to the chase in a very "normal" fashion. Though Handke never explicitly suggests psychological motivation in the novel, Bloch is constantly influenced by the mounting anxiety he experiences as the search for the murder of Gerda T. intensifies. But the anxiety rests not in the search per se but in Bloch's knowledge that in order to avoid apprehension, he must, at least in some instances, *deny* the very semiotic processes that haunt him.

Two objects that figure prominently in the discovery of the identity of the murderer are coins and newspapers. Both are recurring objects of Bloch's attention, but he carefully avoids attaching to either its significance as a clue. Rather, he attempts to make of them ordinary objects that have nothing to do with the way in which the Vienna police perceive them. As though trying to affirm the possibility that these objects may be construed simply as objects in their usual sense, Bloch tests alternative interpretations to the ordinary. Following the method of a tax official, he tries to see objects in terms of their financial worth, but when he asks how much a juke box costs, the proprietor thinks he wants to buy it and cannot understand Bloch's insistence upon knowing the price when he has no interest in acquiring it. Rejecting the usual sequence of numbers, Bloch begins counting at two, but discovers that under the new system he endangers his life each time he crosses the street without allowing for the first car. Bloch appears to be pleased that neither of these approaches proves valid, and once, when he attempts to match the indications on a street map with the realities of the city, he is delighted to discover that in one instance they do not correspond. But Bloch is ultimately unable to deny that the police are decoding these same objects in a quest that will end in a front page headline containing the name of Joseph Bloch.

The anxiety occasioned by anticipation, suggested by the novel's title and reflected in Bloch's behavior, is a key concept at both the semiotic and narrative levels. By its very nature each system of signification—be it of images, gestures, objects, or musical sounds—is anticipatory, depending on a common "language" to reveal meaning. Bloch's recognition of this fact causes him to stop in mid-sentence, convinced that the other person already knows what he is going to say, and to feel a sense of unnaturalness or pretense in the presence of language. Bloch even contends that he knows a moment beforehand that the phone is going to ring or that a customs guard is about to knock on the guesthouse window. As Handke attempts both to dramatize and to upset conventional expectations, Bloch finds himself watching not the hawk circling the field, but the spot on the field toward which the hawk is presumably going to dive; not the drop running down the outside of his glass, but the spot on the coaster it will probably hit; not the dog running toward the man in a field, but the man; not the ants approaching a crumb of bread, but the fly perched atop the crumb.

In the closing pages of narrative, the novel's searches terminate, not arbitrarily but as coincidents that are analogous to Bloch's own climactic search for what might be called "semiotic sanity." The dumb boy missing in the border town where Bloch is staying is discovered drowned, and after a meticulous piecing together of clues, the Vienna police have only to name the murderer of Gerda T. The images of closure suggested by the goalie's cage and the closed border come together in the final scene to complement Bloch's capture, but the image suggested by the dumb boy, now dead, and by Bloch's own inarticulateness seem to dissolve as Bloch's anxiety finally finds verbal expression, which may, after all, have been his quest throughout.

Whether Bloch comes to any permanent reconciliation with language must be left an unanswered question, but the final pages of the novel suggest the emergence of a man who has assessed, rejected, reinvented, and finally affirmed the "normal" semiotic processes of life. Until this point, Bloch is curiously inarticulate. Although occasional mention is made of conversations in which Bloch takes part and a few references to lines of dialogue in those conversations appear, the only instance of an extended conversation in which Bloch participates and speaks directly comes in the final pages of the novel when, moments before the police search is complete, Bloch explains to a salesman watching a soccer match the psychology—or, rather, the semiotics—involved in a goalie's anxiety. In this conversation, Bloch is more articulate than anywhere previously in the novel, volunteering comments on the soccer crowd's behavior and the strategies of the game, and particularly of the goalie. Although he listens as acutely to his own sentences as he might to those of another speaker, and feels as though the conversation is being had for the benefit of a third party, Bloch speaks with authority of the goalie's anxiety, watching as the goalkeeper stands perfectly still and receives the penalty kick directly in his arms. Placing the responsibility of interpretation upon the reader, Handke leaves one uncertain as to whether Bloch will be apprehended or not, but one senses that Bloch now finds solace rather than irritation in his sudden flow of words.

That the reader is finally left with the task of interpretation is a perfectly appropriate conclusion to a novel that has been analyzing the process of interpretation throughout and gradually transferring the responsibility to the reader, who for Handke has always been as much a creator of a novel as the author himself. If any anxiety remains at the end of the novel, it is that of the reader, who, if brought successfully to the level of consciousness toward which Handke has been manipulating him, is now as sensitized as Bloch to the fragile nature of his relationship to the world and to the semiotic processes which inform his every response. The reader has shared with Bloch the misunderstandings, incomprehensions, frustrations, and irritations of failed communication. He has witnessed the continuing transformation of ordinary objects into signs. And in the particularly significant moment during which Bloch sits in his room observing objects, and the words on the printed page of the novel change to images of those objects, the reader has found that regardless of whether Bloch thinks his reception of those objects is immediate, he himself (i.e., the reader) is unconsciously *naming* each outline. It may well be that the "normal hero" of Handke's novel is not Bloch after all, but the reader.

The Goalie's Anxiety at the Penalty Kick may indeed leave the reader with the same uncomfortable feeling he has after reading Kafka, whom Handke considers one of the writers who has changed his consciousness of the world.[18] But if Handke's novel has points of contact with Kafka, they would seem to rest not in the metaphysics which have come to surround Kafka's work but, rather, in the direct experience of the text which both writers achieve. When Handke's novel is viewed as an enquiry into the normal semiotic processes of experience, it becomes clear that the haunting quality of *The Goalie's Anxiety at the Penalty Kick*, the illusive behavior of its protagonist, and the sustained perplexity of its reception are "Kafkaesque" only to the extent that Handke, like Kafka, is seeking the significance of meaning itself in the mysterious world of language.

8

Short Letter, Long Farewell

Like Joseph Bloch, the hero of Handke's fourth novel is the object of a pursuit, conducted this time not by the police in search of a murderer but by an estranged wife propelled by the desire to kill. The unnamed Austrian protagonist of *Short Letter, Long Farewell* (*Der kurze Brief zum langen Abschied*, 1972), who is also the narrator, begins his American experience in New England, where he receives a letter from his wife Judith telling him she is in New York and advising him not to look for her, for to find her "would not be nice." As he continues his travels through New York and Washington to a small town in Pennsylvania, where he teams up with an acquaintance and her daughter, continuing on to St. Louis, and then setting off on his own to Arizona and Oregon, he gradually realizes that Judith is following him. On his thirtieth birthday in St. Louis, a greeting with the world "last" inserted between the printed "Happy" and "Birthday" arrives, followed shortly afterward by an electrically wired package. On the West Coast, pursuer and pursued finally come together and Handke's hero faces the wild eyes and pointed gun of his wife. Though presented in cool, dispassionate terms, the adventure-tale quality of Judith's pursuit effectively sustains the narration, creating an atmosphere akin to that of the detective novel which *The Peddler* analyzes and to which the second part of the title alludes.[1]

Throughout the novel, Handke's hero is not only the pursued, he is himself a pursuer, whose journey through America takes the form less of a flight than of a search. He becomes increasingly conscious of the presence of America, a consciousness which creates an ongoing dialectic between the "outer" world of America and his own elusive "inner" world, between the past, present, and future of this nation and his own experience. The narrator's insistent need to relate the identity of America to his conception of self turns what would otherwise be an intriguing but sparse adventure tale into an exceptionally well-wrought *Entwicklungsroman*. For Handke's protagonist, America becomes a *Versuchswelt*, a world against which he can test his personal fictions and through which he tries to reach some truth about himself and reality.

Throughout his time in America, the hero is constantly aware of his "strangeness." Unfamiliar with his surroundings, he becomes more attentive to them, as when, in New York, he acknowledges how minutely he dissects his activities in order to deceive his sense of ignorance. But even as the consciousness of his unfamiliarity develops, he is struck with the *familiarity* of America, recognizing at every turn images of America he had acquired in Europe. An overweight boy wearing an Al Wilson T-shirt, a Tarzan movie, a picture of a scene in Tucson, Arizona, for example, are transformed into reality as he encounters confirmations of preestablished concepts. The narrator has come to America with a composite picture of that country created by the numerous American imports to which he has been exposed in his native Austria, imports which, as any American who has spent time in Europe knows, derive from American "pop" culture—fast food, jeans, rock and roll, and western movies being among the more prominent. And, like many Europeans, he has come to think of America as a country of surfaces, of people who try to reduce everything to a concept, and in which, as Handke says in an interview with Hellmuth Karasek, "Man fühlt sich im guten Sinne erleichtert, entpersönlicht, als Typus, nicht als Individuum"[2] ("One feels, in a good sense, lightened, depersonalized, as a type, not as an individual"). It is only natural that Handke's hero, attempting to ease the emotional trauma of an intensely personal experience—a slowly deteriorating marriage and, finally, separation—would head for the land which could offer him the oblivion of impersonality, the relief of superficiality, and the surreality of dream.

But this time anonymity is not to be found. Despite his response to America in an earlier visit, Handke's hero now finds that he is no more content with accepting America's image than he is with accepting his own. Throughout the narrative, his experiencing of

America is punctuated by his reading of Gottfried Keller's *Green Henry* (*Der grüne Heinrich*, 1854–55), a nineteenth-century Swiss *Bildungsroman*, the autobiographical hero of which, like Handke's, is in search of self. Green Henry's quest, however, is set in the previous century, when it was still possible to achieve a union between man and nature, between the inner world and the outer, a time when values were grounded not in technology nor in "pop" culture but in a society which was inseparably bound to humanity. On the bus from Providence to New York, a journey which takes him through the wrecked neighborhoods of Harlem to the seamy Port Authority bus terminal, the protagonist begins reading the novel to which he returns throughout. He feels an affinity for the Keller hero, who never wanted to interpret things but to remain as distant as possible; but he also constantly contrasts the worlds to which he and Henry must relate. The delicate counterpointing of past and present, fiction and reality, and image and concept accumulates and intensifies as contemporary America emerges not simply as a backdrop against which the characters move, but as a validating world against which the narrator measures himself.

Already in its earliest pages, the narrative interweaves the levels through which the hero experiences the world. The opening line—"Jefferson Street is a quiet thoroughfare in Providence"—is a quotation from a novel by Patricia Highsmith. Its position as the first sentence in the narration serves not only to connect this novel with detective fiction (as the title already has), but also to suggest the indirect experience which is to color the protagonist's responses to reality. The message he receives from Judith creates anxiety and uncertainty and links his past with his future in the American setting he has just described. But the emotions which the letter invokes themselves become stimulants for a memory of moments of horror and fear in the narrator's rural, European youth: American bombers, the butchering of hares, someone lost in the woods. Minutes after he has checked into a hotel in Providence the narrator finishes reading *The Great Gatsby* (1925), comparing Gatsby's shame and Daisy's cowardliness with similar feelings in Judith and himself. This interplay of fiction and reality, of memories, experiences, and hopes, when juxtaposed with the development of the identity of America, leads Handke's hero to the realization that fiction is an integral part of what most people think of as real. By the time of his climactic confrontation with Judith at the end of the novel, the narrator has sifted through the distortive history of America, seen the points at which that distorting process intersects with his own life, and arrived at an integrated conception of reality.

But the protagonist of *Short Letter, Long Farewell* is not bent simply on sorting out the distinctions between reality and fiction. Like Joseph Bloch, he has a newly acquired but acutely developed consciousness which permits him to concentrate not on the insinuations suggested by objects, as Bloch does, but on correspondences among levels of reality. Though less obsessed with the need to "languagize," the protagonist of *Short Letter, Long Farewell* is every bit as aware as Bloch is of the semiotic processes which constitute—and reconstitute—reality. As Handke remarked in the interview with Karasek, the underlying principle of the novel is "daß also alles das, was der Held sieht, für ihn zu Signalen wird für das, was er erlebt hat, oder für das, was er unternehmen möchte"[3] ("that everything which the hero sees becomes a signal for him for what he has experienced or for what he would like to undertake").

Early in his trip, while still in Providence, the protagonist observes a pair of hotel curtains made of fabric scattered with scenes from American history: Sir Walter Raleigh smoking in Virginia, the Pilgrims aboard the Mayflower, Ben Franklin reading the Constitution, Lewis and Clark shooting Blackfoot Indians, Abe Lincoln offering his hand to a black man. As he continues his travels, he frequently hears modern American folk music: Odis Redding's "Sitting on the Dock of the Bay," Creedence Clearwater Revival, "She Wore a Yellow Ribbon." He listens as an American couple in St. Louis speak of how every state of the union is associated with a particular flower and bird and how Americans see everything as a symbol. Claire, his companion, suggests that the lives of important historical figures have little interest in themselves, but that Raleigh, Franklin, Lincoln, and the others stand as signs for their particular contributions to America's past.

Three years earlier, on the protagonist's first trip to the United

States, America was a composite of inanimate images: "Tankstellen, gelbe Taxis, Autokinos, Reklametafeln, Highways, den Greyhound-Autobus, ein BUS-STOP-Schild an der Landstraße, die Sante-Fé-Eisenbahn, die Wüste"[4] ("gas stations, yellow taxis, drive-in movies, advertising posters, highways, a Greyhound bus, a bus-stop sign on the highway, the Santa Fe Railway, the desert"[5]). But three years earlier, the narrator was not haunted by a failed marriage and by the continuing near-presence of an estranged wife. Where formerly he had a "menschenleere Bewußtsein" (a "consciousness empty of people"), the protagonist is now so preoccupied with rethinking his marriage, and his life, that for him the identity of America becomes analogous to his own. He recognizes both as series of images which, without the human element, can only present an idealized but depersonalized reality. America may well have been a country that valued independence, the pioneer spirit, and rugged individualism, but it is now a breeder of plasticity and waste, whose images of identity are machine-stamped on curtains and exploited by restaurants offering Daniel Boone steaks. The protagonist's life, and particularly his marriage, which once supported certain unnamed but presumably traditional values, has deteriorated into a monomaniacal obsession with the ways in which he and Judith attempted to destroy one another during their marriage and with the anticipation of the ultimate destructive act of murder that Judith now plans.

The narrator, in fact, frequently thinks of death: he experiences the fear of death moments before he calls New York's Delmonico Hotel regarding Judith's forgotten camera; he recalls the death of a man from pollen some years earlier; he speaks of death with Claire, claiming he seldom thinks of his own death, but when he receives Judith's birthday card, he has a "half dream" of death; and, finally, he unhesitatingly follows the implied command of Judith's postcard, on which an *X* marks their coastal meeting place, and faces the inevitable culmination of Judith's search. This steady movement in the narrator's mind toward death grows not simply out of his awareness that Judith is singlemindedly pursuing him across America, but out of his awareness of the deterioration of an idealized nation as well. Benedictine,

Claire's two-year-old daughter, symbolizes what America has become: a nation divorced from nature and humanity, curious only about TV antennae, pedestrian crossings, and police sirens, symbols of the presiding way of life. This way of life has replaced the life of a time when the nation's heroes were neither slick politicians nor mindless jocks, a long-lost world in which man and nature were one, the world of Keller's Green Henry.

America is not, however, an object of criticism, but rather the instrument of awakening for the protagonist. He had previously felt that the symbols of his native Austria were not the symbols of the rest of the world and, more importantly, that they bore no relationship to his internal world. Speaking with Claire, he explains:

Ich hatte nie etwas, womit ich das, was ich täglich sah, vergleichen konnte. Alle Eindrücke waren Wiederholungen schon bekannter Eindrücke. Damit meine ich nicht nur, daß ich wenig herumkam, sondern daß ich auch wenig Leute sah, die unter anderen Bedingungen lebten als ich. . . . Und diese Träume waren in der Umwelt, in der ich lebte, wirklich Schwärmereien, weil es für sie in dieser Umwelt keine Entsprechung gab, nichts Vergleichbares, das sie möglich gemacht hätte. So sind mir Träume und Umwelt nie so recht zu Bewußtsein gekommen, und die Folge davon war, daß ich mich an beides auch nie erinnere. (P. 75)

I never had anything with which to compare the things I saw every day. All my impressions were repetitions of impressions that were already known to me. It wasn't just that I didn't get around much, but also that I didn't see many people whose circumstances were different from mine. . . . In the world I lived in, my dreams were really fantasies, because they had no connection with anything in that world, there was nothing comparable that would have made them possible. As a result, I never became fully conscious of the world around me or of my dreams, and that's why I never remember them. (Pp. 61–62)

The only memories the protagonist has of his childhood are frightening ones, for it was only during moments of terror that his world and his dreams became related. Now, in America, these moments of terror are recreated:

"Ich bemerke, wie sich bei mir in Amerika jetzt die Kindererlebnisse wiederholen", sagte ich. "Alle Ängste, Sehnsüchte stellen sich wieder ein, die ich schon längst hinter mir glaubte. Wieder, wie schon als Kind, kommt es mir vor, als ob die Umwelt auf einmal platzen könnte und sich als etwas ganz andres entpuppen würde, zum Beispiel als das Maul eines Ungeheuers." (P. 96)

"Since coming to America," I said, "I've been having the same experiences as in childhood. Fears and longings that I thought I'd forgotten have been cropping up again. I have the same feeling as when I was little that the world around me might suddenly burst and turn into something entirely different, a monster's maw, for instance." (P. 79)

As a child, the protagonist had only one source of knowledge, and that was fear; for he noticed his surroundings only when he was afraid, looking for a sign which would tell him how the fear would resolve itself. Now, removed in space and time from his childhood Austria, he begins to find correlatives for his own experiences, to reinterpret childhood perceptions, and, consequently, to realize that the ontology of reality rests at the point of intersection between the inner and outer worlds.

If the protagonist claims not to have known people in Austria with whom he could compare his own circumstances and against whom he could measure his feelings, in America he finds several, including Claire, the St. Louis couple, and Claire's daughter, Benedictine. He attempts to interpret their characters or ways of life as correlatives for his own relationship with Judith, seeing in Claire a double for his wife and in the couple a double for himself and Judith when they were living together. In the interview with Karasek, Handke refers to Claire not as a central character, but as a *Gegenfrau,* an opposing double of the protagonist's wife, through whom the protagonist tries to get to know America, and himself, better.[6] And it is clear that for the protagonist, the St. Louis "lovers" function as objects of his observations, from whose way of life he may discover signs which say something about his own.

In the several years of his tender but destructive relationship with Judith, the protagonist was involved in a silent competition in which the loser of each particular psychic battle would suffer humiliation. Each would try to better the other by performing a household chore that the other normally did. Judith, for example, would take out the garbage before her husband could, or he would rewash the dishes she had just done. With Claire, there is no such battle, and when she does not think of taking in the clothes off the line, he voluntarily does so, and she is grateful. With Claire, he is relaxed and nondefensive, and when they talk there are no accusations, reproaches, or explanations. He does not have to suppress the persistent feelings of hostility which the presence of Judith bred, and although he has sex with Claire, physical contact is minimized; their way of being tender is to lie, untouching, side by side. With Claire, the hero discovers a relationship that makes him feel "almost weightless," the idyllic relationship he and Judith once had, or had the potential to have, but destroyed.

The St. Louis couple are singularly devoted and have structured their lives around themselves so carefully that they have virtually lost touch with reality other than their self-created one. The two assist one another in the preparation for their respective jobs, but stop short of encroaching on the other's function. Yet with respect to household chores, they have not delegated duties, necessitating the repeated negotiation of roles. If the two have not organized their lives through their functions, however, they have done so through their possessions. The objects about them are not simply things they own, but signs of their lives together, and their collecting, arranging, and identifying of these objects has come to represent the secret society of their home, which others cannot penetrate. Although they often have guests, visitors remain outsiders and are remembered only in terms of the destruction they leave behind. When Benedictine breaks a glass, for example, the two respond with controlled civility, ritualistically picking up the pieces but quietly mourning the loss. Yet, curiously, none of the couple's possessions is owned in common; from books to napkin rings to sofa pillows, each item belongs individually to one or the other, permitting them a trading relationship which seems to increase their dependency upon one another.

Handke's protagonist realizes that the lovers are perfectly content with one another, despite the extreme intimacy of an affection "so heftig, daß sie sich immer wieder in eine kurze Gereiztheit

verwandelte" (p. 112) ("so violent that it kept shifting into irritation," p. 94). The couple have systematized their existence into a
personally satisfying mode of life which they tenaciously defend,
but which the protagonist, seeing in their marriage systems similar to those on which his and Judith's modeled itself, just as
strongly rejects as oppressive and restricting. When the protagonist observes the St. Louis couple, he recalls the way in which
he and Judith directed their hostilities to their possessions—one
telling the other, for instance, that his chair squeaked—and how
he came to think of Judith herself as a *thing* or, at best, as a *being*.
He recalls how carefully orchestrated their movements had become and how the acts of each were stripped of reality because
their outcomes were already known by the other. The semiotics of
marriage that the St. Louis lovers have invented for themselves
and the contrasting, uncommitted relationship the protagonist
has with Claire become signs for the freedom he seeks and will, in
the novel's climactic scene, finally achieve.

Claire is also the protagonist's practical way of getting to see
America. She travels with him a third of the way across the
country, through Pennsylvania and the midwest to St. Louis,
which has traditionally been known as the gateway to the west and
therefore serves as a symbol of the frontier spirit that is so much a
part of America's heritage.[7] Moreover, the couple with whom
they stay are professional painters who make posters depicting
scenes of the settlement of the west, of covered wagons and
riverboats, for a movie company. Claire and the couple, con-
nected as they are with the American image, serve the protagonist
as a means of both knowing America and realizing independence
in himself. And, since Claire is a university German instructor,
who travels to St. Louis to see a production of Schiller's *Don Carlos,*
she becomes a kind of emissary, transporting the protagonist to
the frontier and to the lost world of eighteenth-century Europe,
to a play world in which freedom is the highest value.

If the protagonist sees signals in Claire and the lovers, so also
does he see them in Benedictine, Claire's now fatherless daughter, and with respect to her his observations become even more
clinical and analytic. Benedictine was not part of his experience
with Claire on his previous trip to America, but this time she is a

real and demanding presence whose odd behavior is particularly interesting to him. The child cannot bear to see anything left open, screaming at the sight of the car trunk being loaded or the unfastened button on her mother's blouse. She insists on the sanctity of an object's name and of her own, reacting vehemently when a synonym or a pet name is used. She rearranges photographs which the protagonist stands on the car dashboard, responding with irritation whenever their order does not coincide with her mental model. The child, like the St. Louis couple, has systematized her life, seeking permanence and order through naming and arranging, but, as a consequence, she has become incapable of coping with any deviation from the pattern.

The protagonist's own memories of his childhood, his negative reactions to the natural beauty that surrounded him but brought only nervousness and misery, strongly suggest that his behavior, like Benedictine's, became systematized into an unchanging pattern against which he could rebel only through fantasy and fiction. Günther Schiwy suggests that Handke's comments on his own youth (in *I Am an Ivory Tower Dweller*, for example) indicate an awareness of this systematizing process.[8] In Handke's case, it was through literature that he was able to rebel against the regulations of his parochial upbringing and to create a private, less fossilized semiology. In the case of the protagonist, his current relationship with Judith causes him to rethink his experiences, not so much as individual events but as parts of the pattern which has become his schema for life; the child's obviously extreme, even neurotic, insistence on order only enhances the challenge to change which his impending confrontation with Judith presents.

Shortly after his arrival in America, when he is still in Providence and has just finished *The Great Gatsby*, the protagonist becomes aware of his need to change. He has a vision of a time that is not past, present, nor future; it is "another" time outside the time in which he normally lives, a time in which significances and feelings are different from those which now occupy, or which have ever occupied, his consciousness. And in that vision is a glance "einer ANDEREN Frau zu jener ANDEREN Zeit" (p. 25) ("of ANOTHER woman at that OTHER TIME," p. 18). That other time exists at the moment of his confrontation with Judith on the Pacific coast, a moment which the protagonist has been imagining as outside of time but toward which the narrative, functioning through time, has been steadily heading.

Handke's hero leaves Claire and Benedictine in St. Louis; flies to Tucson, Arizona, where he is robbed by Judith's henchmen; then heads for a lumber camp in Oregon, where his brother works. There he receives a postcard from Judith on which a spot along the coastal highway in Twin Rocks, Oregon, is marked with an *X*. Correctly interpreting the message to mean that Judith will meet him there, he takes a taxi to the designated point, observes Judith having a pedicure in a nearby shop, and awaits their meeting. Judith arrives, gun in hand, and either shoots or does not shoot her husband:

Sie hatten den Revolver auf mich gerichtet. "Sie nimmt mich ernst!" dachte ich. "Wirklich, sie nimmt mich ernst!" Sie spannte den Hahn. Das Geräusch war so leise, daß man es nur in der Vorstellung hörte und gar nicht daran glauben wollte. Ich war zu Asche verbrannt, aber noch ganz, würde nur bei der kleinsten Berührung auseinanderfallen. Das war es also! Und dafür hatte ich geglaubt, geboren zu sein! Enttäuscht stand ich vom Koffer auf und ging ihr entgegen. Mit götzenhaft starren Gesichtern gingen wir aufeinander zu; auf einmal drehte sie den Kopf weg und schrie, so schrill, daß ihr, wie bei einem brüllenden Kind, die Luft aussetzte. Ich hielt den Atem an bis sie weiterschreien würde, sie mußte gleich weiterschreien, noch einmal so laut; sie blieb aber still, verschluckte sich nur, es würgte sie, und ich nahm ihr den Revolver aus der Hand. (P. 185)

She was pointing the revolver at me. "She takes me seriously," I thought. "By God, she takes me seriously." She cocked the revolver. The sound was so soft that I heard it only in my imagination and refused to believe it. Though burned to ashes, I was still in one piece, but at the slightest move I would fall apart. So that was it! That was what I thought I had been born for! Disappointed, I stood up from my suitcase and went toward her. With rigid, graven faces we approached one another; suddenly she looked away and screamed like a child having a tantrum, so ferociously that her breath gave out. I held my breath, waiting for her to go on screaming; she was sure to start again, twice as loud; but she didn't, she only gulped, as though gagging, and I took the gun out of her hand. (P. 158)

This extraordinary moment is both the perfect climax to Judith's unrelenting pursuit of her husband and the fulfillment of that moment of timelessness which the protagonist has imagined. A film version of the novel, by Herbert Vesely, employs slow motion and replay in this scene to create a sense of another time, to convey the ambiguity the novel suggests, and to enhance the emotional impact of this long-awaited meeting. Unable to decide how Judith's hunt has been resolved, the reader is uncertain of the reality of the entire narration, wondering now whether the journey from St. Louis to the West Coast was merely a speculation on the protagonist's part, an experience lived in its entirety not in chronological time but in the other time he has imagined.

As if in answer to that doubt, Handke takes the protagonist and his wife to California, where they visit director John Ford at his Bel Air estate. The protagonist had seen John Ford's *Young Mr. Lincoln* in St. Louis and found insights in that film into his own sense of an inner reality:

In diesen Bildern aus der Vergangenheit, aus den Jugendjahren Abraham Lincolns, träumte ich von meiner Zukunft und träumte in den Gestalten des Films die Menschen vorweg, denen ich noch begegnen würde. Und je länger ich zuschaute, um so größer wurde die Lust, nur noch Gestalten wie denen im Film zu begegnen, mich nicht mehr aufführen zu müssen, sondern wie sie mich in vollkommener Körper- und Geistesgegenwart unter ihresgleichen zu bewegen, von ihnen mitbewegt zu werden, und doch mit einem Spielraum für mich selber, voll Ehrerbietung auch vor dem Spielraum der andern. (P. 135)

Looking at the images of the past, scenes from the early life of Abraham Lincoln, I dreamed of my own future; the people on the screen prefigured the people I would meet. The longer I watched, the more eager I became to meet only people like those in the picture; then I would never again have to pretend; like them I would be fully present in body and mind, an equal moving among equals, carried along by their motion, yet free to be myself while respecting the freedom of others. (P. 114)

At that moment he had resolved to go to California to meet John Ford. Now, as he and Judith sit on the terrace of the director's home, Ford speaks of moments in his life when he has experienced timelessness, forgetting himself and his existence. He speaks of poses people adopt in the presence of others, which alienate people from themselves and from each other, noting that the moments during which he has felt most like himself have almost always occurred in solitude. He speaks of experiencing a "medieval feeling," during which the world seems to be in a state of nature. And he speaks of his movies about the history of America, insisting that "Nichts davon ist erfunden," that "Alles passierte wirklich!" (p. 193) ("Nothing [in them] is made up," that "it all really happened," p. 165).

The scene with Ford is so realistic that several reviewers have suggested that Handke quite possibly met Ford during his own visit to America. Handke has long been an admirer of the director—in fact, a picture of a log cabin, signed "Directed by John Ford," once hung on the entrance door to Handke's home in Kronberg—but such a visit did not actually take place.[9] This questioning of truth, however, is at the heart of the couple's visit to California, of the narrative itself, and, finally, of all events and experiences that we call real. For Ford making the film and for the protagonist viewing it, postures and stories become an articulated reality in much the same way that the story of Judith and her husband becomes real through Handke's narrative. "Und das ist alles wahr?" ("Is all that true?"), asks Ford, as he listens to Judith tell of the pursuit and the confrontation, "Nichts an der Geschichte ist erfunden?" ("None of it is made up?"), to which Judith replies, "Ja . . . das ist alles passiert" (p. 195) ("No . . . it all happened," p. 167).

The narrative has moved the protagonist steadily along through a ritualistic shedding of the cumulative poses of a lifetime and a marriage toward that ceremonious moment in which he nakedly faces Judith and marvels at the seriousness with which she, who is not yet purged, can take him—or the poses which she considered to be "him." But she too, when disarmed, surrenders her poses in one incredible moment which removes them both from the necessity, and the security, of pretense. The couple's trip to California to see Ford, then, is not a progression in the change they have already experienced but rather an affirmation of that change. Ford articulates for them the significance of a reality removed from, yet realized through, fiction; he pronounces absolution by asking whether it all "really happened," giving Judith the opportunity to reply as she does; and, finally, he bestows a benediction upon them: when they leave California, Judith and her husband are ready to depart—and part—in peace.

9

They Are Dying Out

In 1974, a year after its publication, *They Are Dying Out (Die Unvernünftigen sterben aus)* was produced at the Theatre am Neumarkt in Zürich and the Schaubühne am Halleschen Ufer in Berlin. The Schaubühne, like Frankfurt's Theater am Turm, favored politically involved plays with a leftist orientation, and three years earlier it had shown considerable hesitation with respect to *The Ride Across Lake Constance*.[1] There was no such hesitation with the new play, however. Horst Zankl, who directed both the Zürich and the Berlin productions, undertook it without reservation, apparently feeling its anticapitalistic message was clear. When the Yale Repertory Theatre produced the play in 1979, it was billed as a "biting, wry comment on the cult of mass marketing and its creators," which the translator, Michael Roloff, and the director, Carl Weber, had "Americanized" to reflect the special embarrassments of our homegrown consumerism.[2]

Mr. Quitt, be he the original "Hermann" or the Americanized "Oscar," is by anyone's definition an unconscionable capitalist, who manipulates his colleagues into a position of vulnerability in order to destroy them. And the group of entrepreneurs who gather in his home are unrelenting in their criticism of free enterprise, committing themselves to deception and dissembling while acknowledging that they are cigar-smoking monsters in the public eye.

Nowhere in Handke's work is politics so prominent as in *They Are Dying Out*, yet no critic has satisfactorily accounted for this play's political ideology. Rainer Nägele and Renate Voris, for example, compare the play to Brecht's didactic *St. Joan of the Stockyards (Die Heilige Johanna der Schlachthöfe,* 1932) but conclude that Handke's repudiation of capitalistic practices is ambivalent.[3] And Manfred Mixner carefully examines the political framework

107

of the play but denies the existence of any direct political message.[4] The fact is that the play is not politically convincing, and one is left with the feeling that Quitt's suicide, effected through successive smashings of his head against a massive stone, is something other than—or more than—his disillusionment with life in a capitalistic society. Politics may indeed offer an entry point for the play, but once one gets beneath the surface, one is in a skillfully wrought playworld which has as much to do with alienation as with capitalism, and more to do with aesthetics than with either. Beneath its political mask, *They Are Dying Out* is a dramatized continuation of the aesthetic dialogue which informs all Handke's work, and particularly of the growing feeling of loss suggested in *Short Letter, Long Farewell*.

Like the protagonist of *Short Letter, Long Farewell*, Quitt is a man in search of self. He has invested much time, effort, and capital in building not only an empire but an image, yet he is not content; though seldom given to displays of emotion, Quitt admits he is a lonely man and, in the opening scene of the play, rejects the suggestion of his servant, Hans, to be reasonable. Quitt the businessman suspects there is more to him than his professional pose, and he resolves to prove to Hans—and to himself—that his feelings are "useful."

The entrepreneur becomes preoccupied to the point of obsession with finding the self beneath the camouflage of his businessman's life. In a conversation with Paula Tax, the one female entrepreneur among them, he pleads, "Und wenn Sie mich jetzt ansehen, nehmen Sie bitte einmal mich wahr, und nicht meine Ursachen"[5] ("And if you look at me now, please become aware of me for once and not my causes"[6]), then begs, "Muß ich erst mit dem Kopf auf den Boden schlagen, damit Sie sich nach mir erkundigen?" (p. 45) ("Do I have to bang my head against the floor to make you ask about me?", p. 202). He tells the story of how the egg man came to the door at the same time each week and how he wanted to scream, "Können Sie denn nicht einmal jemand andrer sein?" (p. 44) ("Can't you be someone else for once?" p. 200), and he delights in listening to Kilb relate an event of his (Quitt's) recent past, commenting, "Es ist schön, eine Geschichte von sich selbst zu hören" (p. 16) ("It's beautiful to hear a story about oneself," p. 174), a remark suggesting that he is looking for verification of his existence. He tells of how some young boys once saw him step out of his house and tauntingly cried out, "Ich weiß, wer du bist! Ich weiß, wer du bist!" ("I know who you are! I know who you are!"), "als sei es etwas Schlimmes, daß ich zu identifizieren war" (p. 38) ("as though the fact that I could be identified was something bad," p. 195).

But Quitt's colleagues are disarmed by the unexpected signs of humanization in the entrepreneur. Hearing his long derogatory assessment of the free enterprise system, Koerber-Kent asks, "Was spielten Sie da gerade? Es war doch nur gespielt, oder? Denn in Wirklichkeit sind Sie—" ("What were you playing just now? It was just a game, wasn't it? Because in reality you are—"), to which Quitt sardonically replies, "Ja, aber nur in Wirklichkeit" (p. 29) ("Yes, but only in reality," p. 187). And Kilb, the minority stockholder who faithfully attends all such meetings, asks Quitt, "Können Sie nicht mehr unterscheiden zwischen Ritual und Wirklichkeit?" ("Can't you distinguish between ritual and reality any more?", warning him, "Erkennen Sie Ihre Grenzen, Quitt" (p. 34) ("Know your limits, Quitt," p. 191).

Quitt does indeed have limitations, and they are not only those of the businessman unable to escape society's labels but of a man aware of a self that bears no relationship to the world, to other people, to itself. Quitt longs to be human and speaks to Hans of

richtige Menschen, die ich schmecken und fühlen kann, lebendige Menschen. Weißt du, was ich meine? Menschen! Einfach . . . Menschen! Weiß du, was ich meine? Kein Papierdrachen, sondern . . . Menschen. Verstehst du: Menschen! Ich hoffe, du weißt, was ich meine. (P. 62)

real people whom I can feel and taste, living people. Do you know what I mean? People! Simply . . . people! Do you know what I mean? Not fakes but . . . people. You understand: people. I hope you know what I mean. (Pp. 217–18)

Despite his hopes, Quitt cannot become any more than a "phantom" of himself, one who suddenly notices that he no longer has anything to do with his face. Quitt's quest ends with the discovery that his reality is defined by his fictions, that his very essence is nothing but role.

Quitt, of course, is no real man but a dramatic character, whose search for self must logically end with the cry, "Ich stecke immer noch tief in meiner Rolle" (p. 98) ("I'm still stuck too deep in my role," p. 254), for a dramatic character's freedom cannot be had without annihilation. Quitt, in fact, does have an existence beyond his role as businessman, but it is not to be found in the liberation of a necessarily nonexistent essential self. It resides, rather, in Quitt's identification of himself as artist. As Joseph A. Federico points out, Quitt "sees himself as the hero of a self-authored drama, a 'tragedy'."[7] In Quitt's words, the tragedy is one of business life, in which "ich der Überlebende sein werde. Und mein Kapital in dem Geschäft, das werde nur ich sein, ich allein" (p. 55) ("I will be the survivor. And the investment in the business will be me, just me alone," p. 211). For the artist himself, for Handke, the tragedy expands beyond the world of the play, accounting for Quitt's— and modern man's—loneliness and alienation in terms of no less magnitude than the decline of western civilization and the consequent loss of a poetic language.

In a 1974 interview for *Die Zeit,* Handke remarked of his characters in this play: "Sie spielen, als ob sie tragische Figuren wären. Aber sie bleiben doch im Schatten einer Parodie"[8] ("They play as if they were tragic figures. But they remain in the shadow of a parody"). The comment is central to the play, not because Handke's "wry humor" (as the Yale Repertory Theatre calls it) precludes a serious treatment of Quitt's fate, but because an advanced capitalistic society, such as the one in which Quitt functions, precludes tragedy. Georg Lukács, tracing the decline of narrative in his *Theory of the Novel* (*Die Theorie des Romans,* 1916), and elsewhere, speaks of the utopian age of the Greek epic, a form which emanated from a civilization in which there was no disparity between meaning and essence. Tragedy, he contends, developed when the "inner world" and the "outer world" became opposed, but the form permitted their momentary reconciliation, in the tragic crisis. In more recent centuries, there have been only a few writers who have shared this awareness of the schism between man and his environment and who have attempted to

restore harmony through narrative.[9] Among the writers whom
Lukács regards with especially high esteem (in fact, he has written
a monograph on him) is Gottfried Keller, whose masterpiece is
the autobiographical *Green Henry*, the novel to which the hero of
Short Letter, Long Farewell keeps returning.

Indeed, the same sense of loss which the protagonist in *Short
Letter, Long Farewell* feels whenever he reads Keller's nineteenth-
century novel is expressed by Quitt after Hans reads him a long,
slightly edited, passage from Adalbert Stifter:

Und wieviel Zeit seit damals vergangen ist! Damals, im 19. Jahrhundert, auch wenn man gar keine Weltgefühle mehr hatte, gab es
doch wenigstens noch eine Erinnerung daran und eine Sehnsucht.
Deswegen konnte man die nachspielen und spielte sie den andern vor,
wie zum Beispiel in dieser Geschichte ["Der Hagestolz"]. Und weil man
sie so ernst und geduldig und gewissenhaft wie ein Restaurateur,
Stifter war ja ein Restaurateur, nachspielte, stellten sich Gefühle auch
wirklich ein, vielleicht. Immerhin glaubte man, daß es das gab, was man
spielte, oder daß es möglich war. (Pp. 53–54)

How much time has passed since then! In those days, in the nineteenth
century, even if you didn't have some feeling for the world, there at
least existed a memory of a universal feeling, and a yearning. That is
why you could replay the feeling and replay it for the others as in this
story ["The Bachelor"]. And because you could replay the feeling as
seriously and patiently and conscientiously as a restorer—the German
poet Adalbert Stifter after all was a restorer—that feeling was really
produced, perhaps. In any event, people believed that what was being
played there existed, or at least that it was possible. (Pp. 210–11)

Quitt's nostalgia for a lost literature sounds more like Handke
the poet than Quitt the capitalist, yet Quitt's status as a promoter
of free enterprise has much to do with aesthetics. For Lukács, the
relationship between the decline of western civilization and the
decline of poetry is clear: "The domination of capitalist prose over
the inner poetry of human experience, the continuous dehu-
manization of social life, the general debasement of humanity
—all these are objective facts of the development of capitalism.
. . . The poetic level of life decays—and literature intensifies the
decay."[10]

Hegel, of course, also analyzes the effects of capitalism not in terms of literature but in terms of human relationships, suggesting that mass production prevents the worker from understanding the totality of the events in which he is involved or the product he partially makes. As George Steiner explains Hegel's theory of alienation, capitalism "severs man from the natural rhythms and shapes of creation."[11] The resulting *Verdinglichung*, or reification of life, defines Quitt the capitalist and Quitt the poet as product of the same historical phenomenon. Quitt the capitalist cannot establish contact with the world:

Ich möchte jetzt nach der Welt schnappen und sie aufschlucken, so unerreichbar kommt alles mir vor. Und auch ich bin unerreichbar, krümme mich von allem weg. Jede Geschichte, die ich erleben könnte, verwandelt sich nach und nach zurück in leblose Natur, in der ich keine Rolle mehr spiele. Ich kann davor stehen, wie gerade vor Ihnen, und es ist wieder menschenleere Vorzeit. Ich stelle mir den Ozean vor, die feuerspeienden Vulkane, die Urgebirge am Horizont, aber die Vorstellung gilt nicht mir, ich zittere nicht einmal darin auf als Vorahnung. Wenn ich Sie jetzt anschaue, sehe ich Sie nur, wie Sie sind, und ganz ohne mich sind, aber nie, wie Sie waren oder mit mir sein könnten. Das ist unmenschlich. (P. 46)

I would like to snap at the world now and swallow it, that's how inaccessible everything seems to me. And I too am inaccessible, I twist away from everything. Every event I could possibly experience slowly but surely transforms itself back into lifeless nature, where I no longer play a role. I can stand before it as I do before you and I am back in prehistory without human beings. I imagine the ocean, the fire-spewing volcanoes, the primordial mountains on the horizon, but the conception has nothing to do with me. I don't even appear dimly within it as a premonition. When I look at you now, I see you only as you are, and as you are entirely without me, but not as you were or could be with me; that is inhuman. (Pp. 202–03)

And Quitt the poet can only complain of failed attempts at poetry:

Ich spiele ja nur noch an auf Vergangenes, erzähle alles ernst Gemeinte sofort als Witz, eigene Lebenszeichen rutschen mir höchstens heraus, und es gibt sie auch nur für den Moment, in dem sie herausrutschen. Danach sind sie dann ja: wo man früher das Ganze erblicken wollte, sehe ich jetzt nichts als Einzelheiten. . . . Ich möchte so gern pathetisch sein! . . . Was mir herausrutscht, ist nur noch die Jauche der vergangenen Jahrhunderte. (P. 54)

All I actually do is quote; everything that is meant to be serious immediately becomes a joke with me, genuine signs of life of my own slip out of me purely by accident, and they exist only at the moment when they slip out. Afterward then they are—well—where you once used to see the whole, I see nothing but particulars now. . . . I would so like to be full of pathos! . . . What slips out of me is only the raw sewage of previous centuries. (P. 211)

Handke's own political inclinations may well be Marxist. But if Handke's writing, and particularly *They Are Dying Out*, is political, it is so in the sense that Gottfried Keller has referred to all man's activities as "political," not limiting the definition to ideology but referring to man's communal activities, that is, his relationships with other people and with the world at large. *They Are Dying Out* may indeed echo Lukács's aesthetics, but it stops considerably short of becoming a Marxist platform. For Handke's concern in this play is not to attack capitalism but to portray truthfully the condition of modernism, which, whatever the historical reasons (and the rise of capitalism may be one of them) he sees as a nearly unbridgeable schism between the individual and the world.

Handke has spoken of how history, and particularly the history of the German-speaking world, has destroyed the relationships between nature and language, making the poetic creation of men living together a near impossibility. He expresses the need to narrate the conflict between "die grosse Nature" ("the great nature") of which Hölderlin speaks—for in his time it was still possible to do so—and the modern writer's impotence (see the Interview, pp. 167, 174). Clearly the restoration of a harmonious vision of life is the key for Handke to the restoration of a language which will become the kind of literature Keller and Stifter, as well as Goethe, Schiller, and Hölderlin, were able to create.

The restoration of this vision of life is also necessary to the creation of epic, or even tragic, figures. Where the Greek epic hero felt a continuing sense of union between his inner and outer worlds, and the tragic hero experienced a moment of reconciliation (albeit too late), the modern hero, standing in opposition to his world, can at best be a parody. For Lukács, the prototype of modern literature is the madman, unable to achieve integration. And the characteristic state of the modern artist is impotence. One critic remarked that the world ends for Quitt not with a bang but with a burp, this inarticulate utterance suggesting the final failure of the modern poet.[12]

The extreme pessimism which informs Quitt's fate, however, is not Handke's final comment on modern literature nor the Armageddon of his own writing. For, as Lukács suggests in *The Theory of the Novel*, the grotesque failure of the protagonist in search of himself is inevitable in a world in which no reconciliation is possible, but the work of literature itself can stand as a symbol of the writer's successful integration of matter and spirit. In *They Are Dying Out*, Quitt himself is destroyed, but his servant, Hans, endures. At the end of the play, Hans notices with hope that he is becoming human and, in a parting poem, speaks of learning to dream and of changing the world. If Handke has been using capitalism as a metaphor for the decline of western civilization, then the survival of Hans, the proletarian, would suggest some hope of a return to an age when the integration of man and his environment was still possible. What suggests the possibility of redemption even more strongly, however, is the fact that Hans has been more than just Quitt's servant throughout the play. He has, in fact, been Quitt's *Doppelgänger*. The strong kinship of the two men is suggested in an early monologue, when Hans, hearing Quitt complain of loneliness and detachment, laments:

Ich kann mich an nichts von mir persönlich erinnern. Zum letzten Mal war von mir die Rede, als ich den Katechismus lernen mußte. "Meine Wenigkeit" von "Euer Gnaden". Einmal hatte ich einen Gedanken und vergaß ihn gleich wieder. Bis jetzt versuche ich mich an ihn zu erinnern. So bin ich nie zum Denken gekommen. Aber ich bin bedürfnislos. Immerhin leiste ich mir noch einige Gesten. (P. 11)

I can't remember anything personal about myself. The last time anyone talked about me was when I had to learn the catechism. "Your humble servant" of "Your Grace." Once I had a thought but I forgot it at once. I am trying to remember it even now. So I never learned to think. But I have no personal needs. Still, I can indulge in a few gestures. (P. 169)

Moments later, Hans explains to Kilb that he is only serious when Quitt is serious, and later, when Quitt invites him to tell him about himself, he replies, "Sie nennen mich und bekennen sich" (p. 49) ("You mention me. Yourself you mean," p. 207).

In the second part of the play, Hans speaks of his realization of this connection:

Plötzlich sah ich, daß mir etwas fehlte. Und als ich überlegte, merkte ich, daß mir alles fehlte. Zum ersten Mal gabs mich nicht nur so für mich, sondern als jemand Vergleichbaren, zum Beispiel mit Ihnen. (P. 58)

Suddenly I saw that I lacked something. And when I thought about it I realized that I lacked everything. For the first time I didn't just sort of exist for myself, but existed as someone who is comparable, say, with you. (Pp. 214–15)

And when Quitt asks Hans, "Möchtest du wie ich sein?" ("Would you like to be like me?"), the servant replies, "Ich muß" (p. 59) ("I have to be," p. 215).

From Hans's point of view, the play has rather a fairy-tale quality to it, the story of the poor servant who perseveres and ultimately becomes king. The analogy is a more substantial one than a first mention would suggest, for, in an interview with Heinz Ludwig Arnold, Handke speaks of his familiarity with the Austrian playwrights Nestroy and Raimund, and particularly the fairy-tale plays of the latter, which he says were the basis for *They Are Dying Out:*

Die Märchenstücke von Raimund sind für mich etwas gewesen, was ich immer noch in meinen Stücken zu erreichen versuche. Vor allem im letzten Stück: "Die Unvernünftigen sterben aus" ist im Grunde eine Raimund-Welt da: der unglückliche Reiche und die anderen, seine Genossen.[13]

The fairytale plays of Raimund have been for me what I am still trying to achieve in my plays. Above all in the last play: *They Are Dying Out* is basically a Raimund-world: the unhappy rich man and the others, his comrades.

At one point in the play, a conversation between Quitt and Paula is interrupted by Quitt's wife, who, involved in a crossword puzzle, asks the name of a nineteenth-century Austrian dramatist, seven letters. Quitt suggests Nestroy, she says "no"; he then suggests Raimund, and she replies, "Of course."

Even without the Raimund clue, however, a lover of fairy tales should recognize the familiar tale of the hero in search of an unspecified kingdom, the attainment of which symbolizes "a state of true *independence,* in which the hero feels . . . secure, satisfied, and happy. . . . In fairy tales, unlike myths, victory is not over others but only over oneself."[14] If Quitt, the reigning ruler, fails in his quest, then his *Doppelgänger,* his complementary alter-ego, does not. Hans achieves the freedom of self which Quitt sought.

Hans's achievement suggests Handke's idealized vision of the self as the fulfilling union of man and nature and of his hope for a language which can adequately express a relationship he fears is irrecoverable. His survival turns what might otherwise have been a pessimistic, even nihilistic, vision of the future of literature into an earnest hope for new life. It turns *They Are Dying Out* into both a lamentation and a prophecy, conveying the anguish of modern man in search of self and of the writer in search of a language. At one point in the play, Paula accuses Quitt of thinking of himself as "der Stellvertreter des Allgemeinen" ("the deputy of universal truth"):

Was Sie persönlich erleben, wollen Sie für uns alle erleben. Ihr privat geschwitztes Blut bringen Sie uns Verstockten zum Opfer. Ihr Ich will mehr als es selbst sein. (Pp. 37–38)

What you experience personally you want to experience for all of us. The blood you sweat in private you bring as a sacrifice to us, the impenitent ones. Your ego wants to be more than itself. (P. 195)

Clearly Quitt's ego has become more than itself, transforming itself not only into the noncapitalistic Hans, who poetically envisions a changed world, but into the poet Handke as well, whose own commitment to finding a language which will restore man's relationship to reality is unrelenting.

Die Unvernünftigen sterben aus, the German title of the play, has, unfortunately, been rendered in English as *They Are Dying Out.* By changing "The Irrational" to an indefinite "They," the translator has eliminated the indicator of the play's central concern. Early in the play, Hans cautions Quitt to stay rational (translated as "reasonable"), for a man of his position cannot afford emotion. Indeed, on the plot level, Quitt's actions prove to be far from rational, for he double-crosses his colleagues and commits a particularly violent suicide. Quitt would appear to be the prototypical modern madman whom Lukács describes.

Irrationality is also a key term in German philosophical theory, and a concept of which Lukács is particularly disdainful.[15] For Lukács, irrationality, which opposes Hegelian rationalism and Weimar classicism and was perpetrated by such philosophers as Schilling, Kierkegaard, and Nietzsche, marks the particular course of western civilization over the past two centuries and the corresponding decline in poetic language. It is responsible for the romantic introspection from which has evolved a disintegration of the full human personality, a withdrawal from life, and modern alienation.

In one of the more perceptive essays about this play, "Peter Handkes romantische Unvernunft," Arnold Blumer compares the philosophy of *They Are Dying Out* with that of Novalis, concluding that Handke is himself a "romantic."[16] Blumer's references to Novalis's philosophy, and particularly to his concern with the dialectic between the inner world and the outer world, are well chosen, for there is a kinship between the two writers' *Sehnsucht*, or longing for a reunion between the two worlds. But Novalis is the one romantic for whom Lukács has accolades. In his essay "On the Romantic Philosophy of Life" (1910), Lukács attacks the romantics for being so intoxicated with their egotistical sand castles that they have lost touch with life itself, contrasting them with Novalis, whose poetry preserves the energy of life.[17]

Though much of Handke's work (including his next novel, *A Sorrow Beyond Dreams*) affirms his affinity for the formalism that Lukács reproaches as decadent, this particular play, the last Handke has written to date, suggests a substantial kinship with Lukács. This is not to say that the play supports Lukács's politics nor his affirmation of mimetic literary form; the affinity rests, rather, in the fact that Lukács belongs to Germany's classical-humanist tradition, as opposed to the irrationalist tradition of which fascism allegedly was born.[18] *They Are Dying Out,* which will be echoed by Handke's most recent novels, is the first of Handke's writing to suggest so strongly and explicitly the need for poetic language.

10

A Sorrow Beyond Dreams

In 1967 Handke wrote an autobiographical essay entitled "1957," which, though brief, gives a telling portrait of himself at fifteen, a lad who, unlike the rebellious malcontent of Princeton, seemed always to do what was expected: he stood up when a superior walked into the room, never failed to excuse himself, stayed in bed if the thermometer said he had a fever. When the other boys drew swastikas on the palms of their hands with chalk, then patted another on the shoulder, leaving the imprint, Handke seemed always to be the one whose shoulder was grabbed. When he recalls the inner life of the fifteen-year-old, he creates a picture of a boy who was often ashamed and who felt he wanted to sneak away; who wished for evening to come only moments after he had awakened but at night pulled the covers over his head; who, craving for solitude, sat on the toilet much longer than necessary; and who, even at so young an age, began to be less afraid of death than of not-dying. Though studying to be a priest, the young Handke equated the church with a cold, inner world and began to discover, through forbidden books and through the natural process of maturation, that there was also an outer world. Though he had never yet been in a foreign land, he felt he had always been in one.[1]

Although "1957" is the most explicitly autobiographical of Handke's essays, all his works, and particularly the novels, reveal something of the man behind them. When Günther Schiwy suggested the connection between the protagonist of *Short Letter, Long Farewell* and the author, he was not noting anything new, for any informed reader of Handke's several novels readily recognizes the similarities among the protagonists who appear in each of them and between those characters and their creator.[2] Typically, the protagonist of a Handke novel is characterized by an

119

impenetrable separateness, an apartness not only from his fellow man, with whom he rarely develops any emotional ties, but from the phenomenal reality which surrounds him. The Handke hero sees himself as one destined to question unceasingly the terms of his existence, to analyze continually the systems that define both inner and outer reality, and, finally, to try to come to terms with the conditions of life. He distinguishes himself from others passing through his world by the torment of consciousness, which prevents him from accepting without question even the most basic assumptions of existence. While all Handke's fictional characters undergo this reevaluation of self and circumstance, the most personal of his protagonists is Maria Handke. *A Sorrow Beyond Dreams* (*Wunschloses Unglück,* 1972), written a few months after his mother's suicide on November 19, 1971, reveals a sensitivity, a capacity for understanding, and a sympathy for the need for change which say as much about the author's character and commitments as they do about his subject.

Handke's mother was born in Griffen, Austria, in the house owned by Handke's grandfather, a carpenter and farmer. It was there that her voluntary death, at age fifty-one, also took place. The woman who resolutely lay down on her bed and swallowed the entire contents of a newly filled prescription of sleeping pills bore little resemblance to the woman who thirty years earlier had delighted in running through the Austrian countryside with the man she loved. When Maria became involved with the German soldier who became Handke's father, she was an outgoing, exuberant, spontaneous young woman whose frequent laughter echoed through the village, brightening the lives of her many friends. She was a highly spirited woman who never understood what it was about the older, rather slight, already married soldier that attracted her, but who was proud to introduce him to her parents and to bear his child. When, shortly before the child's delivery, another German, Bruno Handke, offered to marry her, she was persuaded by friends to accept, for even though she did not love the man—indeed, if what Handke says may be believed, was repulsed by him—she did have an obligation to the child.

Handke's recollections speak of the remnants of his mother's gaiety, of the new sense of assurance displayed by the "citified" woman returning from Berlin, of his mother's discovery of herself through literature. But overshadowing these moments is the steadily declining spirit of a woman who had once "begged" her father "etwas lernen zu durfen"[3] ("to let her learn something")[4] and who found herself daily sinking further into the despair of an abysmally empty existence. Handke's stepfather, now working in his brother-in-law's carpentry business, drank heavily and, as the children hid under the covers with pounding hearts, beat his wife. Handke's mother suffered first from headaches, and then from what the neurologist she visited called a nervous breakdown, until finally, writing letters of farewell to her husband and each of her children and sending her eldest son a copy of her will, she decided "Aber an ein Weiterleben ist nicht zu denken" (p. 91) ("But it's unthinkable that I should go on living," pp. 61–62).

Her suicide was the deliberate choice of a woman whose life had already ended some thirty years before, whose every hope for a changed future brought only the certainty of commitment to a house, a family, a place which brought her nothing but pain. Like her son at age fifteen, she had realized there was an outer world, but for her there was no access. Handke's account of her life bears the sadness not simply of a man who has lost his mother, but of a man aware of a life so wasted, a spirit so debilitated that the real tragedy was not death but the choice of death. Though Handke says that "die Ausdrücke sind alle zu milde" (p. 102) "(all words and phrases are too mild," p. 68), he perfectly expresses the enormity of the frustrations, the loneliness, the starvation of a mind with nowhere to go.

When *A Sorrow Beyond Dreams* appeared in English translation, critics applauded it as a significant addition to the "literature of grief." Whereas Handke's previous work had brought adjectives such as "cold," "stark," "remote," and "unfeeling" to the pens of reviewers, now they were calling Handke's work "sensitive," "sympathetic," "moving," and "weighty." Indeed, there is a decided difference in the effect this "life story" has upon its readers and the effect any of Handke's previous novels have had, for *A Sorrow Beyond Dreams* is the first of Handke's works that strikes an emotional chord. In this narration, the intellectual coldness of the earlier novels gives way to a deeply personal retelling of his mother's life and death. The effect, however, has less to do with the intimacy of his subject matter than with the artistic capability that intimacy inspired. Until *A Sorrow Beyond Dreams*, Handke's characters were starkly sketched outlines, with limited accessibility; they fostered detachment rather than empathy. In *Short Letter, Long Farewell*, the protagonist, speaking with the dramaturge at the Schiller play, complains of the difficulty he has in creating roles:

Wenn ich jemanden charakterisiere, kommt es mir vor, als ob ich ihn damit entwürdige. Aus allem Besonderen an einer Figur wird dann ein Tick. . . . [Leute] sind für immer auf einen Begriff gebracht.[5]

When I characterize somebody, it seems to me that I'm degrading him. Everything that's individual about him becomes a tic. . . . I've reduced him to a concept.[6]

Following the Berlin interview (see Appendix 1) Handke expressed dissatisfaction with his own creation of character; like the protagonist of *Short Letter, Long Farewell,* he felt that the very process of portrayal was a betrayal. Only once did he feel that he was able to express character without degradation or compromise, and that was when he wrote of his mother. Maria Handke is the most human of Handke's characters not because she was real but because Handke's art was able to keep her so.

On first reading *A Sorrow Beyond Dreams*, anyone familiar with Handke's previous work is struck by what would appear to be the abandonment, or at least the temporary interruption, of the author's preoccupation with form. Whereas all of Handke's earlier writing had earned such labels as "experimental," "illusive," "inaccessible," and "difficult," in large part because each piece upset traditional expectations for either the drama or the novel, this narration appears to be a straightforward and somewhat disappointing concession to nineteenth-century realism, striving for maximum faithfulness to life. It is only upon a closer reading that one discovers that the narrative of *A Sorrow Beyond Dreams* exists not merely to serve the story of Maria Handke but as an autonomous component of the literary form which is Handke's subject of self-analysis.

Even a first reading should suggest that Handke's concern with form is present in this novella, for on several occasions the story line is interrupted by passages explicitly commenting on the problems involved in the creative process. But because these passages are placed in parentheses, separating them from the main narrative, and because the suicide of Maria Handke has both intrinsic interest and the appeal of a well-told story, the tendency is to consider these paragraphs a distraction, minimizing their significance. In these passages, however, we can most clearly hear the echoing voice of the young rebel at Princeton's Group 47 meeting speaking out against the *Beschreibungsimpotenz* of his "neorealistic" colleagues. For in giving voice to "das bloße Nacherzählen [und] das schmerzlose Verschwinden einer Person in poetischen Sätzen" (p. 44) ("the danger of merely telling what happened and the danger of a human individual becoming painlessly submerged in poetic sentences," p. 28), Handke confronts the central aesthetic dilemma of the "realistic" novelist.

Handke's awareness of the problem of realism is evident in the reasons he gives for writing the story of his mother. Early in the narrative, he explains:

Und ich schreibe die Geschichte meiner Mutter, einmal, weil ich von ihr und wie es zu ihrem Tod kam mehr zu wissen glaube als irgendein fremder Interviewer, der diesen interessanten Selbstmordfall mit einer religiösen, individualpsychologischen oder soziologischen Traumdeutungstabelle wahrscheinlich mühelos auflösen könnte. (Pp. 10–11)

I am writing the story of my mother, first of all because I think I know more about her and how she came to her death than any outside investigator who might, with the help of a religious, psychological, or sociological guide to the interpretation of dreams, arrive at a facile explanation of this interesting case of suicide. (P. 5)

Fidelity to the character of this real life person is obviously a priority for Maria Handke's son, who, like many before him, seeks emotional therapy in the objectification of his grief. But his motives are not purely selfish. As a writer, Handke is urgently aware of his responsibility to make an exemplary case of this VOLUNTARY DEATH, but in a different way than an outside investigator would. The conflict between his need as a writer to give general significance to Maria Handke's life and death and his need as a son to preserve her individuality, that is, not to degrade her to a concept, stimulates his analytical foray into the problems of rendering reality in fiction.

Roman Jakobson, noting that literary realism has little to do with the faithful rendering of phenomenal reality, argues that realism is measured in terms of given artistic norms. Realism is determined by the extent to which a writer tends to conform to or deviate from these norms, or the extent to which the reader views the adherence to these norms as a rendering of reality and the deviation from them as a distortion of reality. Alternatively, one may look to the specific group which has become associated with realistic writing, that is, nineteenth-century novelists, and measure all writing against the literary characteristics of that group. But in any case, what is important is that while writers and readers may feel they are evaluating writing in terms of phenomenal reality, they are in fact evaluating writing in terms of artistic codes.[7]

That realism rests in, not outside of, the text has, of course, been Handke's contention through all of his writing, but when he came to the telling of his mother's life and death, he was undoubtedly even more aware of the frozen conventions available to the "realistic" writer. Hence his narration begins with the printed notice of his mother's death:

"In der Nacht zum Samstag verübte eine 51 jährige Hausfrau aus A. (Gemeinde G.) Selbstmord durch Einnehmen einer Überdosis von Schlaftabletten." (P. 7)

"In the Village of A. (G. township), a housewife, aged 51, committed suicide on Friday night by taking an overdose of sleeping pills." (P. 3)

This objective report of the *Kärntner Volkszeitung* is the same impersonal notice the paper would have published had the woman been anyone other than Maria Handke. Handke continues with a few paragraphs explaining why the need to write of his grief is so strong, returns to the fact of the registered, special delivery letter his mother sent him, then begins the chronological telling of the tale. But he stops himself after the first few words,

"Es begann also damit . . ." (p. 12) ("it began with . . . ," p. 6),
concerned that by using this traditional beginning, he would be
fitting his mother into the mold of the preestablished formulations of literary realism, which would only falsify the woman. As
he later notes:

je mehr man fingiert, desto eher wird vielleicht die Geschichte auch für
jemand andern interessant werden, weil man sich eher mit Formu-
lierungen identifizieren kann als mit bloß berichteten Tatsachen.
(P. 26)

the more fiction we put into a narrative, the more likely it is to interest
others, because people identify more readily with formulations than
with recorded facts. (Pp. 15–16)

As though in deference to this principle of identification, he
proceeds to tell the story of his mother according to the conventions of nineteenth-century realism:

Es begann also damit, daß meine Mutter vor über fünfzig Jahren im
gleichen Ort geboren wurde, in dem sie dann auch gestorben ist.
(P. 12)

Well then, it began with my mother being born more than fifty years
ago in the same village where she died. (P. 6)

The story, predictably, fills in some facts of his mother's background: she was the daughter of a carpenter-farmer of Slovenian
descent; she received praise from a teacher for her neat handwrit-
ing; even after her schooling was over, she had a yearning to
learn; she worked as a cook in a hotel, having run away from
home; she returned; with the others in the village, she experienced the excitement of World War II; she fell in love with a
German army paymaster, but married another; she gave birth to a
son, then settled into the same life the women in her family had
known for generations. But as the narrative continues, it begins
gradually to deteriorate, disintegrating into fragments, single
words, and lists. The women in the village had a game they played
about the stations of a woman's life: "Müde/Matt/Krank/Schwer-
krank/Tot" (p. 17) ("Tired/Exhausted/Sick/Dying/Dead," p. 10).
Handke's narrative plays a similar game, telling us not the whole
story but selecting, condensing, and omitting:

Das Stadtleben: kurze Kleider ("Fähnchen"), Schuhe mit hohen Absätzen, Wasserwellen und Ohrklipse, die unbekümmerte Lebenslust. Sogar ein Aufenthalt im Ausland!, als Stubenmädchen im Schwarzwald, viele VEREHRER, keiner ERHÖRT! Ausgehen, tanzen, sich unterhalten, lustig sein: die Angst vor der Sexualität wurde so überspielt; "es gefiel mir auch keiner". Die Arbeit, das Vergnügen; schwer ums Herz, leicht ums Herz, Hitler hatte im Radio eine angenehme Stimme.

Das Heimweh derer, die sich nichts leisten können: zurück im Hotel am See, "jetzt mache ich schon die Buchhaltung", lobende Zeugnisse: "Fraulein . . . hat sich . . . als anstellig und gelehrig erwiesen. Ihr Fleiß und ihr offenes, fröliches Wesen machen es uns schwer . . . Sie verläßt unser Haus auf eigenen Wunsch." Bootsfahrten, durchtanzte Nächte, keine Müdigkeit. (P. 21)

Auftischen, abräumen; "Sind jetzt alle versorgt?"; Vorhänge auf, Vorhänge zu; Licht an, Licht aus; "Ihr sollt nicht immer im Bad das Licht brennen lassen!"; zusammenfalten, auseinanderfalten; ausleeren, füllen; Stecker rein, Stecker raus. "So, das war's für heute." (P. 66)

City life: short skirts ("knee huggers"), high-heeled shoes, permanent wave, earrings, unclouded joy of life. Even a stay abroad! Chambermaid in the Black Forest, flocks of ADMIRERS, kept at a DISTANCE! Dates, dancing, entertainment, fun; hidden fear of sex ("They weren't my type"). Work, pleasure; heavyhearted, lighthearted; Hitler had a nice voice on the radio. The homesickness of those who can't afford anything; back at the Hôtel du Lac ("I'm doing the bookkeeping now"); glowing references ("Fräulein . . . has shown aptitude and willingness to learn. So conscientious, frank, and cheerful that we find it hard . . . She is leaving our establishment of her own free will"). Boat rides, all-night dances, never tired. (Pp.12–13)

Setting the table, clearing the table: "Has everybody been served?" Open the curtains, draw the curtains; turn the light on, turn the light out; "Why do you always leave the light on in the bathroom?"; folding, unfolding; emptying, filling; plugging in, unplugging. "Well, that does it for today." (P. 43)

Through this paring down process, the reader becomes aware that Handke's disintegrating narrative is simply a more noticeable version of what fiction is: a highly manipulative, selective, reconstituted arrangement of details which are no more an accurate recording of what happened than history is.

For Handke, as for the Russian formalists, art must be destructive in order to be effective, for its first task is to render the familiar unfamiliar in order that our perception may become one of seeing rather than merely recognizing. As Viktor Sklovskij points out in *The Resurrection of the Word* (1914), the creation of literature consists of the repetitious employment of borrowed images, the result of which is "more reminiscence of images than thinking in them."[8] Among the more noticeable instances of the defamiliarization process in Handke's writing is a paragraph in *A Sorrow Beyond Dreams* in which he describes the objects of Maria Handke's life:

die BEHÄBIGE Waschrumpel, der GEMÜTLICHE Feuerherd, die an allen Ecken geflickten LUSTIGEN Kochtöpfe, der GEFÄHR-LICHE Schürhaken, der KECKE Leiterwagen, die TATENDUR-STIGE Unkrautsichel, die von den RAUHBEINIGEN Scheren-schleifern im Lauf der Jahre fast bis zur stumpfen Seite hin zerschlif-fenen BLITZBLANKEN Messer, der NECKISCHE Fingerhut, der TOLLPATSCHIGE Stopfpilz, das BULLIGE Bügeleisen, das für Ab-wechslung sorgte, indem es immer wieder zum Nachwärmen auf die Herdplatte gestellt wurde, und schließlich das GUTE STÜCK, die fuß- und handbetriebene "Singer"-Nähmaschine. (P. 64)

The GOOD OLD ironing board, the COZY hearth, the often-mended cooking pots, the DANGEROUS poker, the STURDY wheelbarrow, the ENTERPRISING weed cutter, the SHINING BRIGHT knives, which over the years had been ground to a vanishing narrowness by BURLY SCISSORS grinders, the FIENDISH thimble, the STUPID darning egg, the CLUMSY OLD flatiron, which provided variety by having to be put back on the stove every so often, and finally the PRIZE PIECE, the foot- and hand-operated Singer sewing machine. (Pp. 41-42)

The passage might have gone without special notice, as a piece of realistic description, had Handke not capitalized the adjectives describing the objects, causing them to stand out like placards. These are the objects of Maria Handke's reality, yet in the story, their reality rests in words. The comment following this descriptive paragraph is: "woran wieder nur die Aufzählung das heimelige ist" (p. 64) ("But the golden haze is all in the manner of listing," p. 42). A paragraph without billboard adjectives follows:

Aber eine andre Methode der Aufzählung wäre natürlich genauso idyllisch: die Rükkenschmerzen; die an der Kochwäsche verbrühten, dann an der Wäscheleine rotgefrorenen Hände; — wie die gefrorene Wäsche beim Zusammenfalten krachte! — ;ein Nasenbluten manchmal beim Aufrichten aus der gebückten Stellung; Frauen, so in Gedanken, alles nur ja schnell zu erledigen, daß sie mit dem gewissen Blutfleck hinten am Kleid selbstvergessen zum Einkaufen gingen; das ewige Gejammer über die kleinen Wehwehchen, geduldet, weil man schließlich nur eine Frau war; Frauen unter sich: kein "Wie geht's?", sondern "Geht's schon besser?" (Pp. 64–65)

Another way of listing would be equally idyllic: your aching back; your hands scalded in the wash boiler, then frozen red while hanging up the clothes (how the frozen washing crackled as you folded it up!); an occasional nosebleed when you straightened up after hours of bending over; being in such a hurry to get through with the day's work that you went marketing with that telltale blood spot on the back of your skirt; the eternal moaning about little aches and pains, because after all you were only a woman. Women among themselves: not "How are you feeling?" but "Are you feeling better?" (P. 42)

But now the solid capitals are no longer needed, for our perception has changed. We are no longer simply recognizing, we are seeing.

When we read the novella more alertly, we discover that Handke continually draws attention to certain words and the images they create, whether through the use of capital letters, italics, quotation marks, or other clichés which he trusts the reader will notice: "ein GERADER Mensch" (p. 37) ("they thought her FRANK and SIMPLE," p. 23); " 'So muß dein Stimmzettel am 10. April aussehen: der größere Kreis unter dem Wort JA ist mit kräftigen Strichen zu durchkreuzen' " (p. 22) (" 'How to mark your ballot on April 10: make a bold cross in the larger circle under the word YES'," p. 13); "viele VEREHRER, keiner ERHÖRT! . . . 'es gefiel mir auch keiner' " (p. 21) ("flocks of ADMIRERS, kept at a DISTANCE! . . . ['They weren't my type']," p. 12). Handke is pointing not only to such images as literary clichés but to the entire concept of realistic literature as a repetition of poetic images. He is, after all, telling us of a VOLUNTARY DEATH, which for him is *not* simply "this interesting case of suicide."

But something else is happening each time Handke deconstructs a cliché, something which has more to do with reality than the GOOD OLD ironing board or the PRIZE PIECE sewing machine. Formalist Boris Tomasevskij, commenting on the relationship between literature and biography, notes the difficulty of determining the exact nature of the relationship between literature and life: "It is sometimes difficult to decide whether literature recreates phenomena from life or whether the opposite is in fact the case: that the phenomena of life are the result of the penetration of literary clichés into reality."[9] The extent to which Maria Handke's life was a cliché is precisely what her son sees as her tragedy. She was a victim of the deadly surroundings into which she was born, a situation which deprived her of a language and a life of her own:

Man kann es aber auch beruhigend nennen: jedenfalls keine Zukunftsangst. Die Wahrsagerinnen auf den Kirchtagen lasen nur den Burschen ernsthaft die Zukunft aus den Händen; bei den Frauen war diese Zukunft ohnehin nichts als ein Witz. (P. 17)

But perhaps there was one comfort: no need to worry about the future. The fortune-tellers at our church fairs took a serious interest only in the palms of the young men; a girl's future was a joke. (Pp. 9–10)

She lived the life of an Austrian farm woman whose story differed only slightly from that of hundreds of others in her circumstance. Unlike her son, who was able to rebel against the systems imposed upon him, finding refuge in literature and fantasy and in creating a semiotics of self, Maria Handke acquiesced. Yet her awareness that the cliché had penetrated her life—indeed, *was* her life—led to her final act of liberation. Ironically, she then became merely a name for a priest to insert in the standard burial service rhetoric: "Unsere Mitschwester . . ." (p. 97) ("Our beloved sister . . . ," p. 65).

The sense of the German title of the novella, *Wunschloses Unglück*, lost in the English translation, is precisely that of the story: the unmasking of the cliché. Not only does the title invert the usual German expression, "wunschlos glücklich," it also suggests a paradox: a wished for, nice, even satisfying misfortune. "DAS WAR ES. DAS WAR ES. DAS WAR ES. SEHR GUT. SEHR GUT. SEHR GUT" (p. 94) ("THAT DOES IT. THAT DOES IT. THAT DOES IT. GOOD. GOOD. GOOD," p. 63). These are the narrator's thoughts as he flies to Austria upon hearing the news of his mother's death. He is filled with pride that she has unmasked the cliché of her life and chosen to end it. But the unmasking process suggested by the title is most prevalent in the artist's effort to portray his mother's life and death truthfully while revealing the fact that what we call "realism" in literature is itself a cliché.

Lukács, examining differing approaches to the selection process in "Narrate or Describe?" (1936), an essay which may well have helped Handke to articulate his objection to Germany's New Realism, attacks the realism of Zola while defending that of Tolstoy.[10] The descriptions of a horse race in *Anna Karenina* (1875–77) and in *Nana* (1880) have both won the praise of literary critics who, using commonly agreed upon relationships between words and the objects or experiences they describe (relationships which the formalists would call arbitrary), recognize in the authors' meticulous descriptions strong correspondences to phenomenal reality. Yet in *Nana* the scene is not, in Lukács's view, an integral part of the narrative but rather a digression used to give the novel a "naturalistic" background and not to further characterization or action. Interestingly, Roman Jakobson also comments on *Anna Karenina,* pointing to Tolstoy's focus on Anna's red purse during her death scene, not because it is or is not an organic part of the action, but because it illustrates the "progressive realism" of writers in rebellion against the recurring norms of literary convention. While Lukács might well denounce focusing on the unessential detail as a decadent realism which obscures the whole in its insistence upon portraying the particular, Jakobson praises Tolstoy's focus on the red bag as a successful attempt to upset the literary formulations which the reader has come to expect of such a scene.

What is more important than the apparent disparity existing between Lukács's praise for the integral element and Jakobson's defense of the unessential detail is the concept of literary language that underlies both critical theories. Handke, after all, rejects as "idyllic" both the GOOD OLD ironing board passage, which creates an image of coziness through describing the objects surrounding his mother, and the passage immediately following it, which focuses on the mother herself, creating an image of his mother's life which is quite alien to that suggested by the cozy kitchen. The integral element of Lukács and the unessential detail of Jakobson necessarily coexist within a realism measured by conformity to or deviation from literary writing.[11]

But another, related concept underlies literary discourse, distinguishing literary prose from nonliterary prose and from poetry, namely the two poles of language that Jakobson studies in his work on aphasia. The metaphoric, which functions on the basis of similarity, and the metonymic, which functions on the basis of contiguity, offer the possibility of a poetics of literature which Jakobson begins to formulate with respect to poetry. He says little, however, about fiction, other than to suggest that a corresponding study of these two modes, and particularly of metonymy, in prose writing would create such a poetics:

It is no mere chance that metonymic structures are less explored than the field of metaphor. May I repeat my old observation that the study of poetic tropes has been directed mainly towards metaphor, and the so-called realistic literature, intimately tied with the metonymic principle, still defies interpretation, although the same linguistic methodology, which poetics uses when analysing the metaphorical style of romantic poetry, is entirely applicable to the metonymical texture of realistic prose.[12]

David Lodge, pursuing and developing Jakobson's suggestion, examines the concept of realism in modern, antimodern, and postmodern novels, pointing to the way in which the distinctive quality of a literary work rests in the manipulation and interplay of these opposing poles.[13] In *Ulysses* (1922), for example, Joyce, in describing Stephen's and Bloom's separate perceptions of a female, attributes the metaphoric mode to the thoughts of the first and the metonymic mode to the description of the second. Stephen, seeing Mrs. Florence MacCabe, the midwife, thinks:

Mrs Florence MacCabe, relict of the late Patk MacCabe, deeply lamented, of Bride Street. One of her sisterhood lugged me squealing into life. Creation from nothing. What has she in the bag? A misbirth with a trailing navelcord, hushed in ruddy wool. The cords of all link back, strandentwining cable of all flesh. That is why mystic monks. Will you be as gods? Gaze in your omphalos. Hello. Kinch here. Put me on to Edenville. Aleph, alpha: nought, nought, one.

    Spouse and helpmate of Admon Kadmon: Heva, naked Eve. She had no navel. Gaze. Belly without blemish, bulging big, a buckler of taut vellum, no, whiteheaped corn, orient and immortal, standing from everlasting to everlasting. Womb of sin.[14]

As Lodge points out, not only is the passage replete with metaphors, but the monologue furthers itself through a series of similarities and substitutions: "It is the perception of a similarity between a telephone cable and the umbilical cord that leads Stephen's thought from the midwife to Eve, from his own birth to the birth of the race, drawing in other similarities and contrasts."[15] On the other hand, when Bloom sees the servant girl standing at the butcher counter, the scene is rendered metonymically:

A kidney oozed bloodgouts on the willowpatterned dish: the last. He stood by the nextdoor girl at the counter. Would she buy it too, calling the items from a slip in her hand. Chapped: washing soda. And a pound and a half of Denny's sausages. His eyes rested on her vigorous hips. Woods his name is. Wonder what he does. Wife is oldish. New blood. No followers allowed. Strong pair of arms. Whacking a carpet on the clothes line. She does whack it, by George. The way her crooked skirt swings at each whack.

    The ferreteyed porkbutcher folded the sausages he had snipped off with blotchy fingers, sausagepink. Sound meat there like a stallfed heifer.[16]

Lodge analyzes the ways in which Bloom's perception is synecdochic, resting in parts of the girl which stand for the whole. Furthermore, he shows how the narrative proceeds through association of contiguous rather than similar items: "The girl is linked with her master (Woods), the master with the mistress, the age of the mistress with the youth of the girl, the youth of the girl with the jealousy and repressiveness of the mistress who forbids her to have male visitors."[17]

Lodge also points to the attempts of postmodern writers to deconstruct the metonymic nature of the narrative process. In *Murphy* (1963), for example, Beckett, who Lodge feels has claim to being the first important postmodern writer, replaces conventional description with a list of Celia's characteristics:

Age	Unimportant
Head	Small and round
Eyes	Green
Complexion	White
Hair	Yellow
Features	Mobile
Neck	$13\frac{3}{4}''$[18]

In *Double or Nothing* (1971), Raymond Federman distorts the linear format of conventional prose:

a very direct form of narration without any distractions
            without any obstructions just plain
                       normal
                       regular
                       readable
                       realistic
                       leftoright
                       unequivocal
                       conventional
                       unimaginative
                       wellpunctuated
                       understandable
                       uninteresting
                       safetodigest
                       paragraphed
                       compulsive
                       anecdotal
                       salutory
                       textual
    PROSE   prose   prose   boring
PROSE   PROSE   prose   PROSE plain PROSE[19]

And in a short story enitled "In the Fifties" (1975), Leonard Michaels presents a near list of events which constituted this period of the narrator's life:

I attended the lectures of the excellent E. B. Burgum until Senator
McCarthy ended his tenure. I imagined NYU would burn. Miserable
students, drifting in the halls, looked at one another.

In less than a month, working day and night, I wrote a bad novel.

I went to school—NYU, Michigan, Berkeley—much of the time. I
had witty, giddy conversation, four or five nights a week, in a homo-
sexual bar in Ann Arbor.

I read literary reviews the way people suck candy.

Personal relationships were more important to me than anything
else.

I had a fight with a powerful fat man who fell on my face and was
immovable.

I had personal relationships with football players, jazz musicians,
ass-bandits, nymphomaniacs, non-specialized degenerates, and numerous Jewish premedical students.

I had personal relationships with thirty-five rhesus monkeys in an
experiment on monkey addiction to morphine. They knew me as one
who shot reeking crap out of cages with a hose.[20]

Handke's expression of the risks involved in the writing of his
mother's biography, that is, the danger of merely telling what
happened (the metonymic mode) and the danger of submerging
her individuality in poetic sentences (the metaphoric mode),
would seem to acknowledge these two poles, as does the preponderance of metonymic discourse throughout the novella. Like the
outside investigator reporting on the events leading to Maria
Handke's suicide, Handke tells of his mother's youth, of the old
age which enveloped her by the time she was thirty, and, finally, of
her decision to end her life. Consistently denying himself the use
of metaphor, Handke relies almost completely on presenting the
raw ingredients of his mother's life in a deconstructed version of
metonymic discourse.

But this metonymic process is contiguous in ways in which an
investigator's report would not be. The most obvious is the relationship each of the events has to this woman who opted for an
understandable, even praiseworthy, VOLUNTARY DEATH,
but the most important is the integral relationship between Maria
Handke's life and her choice of death, on the one hand, and the
narrative process itself on the other, for the emotional impact of
the story rests here. For Handke, his mother's VOLUNTARY

DEATH holds more than mere clinical interest. Through the self-conscious selection process, Handke is able to put in the foreground the correlation between the imprisonment and frustration of Maria Handke, reluctantly committed to the givens of her circumstance, and that of the author, just as reluctantly committed to the established forms of realistic fiction, as well as the correlation between his mother's decision to end her life, unfulfilled, and Handke's to end his story with the admission that he has not found relief in telling it.

If Maria Handke's life has failed, so has Handke's narrative, both ending as they do on a note of the unfulfilled wish. Yet the strange satisfaction which Handke feels when his mother ends her life has a correlative in the reader's response to his narrative. Just as Handke acknowledges his mother's resistence to the way of life imposed upon her, even as she acquiesces to it, so also does the reader feel the pervasiveness of Handke's own resistance to the depersonalizing clichés of fiction even as he uses them. Ultimately, the reader must agree that neither Maria Handke's life nor Handke's story has failed, for Maria Handke's VOLUNTARY DEATH is not just "this interesting case of suicide," and the narrative depicting that death succeeds in presenting it both as an individual life story and as an "exemplary case."

Speaking of the Marxist aesthetics to which his later writing is committed, Lukács measures realism in terms of an "artistically typified essence" that succeeds in creating the "typical" in the "individual," which is the mark of all great literature.[21] As expressed by Russian critic S. Petrov: "A literary type will frequently give us an image of a particular person and at the same time present a generalization that applies, we might almost say, to the whole of mankind."[22] Having omitted the details that would be of no interest to anyone but himself, Handke has touched the generally human in the frustration of a person in search of a place for herself in a world which is oppressive in its indifference, hostile in its passivity, and destructive in its self-perpetuation. No less than Goethe's *The Sorrows of Young Werther* (*Die Leiden des Jungen Werthers*, 1774), Handke's story embodies the profound disappointment of a wish unfulfilled.

Yet Handke's narrative takes on an unexpected character in the final pages of the text. Until then, the author carefully sustained a balance between his mother's life and the form of fiction he had to use to verbalize it. Now, in what might be called a coda to the telling of this life story, he abandons the narrative chronology of Maria Handke's life, slipping into a series of brief anecdotes:

Mit ihrem Speichel reinigte sie den Kindern oft im Vorübergehen schnell Nasenlöcher und Ohren. Ich zuckte immer zurück, der Speichelgeruch war mir unangenehm.

In einer Gesellschaft, die eine Bergwanderung machte, wollte sie einmal beiseitegehen, um die Notdurft zu verrichten. Ich schämte mich ihrer und heulte, da hielt sie sich zurück. (P. 101)

Often, as she passed by, she would quickly wipe out the children's ears and nostrils with her saliva. I always shrank back from the saliva smell.

Once, while mountain climbing with a group of friends, she started off to one side to relieve herself. I was ashamed of her and started to bawl, so she held it in. (Pp. 67–68)

These are the moments too personal to be of interest to anyone but Handke himself, the moments that did not fit into the literary mold. But these are also the moments that offer a new literary possibility, consisting of a montage of isolated memories, the contiguity of which rests not in space or time nor in the relationship of details to the woman they describe but in Handke's own experience and image of his mother.

After trying to find ways of formulating the facts of his mother's life and alternatively trying to search for those facts which fit existing formulations, all in order to achieve an accommodating narrative, Handke can only conclude that writing has not helped his grief and has been "nur ein ständiges Gehabe von Erinnerung" (p. 99) ("merely a constant pretense at remembering," p. 66). Indeed, the narrative that precedes these anecdotal moments is neither a recording of reality nor an act of memory but a shaping of certain raw ingredients of Maria Handke's life into the literary image of a WOMAN WITHOUT A LIFE OF HER OWN. For Handke, it is only now that the possibility of a true act of remembering exists, which can make his story not who Maria Handke was but who Maria Handke was to her son, which is, after all, the only story he can truthfully tell.

11

A Moment of True Feeling

Gregor Keuschnig, the protagonist of *A Moment of True Feeling* (*Die Stunde der wahren Empfindung*, 1975), is readily identifiable with the central characters of *The Goalie's Anxiety at the Penalty Kick* and *Short Letter, Long Farewell*. Though all three are Austrians, Joseph Bloch spends most of his time in a tiny border town away from Vienna, his home city; the protagonist of *Short Letter, Long Farewell* travels through America; and Gregor Keuschnig, with his wife and four-year-old daughter, lives in Paris. As press attaché at the Austrian embassy, it is Keuschnig's job to clip references to Austria from the French newspapers and to promote the image of Austria as a country with more to its identity than Lippizaner horses and skiing. Like the protagonists of the two earlier novels, Keuschnig is a stranger in an unfamiliar land, intensely aware of his surroundings and haunted by the very fact of existence.

In Keuschnig's case, a mental event, occurring outside the boundaries of phenomenal reality, is the source of his alienation. Keuschnig dreams he murders an old woman, and from that moment he feels he must pretend he is himself, even though he has become someone else:

Ab heute führe ich also ein Doppelleben, dachte er. Nein, gar kein Leben: weder das gewohnte, noch ein neues; denn das gewohnte werde ich nur vortäuschen, und das neue wird sich erschöpfen müssen im Vortäuschen des gewohnten. Ich fühle mich hier nicht mehr am Platz, kann mir aber überhaupt nicht vorstellen, irgendwo anders am Platz zu sein; kann mir nicht vorstellen, so weiterzuleben wie bis jetzt, aber auch nicht, zu leben, wie jemand andrer gelebt hat oder lebt . . . Es gibt kein Wie für mich, höchstens, daß ich so weiterleben muß "wie ich".[1]

From today on, he thought, I shall be leading a double life. No, no life at all: neither my usual life nor a new one, for I shall only be pretending to live my usual life, and my new life will consist solely in pretending to live as usual. I no longer feel in place here, but I can't conceive of being in place anywhere else; I can't conceive of continuing to live as I've lived up until now, but no more can I conceive of living as someone else lived or lives . . . I can't live *like* anybody; at the most I can go on living "like myself."[2]

Keuschnig's dream image of himself is irreconcilable with the image of self he has long projected and which others have come to recognize as Gregor Keuschnig; what is more, it is an insufferable identity, to which Keuschnig could not possible conform his behavior without enduring the consequences of society's moral taboos. His commitment, therefore, must rest in living so perfectly in accord with the image of his former self that no one will suspect the "truth." As press attaché for Austria, he devotes his daily activities to revealing to others the fact that there is more to his homeland than they think, but with respect to himself, he must conceal anything which might suggest an identity other than that which others have always associated with Gregor Keuschnig. The paradox lies in the fact that although Keuschnig consciously chooses to retain the outward appearance of his former identity, that identity is no longer available to him. Keuschnig's dream so radically changes his perception of himself that his "usual" behavior becomes an exceedingly self-conscious performance, contrived to prevent others from suspecting he is not who he seems to be.

As a surrogate participant in his own affairs, Keuschnig understands that a pretext has existed all along. For him, every action becomes perfunctory in its predictability, and he begins to perform his daily activities with a sense of ritual. Visiting his lunch-hour mistress, he observes himself "das-den-Korken-aus-der-Flasche-Ziehen," "das-die-Hose-über-den-Stuhl-Legen," "das-das-Glied-in-die-Scheide-Aufnehmen" (pp. 28–29) ("drawing-the-cork-out-of-the-bottle," "laying-his-trousers-over-the-back-of-a-chair," "inserting-the-penis-in-the-vagina," p. 20). He watches a woman and man running toward each other and, turning away in disgust, imagines the rest of this oft-repeated scenario:

Jetzt werden sie ihre äffischen Arme umeinander legen, sich in die jämmerlichen Augen schauen und sich links und rechts auf die kläglichen Wangen küssen, dachte er. Und dann werden sie unbeirrbar ihrer sinnlosen Wege gehen. (P. 40)

Now, he thought, they'll be putting their preposterous arms around each other, looking into each other's pitiful eyes, kissing each other's pathetic cheeks, left and right. And then imperturbably they'll go their senseless ways. (P. 29)

And just before returning home from work, he rehearses the act of seeing his wife and child again and imaginatively enacts the scenarios of life taking place throughout Paris. Overwhelmed by the artifice of experience, Keuschnig sees himself as "der Gefangene von Disneyland" (p. 23) ("a prisoner in Disneyland," p. 15), a victim of "die international bewährten Erlebnisformen als bloße Kurpfuscherei" (p. 66) ("the charlatanism of internationally certified forms of experience," p. 52). He is no longer comfortable with a self-image formulated by others, nor with an interpretation of experience decided for him in advance.

Keuschnig's estrangement following his dream of himself as murderer is similar to that of Joseph Bloch following his actual murder of the movie cashier. But, as in *The Goalie's Anxiety at the Penalty Kick*, Handke is less interested in abnormal psychology than in the existential consequences of the unique vantage point which schizophrenia affords his protagonist. After the murder, Bloch experiences so highly sensitized a consciousness that he is unable, except in rare moments, to see anything as existing outside of systems, particularly those of language and gesture, and he insists upon interpreting the objects of reality as messages for himself. Keuschnig, following his dream murder of an old woman, acquires a similar awareness of systems, similarities, and correspondences, which makes him long for madness as a refuge. But Bloch eventually achieves a kind of semiotic sanity which leaves him interpreting the movements of the soccer game and explaining this system to the businessman. Keuschnig ultimately rejects all systems, reaching a point of readiness for the "unique, never related event" which he finally believes can occur.

For Keuschnig, whose internal transformation is as sudden and as radical as the external metamorphosis of Kafka's Gregor Samsa, the world cannot remain unchanged. Because of the dialectic that constantly haunts him—not the "either/or" but the "neither/nor" in his head—Keuschnig first feels the need to develop a foolproof system which would enable him to redefine himself at will and permanently insulate him from discovery. His attempt to reaffirm life precisely as it has always been, however, is frustrated by his own inability to perceive it as such. Every experience, while leading him deeper into his own schizophrenic negation of self, becomes a deconstruction of the very reality he is attempting to reclaim. Yet this process of rejection is also the means by which Keuschnig will reach the point of readiness for "the moment of true perception."

While returning home from work that day, his mind temporarily calm and clear, Keuschnig sees three objects—a chestnut leaf, a fragment of a pocket mirror, and a child's barrette—lying in the sand. The objects come together in such a way that they suggest an idea, which Keuschnig envisions as the key to the mysteries of the universe.

Er brauchte keine Geheimnisse, wohl aber die IDEE davon—und wenn er nur die Idee eines Geheimnisses hatte, war es unnötig, hinter all den gefälschten Geheimnissen seine Todesangst zu verstecken! (P. 82)

He needed no mysteries, what he needed was the IDEA of a mystery—and if only he had the idea of a mystery, there would be no need to hide his fear of death behind a lot of pseudomysteries! (P. 64)

The number three, traditionally a mystical number (which, as Bruno Bettelheim observes, was considered mystical long before the Christian concept of the trinity[3]), undoubtedly has as much to do with Keuschnig's reaction as the individual objects themselves. Commenting on one of his other novels, Handke refers to a children's book he remembered containing such a combination of three,[4] which, of course, is common to many fairy tales: Grimm's "Von dem Mäuschen, Vögelchen und der Bratwurst," "Der Ranzen, das Hütlein und das Hörnlein," and "Strohhalm, Kohle und Bohne" ("The Mouse, the Bird, and the Sausage," "The Knapsack, the Cap, and the Horn," and "A Straw, an Ember, and a Bean"), for example, among many others. Now, seeing these three seemingly unrelated objects, Keuschnig feels not only the mystery but the possibility of new experiences of reality: "Wer sagt denn, daß die Welt schon entdeckt ist?" (p. 81) ("Who said the world has already been discovered?" p. 63), he cries.

Although this moment of epiphany does not last, it renews itself just before the end of the novel, when Keuschnig, having decided to commit suicide, walks through the streets of Paris to the cliff from which he will throw himself. Now, in the face of the unthinkable, he is "gräßlich wach" (p. 147) ("hideously awake," p. 117), noticing every detail. But he discovers that as he observes others he is experiencing a sympathy for them, for he is seeing people and things in interrelationships: "ein Junge, der mit einer Spielzeugmaschinnenpistole in der Hand heulend hinter der Mutter herlief," "ein Mädchen, das an einem Motorrad mit der Ferse die Stütze zurückstieß und dann losfuhr," "eine große Negerin, die eine gerfüllte Plastiktragetasche auf dem Kopf trug" (pp. 148–49) ("a little boy with a toy tommy gun, bawling as he ran after his mother," "a girl kick[ing] away the prop of a motorcycle with her heel and driv[ing] off," "a big black woman carrying a full plastic shopping bag on her head," pp. 118–19). For Keuschnig, about to embrace the ultimate withdrawal, nothing seems ridiculous any longer; everything coalesces into the mystifying vision of wholeness suggested by the three objects he had earlier seen:

Keushnig wollte nichts mehr für sich. Die gewohnten Anblicke flimmerten vor seinen Augen, als seien sie Erscheinungen—und zwar natürliche—, und jede einzelne davon zeigte ihm eine Fülle, die unerschöpflich war. Er, der nicht mehr zählte, war in die andern gefahren, die in selbstverlorener Energie kreuz und quer gingen, und er glaubte, sie müßten den Schritt wechseln bei dem Ruck, mit dem er das für ihn nutzlose Glück auf sie übertrug. Er lebte noch irgendwie—mit ihnen. Dieser Zustand war keine Laune, keine Augenblicksstimmung mehr, die gleich wieder aufhörte, sondern eine, auch aus all der flüchtigen Augenblicksstimmungen!, gewonnene Überzeugung, mit der man arbeiten konnte. Jetzt erschien ihm die Idee, die ihm gekommen war beim Anblick der drei Dinge im Sand des

Carré Marigny, anwendbar. Indem ihm die Welt geheimnisvoll wurde,
"offnete sie sich und konnte zurückerobert werden. (Pp. 151–52)

Keuschnig wanted nothing more for himself. The usual sights took on
a magical sparkle—for every one of them showed him inexhaustible
riches. He himself had ceased to count, for he had merged with all
those others who were moving this way and that with selfless energy,
and he fully expected the jolt he created by transferring the happiness
he had no use for to these people, to make them change their step. He
was still in a certain sense alive—with them. His state was no longer a
momentary mood; it was a conviction (to which all his momentary
moods had contributed!), a conviction it would be possible to work
with. Now the idea that had come to him on seeing those three things in
the sand of the Carré Marigny seemed usable. In becoming mysterious
to him, the world opened itself and could be reconquered. (Pp. 120–21)

Earlier, when Keuschnig saw the three objects in the sand, he
speculated that the reason he was unable to experience anything
until that moment was that he had decided in advance what an
experience was. Now, moments before his contemplated suicide,
he experiences an unanticipated merger of his feelings with the
people and objects around him, deciding, finally, that his own
conspicuousness, his presence as part of a whole, makes suicide
impossible: "Er könnte sich als Toten ertragen, wenn im selben
Moment auch die übrige Welt mitaufhören würde" (p. 156) ("He
could put up with being dead if the rest of the world would stop at
the same moment," p. 124). For Keuschnig, this new relationship
between the mind and the external world is rich with the promise
of discovery.

As Keuschnig abandons his plan of self-murder, he turns to
find his Austrian writer friend observing him. This persistent fat
man, present since Keuschnig returned home the previous evening, seems to understand exactly how Keuschnig feels. At dinner
he describes how his once active interest in people has been
soured by his awareness of their predictability and how he has
come to despise people who feel secure in their ideas. Though his
heightened consciousness and consequent rejection of conventionalized responses mirrors Keuschnig's own experience, when
the writer asks Keuschnig whether he feels the same way, the
protagonist denies that he does, claiming he feels only the joy of

being alive. Before the evening is out, however, Keuschnig must abandon his pretense, as he listens to the writer's precisely accurate perception of him:

Ich habe dich heute in der Stadt gesehen. . . . Du warst verändert. Wenn ich dich sonst von Zeit zu Zeit traf, sahst du immer gleich aus, und doch erlebte ich dich jedesmal anders—das war ein schönes Gefühl. Aber heute warst du verändert, weil du verzweifelt versuchtest, wie immer auszusehen. Du hast so beflissen gleich gewirkt, daß ich erschrocken bin wie vor jemandem, der gestorben ist und von dem man plötzlich auf der Straße das Ebenbild sieht. (P. 98)

I saw you in town today. . . . You had changed. You always used to look the same when I ran into you now and then, but my impression of you was different each time—I felt good about that. But today you were changed, because you were trying so desperately to look the same as usual. You were so intent on seeming to be your old self that you startled me, it was like seeing a double of someone who's just died walking down the street. (P. 76)

Keuschnig reacts outrageously to the perspicacity of the writer, who has denied him any further possibility of pretense. Feeling immortally disgraced, he spits a peach stone into the writer's face, undresses, runs around the table, jumps on the writer's woman friend, and, finally, thrusting his hand into a plate, smears stew over his own face. Relieved and satisfied, he then confesses to his wife that he made love that afternoon to an embassy employee, whose name he didn't even know.

The writer's relationship to Keuschnig is again the *Doppelgänger,* the physical or hallucinatory double in whom a protagonist sees his own image. For Keuschnig, the psychic split which occurred as a result of his dream and which he has been trying to conceal concretizes in the form of the writer who, in claiming to have rejected conventionalized responses, is articulating the very thoughts Keuschnig must suppress. That the writer attributes these qualities to himself and not to Keuschnig, simply seeking sympathy from his host, suggests the writer is that aspect of Keuschnig's identity which he cannot reveal. Only when Keuschnig does not admit the relationship does the writer make Keuschnig's actions, rather than his own feelings, the subject of his observations, which leads to Keuschnig's realization that he has been exposed.

Like Dostoevsky's Golyadkin in *The Double* (1846), Keuschnig has encountered someone, be he real or an autoscopic hallucination, who is strikingly like him and who does not allow him to take refuge in a dichotomy between the public and the private selves. For both Keuschnig and Golyadkin, this other self is disturbing; like the image of himself which Zoroaster meets in the garden, the double portends death, leading both protagonists to the brink of suicide.

But Keuschnig is able to dismiss his double and to prevent his own death. Having experienced the vision of wholeness which leads him to believe in the plausibility of personal integration, Keuschnig defends his essential self, shouting at the writer from the edge of the cliff, "Du weißt gar nichts von mir!" (p. 157) ("You don't know anything about me!" p. 125). The writer, making faces at Keuschnig, "wie damit ihn Keuschnig endlich für leibhaftig halte" (p. 157) ("perhaps to convince Keuschnig that he was real," p. 125), turns and walks out of Keuschnig's life.

But this novel is not, finally, about the integration of a fragmented self. As Olaf Hansen points out, despite the provocativeness of Keuschnig's changed relationship to reality and to himself, his experience does not "lend itself to an analysis of the individual's alienation in modern society" nor to any other external interpretation. Rather, the text to this point has been working on the assimilation of the reader's imagination with Keuschnig's.[5] The process leading to Keuschnig's rejection of conventionalized reality, which brings him to the point of readiness for "die einmalige, noch nie erzählte Begebenheit" (p. 163) ("the unique, never related event," p. 130) parallels a similar exorcism of formulated perceptions in the mind of the reader, bringing him to the point at which the reconstitution of meaning, through fiction, may occur.

A closer look at the novel reveals that the text is no novel at all, but a process preliminary to the novel, which does not begin—indeed, is not ready to begin—until the final paragraph. Moments after Keuschnig jubilantly acknowledges the possibility that a unique event might occur, he approaches the Café de la Paix, beckoning to someone approaching at the same time. This is the woman whom Keuschnig had telephoned after reading the message she'd scrawled on the sidewalk: "Oh la belle vie!" "Ich bin wie du" (p. 23) (*"Oh la belle vie,"* "I am like you," p. 15). Now, true to their arrangement, the two recognize each other without ever having seen one another before, and *A Moment of True Feeling* ends. In the final paragraph, the text becomes an objective, metonymic narrative of a man in a light blue suit walking across the Place de l'Opera in Paris to meet a woman. The point of readiness for *The Man in the Light Blue Suit,* the originally announced English title of the novel, has been reached.

The text of *A Moment of True Feeling* is a documentation of the literary event itself, which for Handke inheres in the complicity of the text and the reader. In the final pages of *The Goalie's Anxiety at the Penalty Kick,* Handke suggests the significance of the role of the reader through extending Bloch's preoccupation with semiotic processes to the reader's own position as interpreter. In *A Moment of True Feeling,* as in Handke's first novel, *The Hornets* (the hero of which is also named Gregor), the reader's interpretive function prevails as an aesthetic throughout the text, with his reevaluation of the ways in which fiction presents reality forming the counterpart to the dialectic experienced by Keuschnig as he reorders reality in response to his dream.

The Austrian writer becomes even more significant, not as an image of Keuschnig but as the man who is writing "Auf dich, mein lieber Gregor" (p. 96) ("About you, my dear Gregor," p. 75). The author of Handke's work himself appears within the narrative even as he creates it, observing, analyzing, and recording Keuschnig's behavior. But, significantly, Keuschnig never permits him omniscience, denying the author's every conclusion about his character and protesting that the writer knows nothing about him. Resisting the traditionally dominant role of author, Keuschnig will not be turned into art through this one man's version of reality, suggesting that Handke does not believe fiction to be the closed product of a single imagination. Instead, like Umberto Eco, he sees it as an experience very much like an open musical composition: "The multiple polarity of a serial composition in music, where the listener is not faced by an absolute conditioning center of reference, requires him to constitute his own system of auditory relationships. He must allow such a center to emerge from the sound continuum. Here are no privileged points of view, and all available perspectives are equally valid and rich in potential."[6]

As much as Keuschnig, the reader himself has been seeking the continual renewal of cognitive processes through freedom from formulation. Now, as the writer departs from Keuschnig's life, relinquishing his presence within the text, the reader's imaginative role is affirmed, along with the autonomy of the fictional event.

12

The Left-Handed Woman

In 1973, before moving to Clamart, the Paris suburb where he was to remain for five years, Handke lived in a housing community built into a terraced mountainside above the smokestacks of Kronberg, West Germany, an industrial city north of Frankfurt. One day, as the afternoon sun faded and lights illuminated the windows in the community, he noticed the solitary woman behind each window and felt he wanted to write the story of one of these women. After two years of thinking about the story, his thoughts crystallized into two pictures: the woman alone after the child is in bed, eating the leftovers from the child's plate, and the woman at a matinee movie, resting her tired head on her child's shoulder.[1] Filling in the events of a woman's life following her sudden separation from her husband, Handke translated these images into a novella, *The Left-Handed Woman (Die linkshändige Frau,* 1976), and a two-hour film.

The thirty-year-old Marianne fetches her businessman husband, Bruno, at the airport one day while their eight-year-old son waits at home. She listens as he tells of his loneliness while in Finland on business and reaffirms his love for her. To celebrate the homecoming, the couple dine at a nearby restaurant-hotel, rent a room in order to make love as soon as possible, and head home, elated, the next morning. Or at least Bruno is elated, expressing his high spirits by turning somersaults on the lawn. Marianne, however, has had a foreboding vision that her husband will leave her. Anticipating this separation, she tells him to leave without delay. Bruno does so, and Marianne's life as an independent woman begins.

The topos of sudden change which Handke explores in *A Moment of True Feeling* works in a similar fashion here, where Marianne's transformation is engendered not by an external experience but by a dream: "eine seltsame Idee . . . eigentlich keine Idee, sondern eine Art—Erleuchtung"[2] ("a strange idea. . . . Well, not really an idea, more like an—illumination"[3]). Just as the text of *A Moment of True Feeling* begins with a question of a hypothetical experience—"Wer hat schon einmal geträumt, ein Mörder geworden zu sein and sein gewohntes Leben nur der Form nach weiterzuführen?"[4] ("Who has ever dreamed that he has become a murderer and from then on has only been carrying on with his usual life for the sake of appearances?"[5])—so the opening scene of *The Left-Handed Woman* finds Marianne's son reading her an essay he has written for school concerning his idea of a better life. He speaks of a world in which houses would be red, trees and bushes would be gold, everybody would live on islands, he would always have four friends, and everything he didn't know would disappear. After hearing her son's idealistic vision, Marianne rises, walks to the window, and stands for some time as though in a trance, perhaps envisioning her own better life.

From that point on, the narrative may be read as a kind of "what if" story, with the tentative quality of Marianne's life after her vision sustaining itself through her dreamlike withdrawal into long, nearly catatonic silences. In the film version, Marianne does not speak for the first twenty minutes, and when she finally does—to tell her husband of her vision of his leaving—her first lines come as a voice-over, suggesting a transition from the vision itself to the application of that "what if" dream. In fact, this novel may well be the fulfillment of the promise Handke made at the end of *A Sorrow Beyond Dreams*, when he said he would someday write more of his mother's life and death. For Handke, Marianne may be the woman his mother never was, with the narrative suggesting what Maria Handke's life might have been like had she made other choices. In an article in *Le Monde* following the 1978 Cannes Film Festival, Handke speaks (in French) of the creation of his heroine:

Parce que j'avais derrière moi *le Malheur indifférent*—ce livre où j'ai tenté de décrire la vie et la mort de ma mère,—j'ai pu avoir l'énergie spirituelle de me représenter une femme entièrement fictive. . . .

J'avais besoin de faire vivre, et survivre, cette femme rêvée. Un besoin fondé sur mes propres certitudes, ma propre culpabilité. A la mort d'un proche, je crois qu'on se sent toujours métaphysiquement coupable, je veux parler de cette culpabilité éternelle qui donne envie d'esquisser un monde meilleur que le monde vécu.[6]

Because I had *A Sorrow Beyond Dreams* — the book in which I attempted to describe the life and death of my mother — behind me, I had the spiritual energy to represent an entirely fictive woman. . . .

I needed to make this dream woman live, and survive: a need based on my own certainty, my own guilt. At the death of someone close to you, I believe you always feel guilty in a metaphysical sense. I wanted to speak of this eternal culpability, which gives one the wish to create a better world than the world [in which the loved one] lived.

But just as his story of Maria Handke's life embraces both the particular and the general, so also does his story of Marianne's life suggest not only what is possible for "the woman" — as the narrative almost always calls her — but, as with Kaspar, what is possible for someone. Judging from the fact that *The Left-Handed Woman* held a place on Germany's best-sellers list for many weeks, its readership undoubtedly included a fair percentage of women who, like Marianne, have themselves contemplated the idea of independence. But those who look to Marianne as a prototype of the emancipated woman must finally confront the limitations of this reading.

At thirty, Marianne has reached a point in life considered by many to be a milestone, engendering reevaluations of self and, in many cases, a rejection of husband, children, and home, which she suddenly sees as detriments to her individuality. Typically, the woman who emerges from her "delayed adolescence" to face maturity turns to ways of self-discovery such as those Marianne's friend Franziska offers. But Marianne does not join the women's group in which "more than recipes are discussed." Nor does she accept Franziska's receptive ear and confide in her friend about her problems. When a publisher-friend brings her a book to translate, Marianne does not share anything personal with him and does not even seem to be aware of his kindnesses. In fact, there is very little in Marianne's behavior to suggest that she is a woman in search of a potential self. Just prior to her telling Bruno of her vision, her husband tells her of an English novel he read on the return flight, concerning a feudal master-slave relationship, but Marianne says nothing in response. The novel she translates contains a passage which might well express a manifesto for the housewives' slave rebellion, but Marianne only shrugs her shoulders when she reads it.

If we associate Marianne too solidly with the quest for self so common among suburban wives, we find that we are doing so not because it is suggested by Marianne's behavior, but because all the expectations of women's liberation automatically accompany the thirty-year-old's decision to end her marriage. Furthermore, the text itself, from Bruno's remark that he has never known a woman who has made a lasting change in her life, to the novel that Marianne translates, contributes to the cliché. The identity of Michele, the protagonist in the French novel Marianne translates, is obviously measured in terms of her husband, and her expression of discontent obliquely suggests an association with Marianne:

"Bis jetzt haben alle Männer mich geschwächt. Mein Mann sagte von mir: 'Michèle ist stark.' In Wirklichkeit will er, daß ich stark sei für das, was ihn nicht interessiert: für die Kinder, den Haushalt, die Steuern. Aber bei dem, was mir als Arbeit vorschwebt, da zerstört er mich. Er sagt: 'Meine Frau ist eine Träumerin.' Wenn träumen heißt, das sein wollen, was man ist, dann will ich eine Träumerin sein." (P. 57)

"Up until now all men have weakened me. My husband says: 'Michèle is strong.' The truth is that he wants me to be strong in connection with things that don't interest him: the children, the household, taxes. But when it comes to the work I hope to do, he destroys me. He says: 'My wife is a dreamer.' If wanting to be what I am is dreaming, then I want to be a dreamer." (P. 36)

Although Handke apparently manufactured these lines, the book in the film version is Flaubert's *A Simple Heart* (*Un Coeur simple*, 1877), a classic story of a servant woman's exploitation, which further supports the cliché. But Marianne's behavior simply does not follow the pattern of the quest for self, confirming that Handke is not constructing a feminist myth so much as he is deconstructing it.

Marielouise Janssen-Jurreit, an active feminist and author of *Sexismus: Über die Abtreibung der Frauenfrage (Sexism: Concerning the Abortion of the Women Question)*, speaks in *Der Spiegel* of how offended she was when she first read *The Left-Handed Woman*, singling out such sentences as, "Die Augen der Frau schimmerten von Tränen" (p. 32) ("The woman's eyes glistened with tears," p. 19). Annoyed, she asks: "Laßt er uns also seine sprachliche Überlegenheit diesesmal nur auf andere Weise fühlen, indem er uns mit Unbeholfenheiten und Kitsch irritiert und uns mit Sätzen wie aus schlechten bürgerlichen Romanen verlegen macht?"[7] ("Does he this time let us feel his linguistic superiority only in other ways, in which he irritates us with awkwardness and kitsch and embarrasses us with sentences out of bad bourgeois novels?"). But she then reconsiders her annoyance, evaluating Handke's technique of character presentation and concluding that such sentences have nothing to do with either a masculine inability to create female characters or a biased, chauvinistic vision of women. As in *A Sorrow Beyond Dreams*, the cliché is a staple of the unmasking process, working here to destroy any associations with a feminism with which the left-handed woman has little to do.

In the *Le Monde* article, Handke expresses the feeling that his character stands outside any historical movement, maintaining that Marianne's decision to end her marriage is not the expression of a feminist quest for identity but rather of "un retour à une autonomie un peu enfantine"[8] ("a return to a kind of childlike autonomy"). With the determination and carelessness of a child, she stands staring at her reflection in the mirror and says aloud: "Meint, was ihr wollt. Je mehr ihr glaubt, über mich sagen zu können, desto freier werde ich von euch" (p. 37) ("I don't care what you people think. The more you have to say about me, the freer I will be of you," p. 23).

Marianne's one continuous contact is her child, with whom she picnics on the living-room floor, goes hiking in the woods, and takes a bath. In the film version, when Marianne first tells her husband to leave her, she returns home and climbs on Stefan's stilts, parading around the living room as her son watches from the stairs. Although Marianne's relationship with her son does not appear to grow in warmth or psychological closeness as the two live their lives without Bruno, the affinity of the two characters becomes increasingly stronger as Marianne defers increasingly less to social demands, an affinity strengthened by a visit from Marianne's father. Marianne seems to have carved out an impenetrable space for herself which admits nothing of the adult world. And unlike her feminist counterpart, she does not turn frantically toward human contact but withdraws instead into the peace of an asocial world.

The movement of the narrative appears to be regressive, with Marianne's every action further confirming her near-total physical withdrawal and complete psychological withdrawal from social contact. But Handke is observing, collecting, and displaying the movements of the left-handed woman with the care of an insect collector, then reassembling them in order to reveal what he calls a "gaieté originelle"[9] (a "primordial joyfulness"). If Marianne's solitude is "a better way of life," it is so not because she rejects social roles but because she returns to a pure self, a symbolic childhood representative of a self which has not yet been subsumed by the demands of civilization. Maria Handke sacrificed this purity of spirit to her marriage, and the protagonist of *Short Letter, Long Farewell,* reading *Green Henry,* laments its loss. As Handke explains:

Et cette nature, que l'on dit morte depuis Rousseau, existe toujours dans chaque individu (homme ou femme) qui surmonte l'idéologie aveugle du regard purement sociologique.[10]

And this nature, which since Rousseau is said to be dead, exists all the same in every individual (whether man or woman) who surmounts the blind ideology of a purely sociological view.

Yet *The Left-Handed Woman* is also a study in solitude itself, a still life of a woman who simply is. Like the protagonists of Handke's other novels, only more so, Marianne is a loner, more prone to silence than to conversation, more willing to slip into solitude than to embrace the activity of life. Handke has spoken several times of the danger implicit in writing, since it is a self-enclosing activity which fosters, and offers the comfort of, social withdrawal. It would seem that Marianne, too, in her ideal world, prefers such unassailable aloneness. At the end of the novel, she congratulates herself on not having given herself away. Unlike the left-handed woman in a record of that name which she plays repeatedly one night, Marianne has left no signs; she has preserved the purity of her silent self.

Yet, finally, whatever we say about Marianne must remain somewhat speculative, for aside from her brief mirror monologues, we are given little insight into the left-handed woman's motivation. Unlike Maria Handke—but like Gregor Keuschnig, about whom we know nothing prior to the dream which transforms him—Marianne is a woman without a past. Nearly all we know of her circumstances appears in the novel's first paragraph: she is thirty, she has brown hair and gray eyes, she lives in a rented bungalow in West Germany (Clamart, France, in the film version) with her businessman husband and eight-year-old son, she is comfortably well off financially. Later we learn that until ten years earlier she had done translation work for a publisher.

More significant than what we don't know of her past, however, is what we don't know of her present inner world. Handke consistently refuses to offer any glimpses into Marianne's psyche, and comments in a *Der Spiegel* article covering the film-making: "Ich weiß nicht, wie sie ist—und will es auch nicht wissen"[11] ("I don't know who she is—and don't want to know"). This unwillingness to suggest motivation, also evident in *The Goalie's Anxiety at the Penalty Kick*, acquires particular strength in *The Left-Handed Woman*, in which Handke expresses Marianne's entire psychic response to her new situation through a narration focusing completely on surface impressions. Writing about the genesis of this novella, Handke comments:

Daß ich das Drehbuch dann in eine Erzählung umschrieb, hatte folgenden Grund: nach einigen Büchern, in denen das "Er dachte", "er fühlte", "er empfand" viele Sätze eingeleitet hatte, wollte ich eine Prosa ausprobieren, in der das Denken und Fühlen der Figuren nie beschrieben würde: wo also statt: "Sie hatte Angst" stünde: "Sie ging", "sie schaute aus dem Fenster", "sie legte sich neben das Bette des Kindes", usw.—Und diese Art Beschränkung empfand ich, was meine literarische Arbeit betrifft, als befreiend.[12]

I rewrote the filmscript in the form of a narrative for the following reasons: after several books in which "he thought," "he felt," "he perceived" introduced many sentences, I wanted to make full use of a prose form in which the thinking and the feeling of the figures would not be described, where, therefore, instead of "she was afraid," we would have "she went," "she looked out the window," "she lay down next to the bed of the child," etc. And I perceived that this kind of limitation with regard to my literary work was liberating.

Though appearing first as the novella, *The Left-Handed Woman* was conceived originally as a screenplay, which may account for Handke's reliance on visual rather than psychological presentation of scenes and for the many starkly sketched scenarios. But the prose narrative he describes also has affinities with earlier comments on the drama emphasizing the preeminence of action and gesture. To a great extent, our conclusions regarding Marianne's psychic life must be drawn from our observations of her behavior. But this is precisely what other characters are continually doing. Stefan, for example, sees his mother bow her head and responds, "Ich bin auch traurig" (p. 59) ("I'm sad too," p. 38). When Marianne takes the child on her lap during the publisher's visit, the publisher asks, "Sind Sie nicht gern mit mir zusammen?" (p. 49) ("Don't you like my company?", p. 30) suggesting she preoccupies herself with the child as a defense. The reader of *The Left-Handed Woman* is in a position very much like that of Joseph Bloch or the audience watching *My Foot My Tutor:* he must translate signs for which Handke offers no verification of meaning. In the absence of psychological insight, the reader focuses more on action, gesture, and objects, noticing what he would not otherwise notice and creating meaning he would otherwise be given.

Again, Handke hopes by this method to make the familiar strange, to bring things into new relationships. In *Le Monde,* Handke speaks of a children's book, *The First Pictures (Les Premières Images),* in which three usually unrelated objects—a hammer, a globe, and an apple—play a significant role, and how, recalling that unexpected relationship, he hoped to achieve a similar rearrangement of perceptions here[13]—which is, of course, what he attempts in *A Moment of True Feeling* as well.

In the Berlin interview, Handke defined a story not as a series of events leading to a climax and dénouement, but rather as a reordering of daily occurrences in order that something of the truth of experience might be revealed (Interview, pp. 164, 172). In an early theoretical essay, he observed that conventional plot contributes nothing to the progress of literature, which consists "in einem allmählichen Entfernen von unnötigen Fiktionen" ("of the gradual removal of unnecessary fictions"):

Immer mehr Vehikel fallen weg, die Geschichte wird unnötig, das Erfinden wird unnötig, es geht mehr um die Mitteilung von Erfahrungen, sprachlichen und nicht sprachlichen, und dazu ist es nicht mehr nötig, eine Geschichte zu erfinden.[14]

More and more vehicles fall by the wayside, the story becomes superfluous, invention becomes superfluous, what matters more is the communication of experiences, linguistic and nonlinguistic ones, and for that it is no longer necessary to invent stories.

In *The Left-Handed Woman,* in which there is no evidence of plot development and no sense of an ending but merely presentation of scenes, the story in the traditional sense becomes "superfluous."

As in *A Sorrow Beyond Dreams,* Handke fragments his presentations of particular incidents in the protagonist's life, presenting spare, highly selective details. In both novellas, even as he uses the cliché, he creates a dialectic between the cliché and the truth of experience, challenging the reader, in effect, to choose between them. Like *A Sorrow Beyond Dreams, The Left-Handed Woman* is deceptively simple, but like everything Handke has written, it is supremely concerned with the aesthetics of fiction.

13
The Forthcoming Handke

In the fifteen years since the appearance of his first novel, Handke has published eight additional novels and nine plays, not to mention several books of poetry, short stories, radio plays, scripts for television and the screen, and numerous essays on literature and other subjects. Handke is widely read in Europe, with translations of his plays and novels available in most western countries; in America, many of his poems, all of his plays, and all but the first two of his novels are either available or forthcoming in English translations. Nine book-length critical studies of Handke's work have been published to date in German, as have special issues of a literary journal and a 400-page collection of essays devoted solely to his work. In 1967, Handke was awarded the Gerhart Hauptmann Prize by the Freie Volksbühne in Berlin; in 1973, he received the prestigious Georg Büchner Prize; and in 1979, he won (though declined) Austria's first annual Kafka Prize.[1] Fifteen years after his Group 47 attack on the writers who might have been his literary mentors, the *enfant terrible* has more than met the challenge of his assault.

More significant than the sheer volume of his productivity, of course, or than his growing critical recognition, is the progress Handke has made in redirecting literary tradition. Throughout his writing, he has remained constant to his early statement that language is all that concerns him when he writes, but over the years his vision of language, and hence of literature, has matured. In the drama of the 1960s, Handke's preoccupation with language was so intense as to be dogmatic, virtually precluding the communication of nonlinguistic experiences, which he claimed was part of the task of literary discourse. In the fiction of the 1970s, however, Handke's angry attack upon the "idiocy of language" acquired a more temperate character, with his obsession

156

with the impossibility of saying anything deferring to the necessity to say. Handke's fiction touches a range of linguistic, philosophical, and aesthetic possibilities only suggested by the early plays. And while the drama significantly contributed not only to the German stage but to "world theater" as well, the narrative form, in which Handke says he has always "felt freer," would seem to offer far richer potential.[2] Handke continues to pursue that form, with each new piece of fiction contributing further to his advancement of literary form.

Since *The Left-Handed Woman,* Handke has published two additional prose works in German: *The Weight of the World (Das Gewicht der Welt,* 1977) and *Slow Homecoming (Langsame Heimkehr,* 1979).[3] Though written as a journal, *The Weight of the World* does not depend on a fictionalized story, historical events, or travel as a unifying principle, as do more traditional examples of diaristic writing such as Max Frisch's *Diary with Marion (Tagebuch mit Marion,* 1947), or Günter Grass' *Diary of a Snail (Tagebuch einer Schnecke,* 1972). Instead, each entry stands independently as a fragment of experience. The seemingly random images, observations, memories, and thoughts of the journal (which recalls the last passages of *A Sorrow Beyond Dreams*) are held together only by the central consciousness of the author-narrator, who remembers and creates a mélange of outer- and inner-world experiences, mingling present and past, real and surreal, convictions, speculations, impressions, and ideas.

In a foreword to the German edition of the novel, Handke speaks of *The Weight of the World* as a completely new literary possibility for him. Apparently he had not originally planned on using journal form, intending rather to give order to his daily experiences through a story or a (silent) theater piece. But as he wrote, he became aware of the necessity of selectivity, which forced him to ignore those experiences which did not fit the mold of his purpose. Deciding not to sacrifice spontaneity, he abandoned his original plan, discovering in the process not only a new sense of freedom from established literary form but a *Sprachlebendigkeit,* a moment during which language acquired such immediacy that the gap between experience and expression disappeared. As he suggests in his entry of January 1977: "Das Gipfel der

Schönheit: Wenn ich zu mir selber sage, und zwar unwillkürlich: 'Schön war das!'" (p. 295) ("The height of beauty [is] when I say to myself, spontaneously, 'that was beautiful!' ").

Handke's most recent novel, *Slow Homecoming*, confirms that his thinking and writing are entering a new, though not unanticipated, phase, which celebrates the redemptive power of poetic language. In *Short Letter, Long Farewell*, Handke spoke of how a child's language is molded by a technology-oriented culture which denies man's relationship to nature. In that novel, he counterpointed the protagonist's experience with that of the hero of Gottfried Keller's *Green Henry*, suggesting the distance which has developed over the past century between man's inner and outer worlds. He expressed this same sense of loss in *They Are Dying Out*, pitting the poet against a society whose reigning language is advertising slogans. As Quitt listens to a passage from the nineteenth-century Austrian writer Adalbert Stifter, he laments the loss of a language which could restore man's relationship to nature. Seeing little possibility for such a restoration, Quitt finally chooses suicide, the ultimate withdrawal.

Slow Homecoming, which Handke prefers to call an epic poem (Interview, pp. 170, 176), is the odyssey of Sorger, a European self-exiled in a lonely Alaskan village, tracing his travels across America, and into his own soul, as he decides to satisfy his longing for home. The novel is the culmination of Handke's belief in the potential of poetic language, attempting to reach a world harmony and a universality of self through narrative. As he explains in the 1979 interview, immediately after his completion of this novel, "Ich wollte die Schönheit . . . herstellen mit Sprache und merkte dann, daß ich in Konflikt kam mit der Geschichte meiner Vorfahren, die auch in mir ist" ("I wanted to create beauty . . . with language, and then I noticed that I came into conflict with the history of my ancestors, which is also in me") (Interview, pp. 170, 177). But Handke was able to narrate this conflict and to bring history, nature, and self to a new beginning in the "quietness" of form. With *Slow Homecoming*, it becomes clear that for the more mature Handke, the poet is the messiah of hope.

Fifteen years ago, it would have been impossible to predict that the invective of Handke's first play would develop into the poetic lament of his most recent narrative. So also is it difficult today to guess at the direction Handke's future writing will take. There is little doubt that his commitment to language and to the revitalization of literary form will continue, but this most recent Goethean foray into the ways of world harmony suggests that Handke's interests now lie less in the limitations of language than in its possibilities. Perhaps one of Handke's journal entries in *The Weight of the World* might be offered as the writer's own vision of his coming work:

Guter Schriftsteller: die Sprache bemerkt sich selber; großer Schriftsteller: die Sprache wird darüber hinaus frei für was andres als sich selber (P. 306)

Good writer: language aware of itself; great writer: language opens up to something other than itself.

Judging from the maturing process Handke's writing has already undergone, his forthcoming work will, by both conventional standards and his own, make Handke one of the "great" writers of our time.

Appendices

Notes

Bibliography

Index

Appendix 1
An Interview
with Peter Handke,
Berlin, July 23, 1979

JUNE SCHLUETER: Der Untertitel Ihres neuen Romans, *Das Gewicht der Welt,*
der auf englisch als *Fantasies and Prejudices* erscheinen wird, zeigt mir, daß
Sie jeden Tag während der Zeit von einem Jahr und fünf Monaten, d.h.
von November 1975 bis März 1977, dieses Buch geschrieben haben.
Stimmt das?

PETER HANDKE: Ja. Es gibt vielleicht zwei oder drei Tage, wo ich etwas zu-
sammengezogen und zusammengefügt habe, aber im grossen und ganzen
stimmen alle Tagesangaben. Zu einem Journal gehört es ja, daß es täglich
geführt wird, daß kein Tag ausgelassen wird in einem Jahr.

JS: Waren die täglichen Ereignisse Ihres Lebens während dieser Monate die
spezifischen Stimuli für Ihre Journalnotizen?

PH: Ja, nur diese.

JS: Aber in der Vornotiz zu diesem Buch sagen Sie, daß dieses "eine mir bis
dahin unbekannte literarische Möglichkeit" sei. Glauben Sie, daß Sie dieses
Buch falsch darstellen, wenn Sie es ein Journal nennen, und es als Fakt
ausgeben, obgleich es Fiktion ist?

PH: Ich sehe keinen Widerspruch zwischen "Journal" und "Fiktion". "Journal"
ist ja nur eine sachliche Beschreibung von Aufzeichungen, die Tag für Tag
gemacht werden. "Journal" ist auch eine Verlegenheitsbezeichnung. Es ist
eher ein Roman, glaube ich. Für mich ist es eine Art Roman—oder Epos
sogar—von Alltäglichkeit. Aber das kann man erst im nachhinein sagen,
wenn man das Ergebnis sieht.

JS: In "Die Literatur ist romantisch" [1966] schreiben Sie über eine neue
Definition der Literatur, einer Literatur ohne Fiktion, ohne Wortspiel,
ohne Rhythmus, ohne Stil. Und Sie sagen, nur für eine solche Literatur
wäre das Wort "realistisch" zutreffend. Halten Sie *Das Gewicht der Welt* für
eine solche realistische Literatur?

PH: Nein.

JS: Halten Sie Ihre anderen Werke für "realistisch"?

PH: Ich versuche, solche Unterscheidungen wie "realistisch" und "romantisch"
zu vermeiden, denn in der Arbeit der Praxis kommen diese nicht mehr
vor. Diesen Aufsatz habe ich einmal geschrieben, er wird schon seinen Sinn
gehabt haben, denke ich, und ich glaube, daß das alles klar ist in dem

Aufsatz. Aber man kann nicht nach einem Programm schreiben. Es war auch kein Programm, es war ein Versuch der Klärung damals. Ich weiß auch nicht, was "realistisch" ist.

JS: Sie haben einmal Ihr Stück *Der Ritt über den Bodensee* "realistisch" genannt.

PH: Ja. Wo habe ich das gesagt?

JS: Es war vor wenigen Jahren in einem Interview für die Münchener "Abendzeitung".

PH: Ja, da kommen sicher solche Wörter vor, man müßte dann die Sätze und Schwingungen, die Situation kennen. Es gibt Zeiten und Orte, wo jedes Wort verwendbar ist, aber es ist nicht allgemein verwendbar. Ich kann mir vorstellen, daß man eines Tages an diesem Ort zu diesem Thema sagt, es ist realistisch, und daß dieses Wort dann ganz dinghaft für ein Problem steht. Ich weiß nicht, wo man da hinkommt, denn "realistisch" zu hören, sperrt mir sofort jede Phantasie ab. Ich möchte nicht, daß man immer wieder fragt, ob ich auch danach schreibe oder ob das, was ich jetzt schreibe, die Praxis dessen ist, was sozusagen die Theorie gewesen ist. Da gibt's keine Theorie und Praxis, da gibt's nur Praxis. Und in der Praxis entsteht in jedem Satz eine neue Theorie. Aber die ist sofort wieder ungültig.

JS: Sind Sie derselben Meinung über "Ich bin ein Bewohner des Elfenbeinturms" [1967], den Aufsatz, in dem Sie Ihren Angriff auf die Beschreibungsimpotenz Ihrer Kollegen zur Tagung der Gruppe 47 in Princeton erklären?

PH: Ich bin froh, daß ich das geschrieben habe. Natürlich gibt es theoretische Äußerungen, Erklärungen von Zielen oder Vorstellungen. Die sind, wie ich gemerkt habe, immer sehr gefährlich, weil ein Zwang entsteht, nicht bei allen, aber bei denen, die das Lesen und die Erzählungen oder Gedichte dann auf solche Erklärungen beziehen. Da bin ich auch selber Schuld, wenn ich das geschrieben habe.

JS: Wenn Sie heute diese Aufsätze schreiben würden, wäre Ihre Argumentation dann anders?

PH: Ja, ganz sicherlich. Ich will auch keinen Aufsatz mehr schreiben.

JS: In dem Aufsatz "Ich bin ein Bewohner des Elfenbeinturms" sagen Sie, daß nach Ihrer Meinung eine Geschichte in der Literatur nicht länger nötig sei, und daß immer mehr Vehikel der Fiktion wegfallen. Das stimmt für *Das Gewicht der Welt* und für Ihren ersten Roman *Die Hornissen*, aber mir scheint, andere Ihrer Werke, zum Beispiel, *Der kurze Brief zum langen Abschied*, *Wunschloses Unglück*, und *Die linkshändige Frau*, sind traditionellere Erzählungen. Sind Sie mit dieser Beobachtung einverstanden?

PH: Diese Erzählungen und Romane haben eigentlich gar keine Geschichte. Das sind nur in eine neue Ordnung gebrachte Alltäglichkeiten. Was daran "Geschichte" oder "Fiktion" ist, ist immer nur der Schnittpunkt zwischen den einzelnen Alltäglichkeiten. Das erzeugt den Eindruck von Fiktion. Und deswegen glaube ich, daß sie gar nicht traditionell sind, sondern daß die unarrangierteste Alltäglichkeit nur in eine neue Ordnung gebracht ist, wo sie plötzlich wie eine Erfindung aussieht. Ich will auch nie etwas anderes machen. Ich trau mir einfach keine groteske Fantasie zu, oder eine fres-kenhafte Darstellung der Gesellschaft in einem grossen Epos. Ich dachte einmal, das könnte ich, aber ich denke nun, das ist auch nicht mehr richtig, das geht nicht mehr. Mit meiner größten Anstrengung kann ich mich erweitern. Ich kann mich immer weiter machen. Das ist meine einzige epische Fähigkeit. Aber ich kann nicht verschiedene Personen aufschlüs-seln, Sie wissen, diese Romanciertricks. Das kann ich nicht machen. Was ich kann, ist ein episches Gedicht schreiben, eine Erzählung, die immer etwas sehr lyrisches an sich hat, weil eben alles, was ich schreibe, durch mich erst beglaubigt. Ich finde es albern, einen Gesellschaftsroman zu schreiben—für mich. Es mag sein, daß das irgend jemand möglich ist, aber es muß alles, jeder Baum, den ich beschreibe, das muß auch ich sein. Anders kann ich mir das Schreiben gar nicht vorstellen, als daß ich ein ganz weites "ich" bekomme. Goethe hat auch gesagt, es gibt in Deutschland—oder vielleicht auch überall—ein dumme Diskussion über eine subjektivis-tische neue Sensibilität. Es gibt einen schönen Satz von Goethe: wenn man sich nur auf sein gutes "Ich" verlässt, dann ist das schon richtig, jede Handlung und jede Nicht-Handlung sind dann richtig. Er meint nicht, daß ein spezielles "Ich" gut ist, sondern daß das "Ich" des Menschen gut ist. Das gibt's immer, das gab's immer in der Literatur. Ich meine, das muß ja nicht das Thema sein, aber wenn ein Autor sich auf sein gutes "Ich" verlässt, dann wird er andere Menschen nicht unbedingt gut beschreiben, aber ihnen gerecht werden können, auch wenn sie noch so fragmentarisch in seinen Erzählungen oder in seinen Gedichten vorkommen.

JS: Der amerikanische Kritiker Lionel Trilling und anderer haben behauptet, der Roman als Genre habe sich selbst erschöpft, seine Zeit sei abgelaufen. Halten Sie das für richtig?

PH: Das hat man schon oft gehört. Ich glaube, jede Generation und jedes Zeitalter hat es nötig, Erzählungen zu lesen, die über den bloßen Bericht, über die bloße Beschreibung, über das Journalistische hinausgehen, näm-lich einen Entwurf vom Menschen zu lesen, der nicht eine Wiederholung der Alltäglichkeit ist, die man Zeitungen oder Fernsehen entnimmt. Und ich denke, daß vielleicht der Roman—nun weiß ich nicht, was Roman wieder ist, aber daß eine bestimmte erzählende Haltung—der Gesellschaft sehr gerecht werden kann. Ich sage nicht "Roman", sondern die Haltung des Erzählens, die Mitvergangenheit: es war einmal, oder ich ging, oder er ging, sie, die Frau ging. Ich stelle mir vor, daß das eine ewige und auch die freieste Sprache ist. Das heißt ja nicht "Roman", das heißt die erzählende Sprache, und ich habe Ihnen vorhin gesagt, daß alle meine Erzählungen—oder wie man das nennt—oder Romane—eher epische Gedichte sind. Und das, glaube ich, ist eine Form, die dem Zeitalter entspricht: keine Aufschlüsselung in Personen und in Handlung, sondern ein Ich schreibt sozusagen ein erzählendes Gedicht über die Zeit, in der es lebt, über das "ich" und über die anderen. Ich glaube, so war es aber auch immer, daß nämlich der Roman, wie man ihn versteht, ein Bastard war, eher eine Unterhaltungssache, und das wird er auch immer bleiben, so wird es ihn immer geben. Aber ich glaube nicht mehr, daß er sich in der Mitte der Sprache als der Ausdruck einer Gesellschaft und einer Zeit behaupten kann.

JS: Sie haben oft gesagt, daß das einzige, was Sie als Schriftsteller betrifft, die Sprache sei. Ist das noch immer so?

PH: Ja, ich meine, daß es ein ganz kostbarer Lebensbeweis ist, nicht nur für mich als Schriftsteller, daß ich Sprache habe. Die meiste Sprache, die es gibt, die sich als Sprache geriert und auftritt, ist gar keine Sprache mehr. Es gibt fast keine Sprache mehr. Erst dann, wenn ich lebe oder wenn ich ein Gefühl habe, daß es eine Zukunft gibt, erscheint auch die Sprache, nicht nur für mich als Schriftsteller. Die Sprache ist das Kostbarste, was es gibt. Die meisten Menschen haben überhaupt keine Sprache. Es geht ein Aufatmen durch die Massen, wenn irgend jemand da ist, der eine Sprache hat. Was ist diese Sprache? Ich glaube, diese Sprache ist nur die poetische Sprache. Das heißt Sprache. Alle anderen Sprachen sind Übereinkünfte, sind Routinen. Im besten Fall ist es eine Lebensroutine, im besten Fall. Aber im Normalfall ist es etwas Tötendes und Abschließendes und etwas Aggressives, etwas Böses. Selbst wenn ich mit Psychoanalytikern oder auch mit Theologen rede, fast mit allen, deren Sprache, denke ich, ist eine böse Sprache. Nur jemand, der einen Entwurf hat vom Menschen, der hat auch eine freundliche, eine offene, eine genaue Sprache. Es gibt natürlich einige wenige Theologen oder Philosophen, die das wissen, die wissen, daß ihre Sprache in Konventionen steckt. Das einzige, was gilt für mich, und wo ich mich dann auch ganz mächtig fühle, mächtig ohne Macht, ist, wenn es mir gelingt, eine Sprache mit Form zu finden. Ich meine, Sprache heißt für mich Form und Form heißt für mich Dauer, weil es sonst keine Dauer gibt in der menschlichen Existenz.

JS: Wie wichtig sind die Werke von Roland Barthes für Sie?

PH: Es ist für mich schon wichtig gewesen, vor fünfzehn Jahren, um die Strukturen. Es hat mir geholfen, auch Strukturen zu sehen, und das ist ein Vergüngen, es macht einen heiter; denn die Formlosigkeit, die sich einem bietet, ist in allen Phänomenen, jedes ist für sich und alle sind durcheinander. Es hat mir damals geholfen, eine Ordnung zu sehen, und zwar keine hierarchische, sondern eine strukturelle, ein ungewertete und fast sportliche Ordnung. Aber das ist alles lang vergessen und trotzdem bin ich dankbar. Das poetische Schreiben muß weit darüber hinausgehen.

JS: Halten Sie sich zunächst für einen österreichischen Schriftsteller?

PH: Ich halte mich für einen deutschsprachigen Schriftsteller und ich bin Österreicher. Das ist die Antwort. Und ein anderer kann mich ruhig einen österreichischen Schriftsteller nennen. Das ist auch richtig. Aber ich kann sagen, ich bin ein deutschsprachiger Schriftsteller, und ich bin Österreicher.

JS: In "Ich bin ein Bewohner des Elfenbeinturms" sagen Sie, Kleist, Flaubert, Dostojewski, Kafka, Faulkner, und Robbe-Grillet haben Ihr Bewußtsein von der Welt verändert. Sie haben diese Aussage 1967 gemacht. Würden Sie heute dieser Auflistung weitere Namen hinzufügen?

PH: Es gibt so viele und so wenige Grosse. Ich bin vielleicht weiter in die Geschichte zurückgegangen und habe versucht von Anfang an wieder zu lesen. Ich war in der Schule begeistert von Homer oder von Pindar, von Heraklit, und ich habe ebenfalls alles, was ich, was vielleicht viele, viel zu früh lesen, noch einmal gelesen. Nur in einem Wort: langsamer. Goethe. Aber es gibt einen, den ich jetzt erst ganz begreife, und der mir eine heilige Schrift ist in einem ganz sachlichen Sinn, das ist Hölderlin. Das habe ich vorher nicht so verstanden. Aber jetzt kann ich ihn lesen wie eine weitaus besser geschriebene und moralisch ebenso hochstehende heilige Schrift, wo man nicht gezwungen ist, etwas zu glauben, sondern, dadurch daß die Sätze stehen wie Gebirge, einfach glauben kann, zumindest ein Vorbild sieht. Ich lese auch inzwischen viele naturwissenschaftliche Abhandlungen, weil das auch eine seltsame Konzentration und Ruhe und Phantasie vor allem gibt, eine ganz sachliche Phantasie. Ein Schriftsteller ist immer bedroht von einer Phantasie, die ganz beliebig überall hingeht, während beim Lesen von zum Beispiel geologischen Beschreibungen meine Phantasie begrenzt bleibt und doch ganz stark. Die Phantasie wird nicht zu Bildern, sondern geht sozusagen in die Grammatik hinein und belebt die Grammatik ganz neu.

JS: Sie und Wim Wenders haben zusammen Filme gedreht, und Sie selbst haben Ihre Erzählung *Die linkshändige Frau* verfilmt. Ich weiß, daß Filme Sie immer interessiert haben. Ist es möglich, daß Sie in Zukunft lieber Filme machen möchten als Bücher schreiben?

PH: Ich denke schon, daß ich einen Film machen werde, oder zwei vielleicht, wenn ich das kann. Aber die große Schwierigkeit ist die, daß das keine beliebige Grenzüberschreitung sein kann, denn sehr leicht verliert man die Identität dessen, was man ist, eine Identität die man als Schriftsteller ohnedies sehr schwer hat. Mir fällt es sehr schwer zu sagen, "Ich bin Schriftsteller." Nur manchmal, in Momenten wo ich weiß, was ist, wo ich also sagen kann, was ist, indem ich schreibe, dann bin ich . . . "I'm a writer." Das ist viel schöner in English. Aber die Identität ist nicht alltäglich, wie bei einem Arzt oder bei einem Germanisten, wem auch immer. Als ich diesen Film gemacht habe, habe ich mir gar keine Rechenschaft darüber gegeben, daß ich nah daran war, meine Identität, die ohnedies so fragil ist, zu verlieren. Und lange Zeit danach war ich gar nichts. Man muß schon sehr philosophisch sein, um zu ertragen, daß man gar nichts ist. Verstehen Sie, man kann nicht so einfach sagen, jetzt mache ich wieder einen Film und jetzt schreibe ich wieder ein Buch, so geht das nicht. Das ist eine sehr, sehr gefährliche, abenteuerliche Sache. Wenn ich wieder einen Film mache, weiß ich, daß ich sehr, sehr aufpassen muß. Das war ganz, ganz schwierig, dann wieder zurückzufinden zu den Sätzen, zum Schreiben. Mich jetzt nicht völlig als Dilettant zu fühlen oder als Anmaßender, als ich wieder versucht habe, eine Geschichte zu schreiben, oder wie gesagt, ein erzählendes Gedicht. Daß überhaupt zwei Sätze dann aneinander kommen, das ist ein ganz grosses Problem. Was heißt das, daß ein Satz dem anderen folgt? Es war als ob alles wie isoliert wäre und ich schwindle, indem ich einen Satz an den anderen füge. So ging es mir dann mit dem Schreiben.

JS: Obgleich Sie Ihren ersten Erfolg als Dramatiker hatten, haben Sie seit *Die Unvernünftigen sterben aus* [1973] kein Theaterstück geschrieben. Glauben Sie, daß Sie für sich selbst das Drama als Genre erschöpft haben?

PH: Ich habe schon eine gewisse Vision von einem Stück, die wäre, daß ein Mensch auf der Bühne drei Stunden die Leute anredet. Das ist meine Dramavorstellung, wenn man das schreiben könnte, aber ganz ernst und mit Leidenschaft. Das wäre dann Drama. Alles andere kommt mir so trickhaft vor beim Theater. Ich habe mich einmal ganz identisch gefühlt als Stückeschreiber, als ich *Der Ritt über den Bodensee* geschrieben habe. Da habe ich gedacht, das ist reines Theater und das ist ganz neues Theater, das ist auch ganz vollkommen. Und seitdem habe ich das verloren. Das kann man auch nur einmal. Ich konnte das nicht weiterführen. Und dann stelle ich mir noch so ein reines Drama vor, ein Mann oder ein Mensch auf der Bühne, der die Leute anspricht. Also wieder etwas wie *Publikumsbeschimpfung,* aber anders. Aber das aufschlüsseln in Auftritte? Dann müßte ich das Drama erträumen, ganz vernünftig, Szene für Szene. Das, was dem Schreiben die Wahrheit gibt, muß in der Phantasie erschaffen werden, nicht durch Denken, nicht durch Planen, nicht durch Sammeln, nicht durch Beobachten. Dieses muß schon vorher irgendwann passiert sein, aber erst die Phantasie erzeugt die Wahrheit. Bei dem meisten Geschriebenen, das man liest, merkt man, daß es nicht durch die verifizierende Phantasie hindurchgegangen ist. Das ist gemacht, das ist nach einem Muster, aber es ist nicht dieses Aufregende, dieses Wärmende, dieses Befreiende. Ich meine nicht, daß die Phantasie besondere Bilder erzeugt, Groteskheit oder was auch immer, sondern daß erst die Sprache, die die Phantasie erzeugt, schreibenswert ist. Wenn es in der Phantasie sozusagen aufgestiegen ist wie ein versunkenes Land, dann kann es geschrieben werden. Und bei Stücken geht's mir so. Man kann wirklich das Schreiben nur erträumen. Alles was geschrieben ist—wenn es gut sein soll—muß vernünftig sein, und das Schreiben ist ein ungeheuer vernünftiger Akt. Jeder Satz ist vernünftig insofern, daß man versucht zu vermeiden, und Vermeiden ist vernünftig. Also nicht in positiven Sätzen, sondern im Vermeiden ist das Schreiben vernünftig. Aber in positiven Sätzen muß es erträumt sein. Das ist ganz, ganz schwierig. Deswegen versteht auch niemand, fast niemand, was Literatur ist, was das für ein erschöpfender Prozess ist, jeder einzelne Satz. Wie gesagt, bei Stücken im Theater gelingt mir das eben nicht mehr. Es gibt Ansätze, die in mir sind, die aber irgendwie steckengeblieben sind—vielleicht wieder aufsteigen werden. Es muß alles sozusagen ins Schweben kommen. Oder vielleicht geht das einem

Menschen überhaupt verloren im Laufe seines Lebens, das Schreiben hört dann auf.

JS: Bitte noch zwei Fragen. Ein Kollege von mir hat neulich gesagt, daß die Studenten in Amerika heute Handke lesen, wie *seine* Generation Hesse gelesen hat, bevor nämlich Ihre Werke an der Universität gelehrt wurden. Können Sie erklären, weshalb die jungen Intellektuellen in Amerika eine solche Affinität zu Ihren Werken empfinden?

PH: Ich glaube, weil es unabhängige Menschen sind. Ich weiß, auch hier gibt es Leute, die das lesen, aber es sind keine Gemeinden, wie das früher war, es sind die unabhängigen Menschen, die keine Ideologie haben, die skeptisch sind und gleichzeitig Sehnsucht haben, die sachlich sind, gleichzeitig aber in der Sachlichkeit nicht untergehen wollen. Das wird wohl überall so sein. Und so viele sind es auch nicht. Es schmeichelt mir natürlich, aber ich habe nicht den Eindruck, daß es in Amerika viele sind. Ich bin stolz, daß es überhaupt so ist. Es gibt einen schönen Ausspruch von Ingeborg Bachmann, der heißt, "es verlangt mich nach Dir, Leser". Ich verachte die Leser nicht. Alles, was ich will, ist gelesen zu werden. Es ist etwas ungeheuer Schönes bei einem Menschen, der Leser ist. Ich sage nichts von den amerikanischen Kritiken, aber ich möchte eigentlich, daß gar nicht kritisiert, sondern daß nur gelesen würde. Aber andererseits muß ich sagen, manchmal gefällt es einem auch, etwas Genaues, Einfühlendes, Tiefes zu lesen als Kritik über das, was man geschrieben hat. Das tut einem, der schreibt, auch sehr, sehr gut. Und überhaupt nicht ermutigt zu werden, sondern immer nur als ein Feind gemalt zu werden, das schadet sehr dieser guten Phantasie, die ein Schriftsteller braucht. Diese träumende Phantasie ist das Kostbarste, was der Mensch überhaupt haben kann. Das weiß ich inzwischen. Da erst fühle ich mich sozusagen, da erst fühlt man das Göttliche in sich. Und in der Literatur—in diesem Betrieb —kann man sehr leicht vernichtet werden, auch wenn jeder glaubt, das sei nur ein kleiner Betrieb; da werden die kostbarsten Phantasien vernichtet. Wenn ich etwas gelernt habe, ist es eben, daß ich aufpassen muß auf meine Phantasie, auf diese Schwierigkeit, die vielleicht jeder hat, auf diese gute, auf diese entwerfende, auf diese die Welt neu schaffende Phantasie, wo dann alles sozusagen Sprache werden kann, und wo man denkt, man könnte mit der Sprache die Welt zum Glänzen bringen und nicht sie verraten, wie das meist mit Sprache passiert. Alle Schönheit wird durch Sprache eigentlich vernichtet. Was man mit dem Schreiben will, ist ja, daß die Schönheit Dauer kriegt. Ja, ich rede jetzt etwas weitschweifig. Sie haben mit Hesse angefangen, daß ist ein sehr ehrenwerter Schriftsteller, glaube ich. Aber man kann das nicht vergleichen.

JS: Könnten Sie mir zum Schluß etwas über Ihre neue Erzählung *Langsame Heimkehr* sagen, die Sie kürzlich beendet haben?

PH: Ich kann nur sagen, da habe ich mich so weit gemacht wie noch nie, mit dem Schreiben. Das ist ein Versuch gewesen, eine Harmonie über die Welt und dennoch eine Universalität für mich als Schreibenden zu erreichen, ein Versuch, der vielleicht vermessen war. Das ist manchmal so bei dieser Erzählung oder bei diesem epischen Gedicht, wie Sie es sicher nennen. Ich habe das Gefühl, es ist seit Jahrhunderten nicht so versucht worden, diese Harmonie festzuhalten mit Sprache und auch ansteckend weiterzugeben, weil wir hier vor allem im deutschsprachigen Raum das Problem mit unserer Geschichte haben. Wir haben fast keine Zukunft durch das, was passiert ist vor etwa 40 Jahren, wir haben fast keine Kraft zur Schönheit, niemand kann richtig leben hier und es gibt keine Natur. Auch wenn es eine Natur gibt, aber es gibt keine Sprache für die Natur, was aber Hölderlin nennt, ist doch die grosse Natur, noch bei ihm. Auch für Österreich gilt das natürlich, da ist kein Unterschied. Es ist das grosse Problem mit der Geschichte, dadurch mit der Zukunft, und dadurch das Problem mit dem poetischen Entwurf vom menschlichen Zusammenleben. Und bei diesem, was ich geschrieben habe, kam es, ohne daß ich das wollte, zu dem Konflikt zwischen diesen beiden. Ich wollte die Schönheit, die stille Schönheit, herstellen mit Sprache und merkte dann, daß ich in Konflikt kam mit der Geschichte meiner Vorfahren, die auch in mir ist. Ja, ich weiß nicht, ob die Geschichte nicht daran zerrissen ist, aber jedenfalls habe ich diesen Konflikt noch erzählen können. Ich habe das in der Ruhe getan, in der Form. Ich glaube, daß es eine Form hat, das ist ja das Wichtigste überhaupt. Kurz sind die Gefühle und lang sind die Formen. [Lachen] Es wird dadurch aber fragmentarisch, die Geschichte bricht dann ab. Ich habe mit der äußersten Anstrengung, zu der ich überhaupt fähig bin, alles in der Geschichte auf einen Anfang gebracht und damit hört die Geschichte auf. Alle Probleme mit Heimat, mit Sprache, mit Familie, mit Geschichte, mit Natur habe ich auf einen neuen Anfang zu bringen versucht, aber nicht philosophierend, nicht abhandelnd, sondern eben erzählend, in der erzählenden Sprache. Und dann habe ich plötzlich gemerkt, daß die Geschichte zu Ende ist. Da war ich ungeheuer erleichtert, und zugleich war es ein großer Schock für mich, weil ich dachte, es würde eine Geschichte von 300 Seiten werden und es sind 200. Ich wollte eigentlich, daß es in Amerika anfängt, in Alaska, 10 Seiten, und daß dann der Rest quer durch Europa vor sich geht. Und jetzt spielen die 200 Seiten alle dort, und es hört im Flugzeug über Europa auf. Es wird auch so seinen Sinn haben, aber das ist auch ein großer Schock. Was heißt "großer"? Es ist ein Schock.

Note: This translation was prepared by the author and Dietrich Büscher.

JS: The subtitle of your recent novel, *The Weight of the World,* which is tentatively scheduled to appear in English as *Fantasies and Prejudices,* suggests that you wrote this book every day over a period of one year and five months, from November 1975 to March 1977. Was this so?

PH: Yes. There are possibly two or three days which I combined, but for the most part all these dates are accurate. It is the nature of a journal that it be written daily and that nothing be left out for any day in a year.

JS: Were the daily events of your life during those months the specific stimuli for your journal entries?

PH: Yes, only these.

JS: Yet in the preface to this book, you say that it is a previously unknown literary possibility for you. Do you think you are misrepresenting the book by calling it a journal, making it appear to be fact when it is fiction?

PH: I see no contradiction between "journal" and "fiction." "Journal" is only an objective description of notes which are made day by day. "Journal" is also a term I used because I did not find any better term. It is, I believe, more a novel. For me it is a sort of novel or epic of everyday occurrences. But this can only be said afterward, after one sees the result.

JS: In "Literature Is Romantic" [1966], you write about a new definition of literature, a literature without fiction, without wordplay, without rhythm, without style. And you say that the word "realistic" would only be applicable for such a literature. Do you consider *The Weight of the World* "realistic"?

PH: No.

JS: Do you consider any of your writing "realistic"?

PH: I try to avoid distinctions such as "realistic" or "romantic," for in the process of writing these distinctions no longer occur. When I used the term "realistic" in this essay it must have made sense, and I think that everything in this essay is clear. But one cannot write according to a set of rules. The essay was not a set of rules; it was an attempt to make things clear at that time. I really don't know what "realistic" is.

JS: You once called your play *The Ride Across Lake Constance* "realistic."

PH: Where did I say that?

JS: It was some years back, in an interview for the Munich *Abendzeitung*.

PH: Such words certainly do get used, but one would have to know the sentences, the vibrations, the situation. There are times and places in which any word can be used, but it is not applicable in general. I can imagine that one can say "realistic" *this* day in *this* place on *this* topic, and that the word is then completely appropriate. I have no idea where one gets then, for to hear the term "realistic" immediately stops my every creative impulse. But I really don't like being asked whether what I write now is the practice of what was, so to speak, the theory. When writing, there is no theory and practice; there is only practice. And in practice, a new theory is generated in every sentence. But at the same moment that it comes into being, this theory is immediately invalidated.

JS: Do you feel the same way about "I Am an Ivory Tower Dweller" [1967], the

essay in which you explain your attack upon the impotence of the descriptive language used by your colleagues at the Group 47 meeting in Princeton?

PH: I am glad that I wrote that essay. Naturally, there are theoretical expressions or explanations of aims and imaginations. They are, as I found out,
always very dangerous because for those who read them they create a
pressure to relate narratives or poems to such explanations. But I am also
to blame, if I have written such an essay.

JS: Were you to write these essays today, then, they would be different.

PH: Yes, definitely. I don't want to write any more essays.

JS: In "I Am an Ivory Tower Dweller," you say that in your opinion, a story is
no longer necessary in fiction and that more and more of the vehicles of
fiction are falling away. While this is the case in *The Weight of the World* and
your first novel, *The Hornets,* it seems to me that some of your other
work—for example, *Short Letter, Long Farewell, A Sorrow Beyond Dreams,* and
The Left-Handed Woman—have more of a traditional narrative. Do you
agree with this observation?

PH: These narratives and novels really have no story. They are only daily
occurrences brought into a new order. What is "story" or "fiction" is really
always only the point of intersection between individual daily events. This
is what produces the impression of fiction. And because of this I believe
they are not traditional, but that the most unarranged daily occurrences
are only brought into a new order, where they suddenly look like a fiction. I
never want to do anything else. I don't think I could do a grotesque fantasy
or a frescolike representation of society, presenting a great many people
who all come together, in a great epic. I once thought I could do that, but I
now think that this is no longer right, that it no longer works. With my
greatest effort I can expand myself, I can continue to expand myself. This
is my only epic ability. But I cannot do this with various characters, these
tricks of the novelist. I cannot do that. What I can do is write an epic poem,
a narrative, which always has something lyric about it, because everything I
write is first verified through myself. I find it silly to write a social novel—
for me. It may be that this is possible for someone, but everything, every
tree that I describe, must also be myself. I cannot imagine writing any other
way than that through which I achieve an expansion of self. Goethe also
said that in Germany, or perhaps everywhere, there is a stupid discussion
about new, subjective sensibilities. There is a beautiful sentence by Goethe:
if one relies only on one's own good "ego," then that is already right, and
then any action or nonaction would be right. He doesn't mean that a special
"ego" is good, but that the "ego" of mankind is good. That is always so; that
was always so in literature. This need not be the theme, but as long as a
writer relies on his own good "ego," he will also be able not to describe other
people well but to do them justice, even when they are presented as
fragmentary in his narratives or poems.

js: The American critic Lionel Trilling, as well as others, remarked that he feels the novel as a genre has exhausted itself, that its time is up. Do you think this is so?

ph: I have often heard this. I believe every generation and every time has the need to read narratives which go beyond a mere report, beyond a mere description, beyond journalism, to read a creation of man which is not the repetition of daily occurrences one finds in newspapers or on television. And I think that perhaps the novel—and I really don't know what "novel" is, but that a definite narrative posture—can do justice to society. I don't say "novel," but the posture of narrating the common experiences of the past—there once was, or I went, or he went, or the woman went—I imagine that this is an eternal language and that this is also the freest language. That does not mean "novel," but the narrating language, and I've already told you that all my narratives, or whatever one calls them—novels—are more epic poems. And I think this is a form that suits our time. There is no expansion of character or plot, but an "I" is writing a narrative poem about the time in which he lives, about the self, and about others. But I think this was always so, that the novel, as it is understood, has been a bastard, more something to entertain people, and it will always remain so, and it will always exist. But I no longer think that the novel can continue to hold its place as the expression of a society and of a time.

js: You have said many times that the only thing that concerns you as a writer is language. Is this still true?

ph: Yes. I mean that it is a very valuable proof of life, not only for me as a writer, that I have language. Most language that presents itself as language is no longer language. There is almost no language any more. It is only when I live and have a feeling that there is a future that language appears, not only for me as a writer. Language is the most valuable thing there is. Most people have no language at all. There is a sigh of relief through the masses when there is someone who has a language. What is this language? I believe this language is only poetic language. That is what language means. All other languages are a set of rules, routines. At its best such language is a routine of living, at its best. But normally it is something that kills and closes in; it is something aggressive, something evil. Even when I talk with psychoanalysts, or theologians, or with almost everyone, I think that what they have as language is evil. Only someone who has a design of man also has a friendly, an open, a precise language. There are, of course, a few theologians and philosophers who know this, who know that their language is stuck in conventions. The only thing which is valid for me, where I feel very powerful—powerful without power—is when I succeed in finding form with language. I think language for me is form, and form is permanence, because otherwise there is no permanence in human existence.

js: How important is the writing of Roland Barthes for you?

ph: It was important for me fifteen years ago, for structures. It helped me to see structures, and that is a pleasure, because there is formlessness in every phenomenon, everything for itself, and all are confused. It helped me at that time to see an order, not a hierarchical order but a structural order. But all that is long forgotten, and in spite of that I am grateful. Poetic writing must continue on much further.

JS: Do you consider yourself primarily an Austrian writer?

PH: I consider myself a German-language writer and I am Austrian. That is the answer. And somebody else can by all means call me an Austrian writer. That is also true. But I can only say I am a German-language writer and I am Austrian.

JS: In "I Am an Ivory Tower Dweller," you say that Kleist, Flaubert, Dostoevsky, Kafka, Faulkner, and Robbe-Grillet have changed your consciousness of the world. Since 1967, when you made that statement, would you add any new names to this list?

PH: There are so many and so few greats. Perhaps I have gone a little bit further back into history and tried to reread from the beginning on. Years back in school I was fascinated by Homer, by Pindar, by Heraclites, and I have reread everything which I, and perhaps many others, read too early, this time more slowly. Goethe. But there is one whom I only now totally comprehend and who for me writes a holy scripture in a completely objective sense, and that is Hölderlin. I had not understood him in this way before. But now I can read his work as a far better written and morally highstanding, holy scripture, where one is not forced to believe but, because sentences stand like mountain ranges, can simply believe, or at least see an ideal. At the moment I am also reading many scientific essays, because this gives one such a strange kind of concentration and quietness and, above all, a creative impulse, a completely objective creative impulse. A writer is always threatened by a creative impulse which goes anywhere it likes. While I am reading geological descriptions, for example, my creative impulse remains contained and, in spite of that, very strong. This creative impulse does not become pictures, but goes, so to speak, into grammar, giving grammar new life.

JS: You and Wim Wenders have made films together and you personally made a film of your novella *The Left-Handed Woman*. I know that films have always been an interest of yours. Is there any possibility that you will in the future prefer filmmaking to writing?

PH: I think I will make a film, or perhaps two, if I can. But the greatest difficulty is that there cannot be any arbitrary crossing of borders, because one loses one's identity very easily, an identity which as a writer is difficult to have anyhow. It is very difficult for me to say, "I am a writer." Only sometimes, in moments where I know what is, where I can say what is by writing, am I a writer. But this identity is not an everyday one, as with a doctor, or a German professor, or whatever. When I made this film, I didn't count on coming so close to losing my identity, which is fragile anyhow. And there was a long time afterward when I was nothing. And one must be very philosophical to endure the fact that he is nothing. You understand, one cannot simply say, now I'll make a film again, and now I'll write a book again; it doesn't work like that. It is a very, very dangerous and adventurous thing. If I make a film again I know that I have to be very, very careful. It was very, very difficult then to find my way back to sentences, to writing, and not to feel totally like a dilettante or a pretender when I afterward tried again to write a story or, as we said, a narrative poem. It is also a great problem that two sentences come together. What does it mean, that one sentence follows another? It was as though everything were isolated and I were lying by adding one sentence to the other. That is how I felt then when I was writing.

JS: Even though your first success was as a dramatist, you have not written a play since *They Are Dying Out* in 1973. Do you feel you have exhausted drama as a genre for yourself?

PH: I have a certain vision of a play, that would be one person who addressed the people for three hours. That is my conception of drama, if it could be written, but very serious and with passion; this would be drama. Everything else in the theater strikes me as tricky—for me. At one time I felt very identifiable as a playwright: when I wrote *The Ride Across Lake Constance*. Then I thought that this is pure theater, this is totally new theater, totally perfect, but since then I have lost that. That can be done only once; I could not go further with that. Then I imagine still another pure drama: one person onstage who addresses the people: something like *Offending the Audience* again, but different. But to reveal this in scenes, I would have to conceive the whole drama very rationally, scene for scene. What gives writing truth has to be created in the imagination, not through thinking, not through planning, not through collecting, not through observing; all these things have to happen before, but the imagination creates truth. With most writing one reads, one notices that it has not gone through the verifying creative impulse. It is worked out according to a pattern, but that is not what is exciting, warming, liberating. I don't mean that the imagination creates special pictures, grotesqueries, or whatever, but that the language which the creative impulse makes is worthy of being written. If it has, so to speak, risen up through the imagination like a sunken land, then it can be written. It is that way with me with plays. One can really only dream writing. Everything that is written, if it is to be good, must be rational, and writing is an extremely rational act. Writing is rational not in positive sentences but in avoiding. But positive sentences must be created through dream. That is very, very difficult. That is why almost no one understands what literature is, what kind of an exhausting process it is—every single sentence. As I said, with theater pieces this does not come to me any more. There are beginnings in me, but they somehow stay stuck. Perhaps they'll come up again; everything has to come into floating. Or perhaps a man loses this in the course of his life and writing then stops.

JS: Two last questions please. A colleague of mine recently commented that students in America today are reading Handke the way his generation read Hesse, even before their works were being taught in the university curriculum. Can you explain why the young intellectuals of America feel such an affinity for your work?

PH: I believe because they are independent people. I know that there are also people here who read what I write, but they are not a congregation as they were in the past. They are independent people. They have no ideology, they are skeptical, and at the same time they have longing, and they are objective and at the same time they don't want to perish in objectivity. This might be the case everywhere. But there are not so many. That flatters me, of course, but I don't have the impression that there are many in America. I'm proud that this is so anyway. There is a nice saying by Ingeborg Bachmann which goes, "I long for you, reader." I don't look down upon readers. All I want is to be read. I think it is something extremely beautiful for a human being to read. I don't want to say anything about American literary criticism, but what I really want is not to be criticized but only to be read. On the other hand, I must say that sometimes I am pleased to read something precise where I can see that this critic has a sympathetic understanding of what I have written. That is very, very good for one who writes. I believe that to receive no encouragement but to be portrayed always as an enemy is very, very damaging to the good creative impulse which a writer needs. This creative impulse is the most valuable thing one can have; this I have learned. It is only there when one feels the divine in oneself. And in the literary world this valuable creativity can easily be destroyed. If I have learned anything at all, I have learned that I have to be careful of my creative impulse, of this difficulty, which perhaps everyone has, of this good, of this new-world-creating creative impulse, where everything, so to speak, can become language and where one thinks one can bring the world to shine with language, and not to betray it as it almost always happens with language. Every beauty is destroyed by language. What one really wants with writing is the fact that beauty achieves permanence. But I'm going on too long. You began with Hesse, and I think he is a very honorable writer. But a comparison is not possible.

JS: And finally, can you tell me something about your new novel, *Slow Homecoming*, which you recently completed?

PH: I can only say I have expanded myself as never before with this writing. It is an attempt to reach a world harmony and at the same time to reach a universality for myself as someone who writes, an attempt which may have been too daring. Sometimes this is so in this narrative—or in this epic poem, as you will surely call it. I have the feeling that for centuries this has not been tried: to capture this harmony with language, and to pass it on contagiously, because we have, especially in the German-language part of the world, the problem with our history, and because of this we have almost no future. Because of what happened forty or so years ago, we have no more power for beauty; no one can really live the right way here, and there is no nature. Or there is nature, but there is no language for nature, what Hölderlin speaks of as the great nature, which was still possible in his time. In Austria, too, there is, naturally, no difference. This is the great problem with the past and, because of the past, with the future. And because of this we have the problem with the poetic creation of human beings living together. And in this which I have written, without wanting it, it came to the conflict between these two. I wanted to create beauty, so to speak, the quiet beauty, with language, and then I noticed that I came into conflict with the history of my ancestors, which is also in me. This is how it happened. I don't know whether the story is torn into pieces by this, but in any case I was able to narrate this conflict. I did this in the quietness in the form. I think that it has a form, which is the most important thing. Short on feelings and long on form. [Laugh]. And because of this it became fragmentary; the story stops abruptly. With the greatest effort of which I am capable, I brought everything in this story to a beginning, and with that the story ended. All problems with home, with language, with family, with history, with nature, I have tried to bring to a new beginning, but not in a philosophizing way, not in an essayistic way, but in a narrative way, in the narrative language. And then I suddenly noticed that the story was ended. I was immensely relieved and at the same time it was a great shock for me, because I thought it would be a story of 300 pages and it is only 200. What I really wanted was that it start in America, in Alaska, for ten pages, and that the rest happen across Europe. And now all 200 pages take place there, and it stops in the plane above Europe. It will make sense, but that too is a great shock. What do I mean "great"? It is a shock.

Appendix 2
Chronology

1942	Born December 6, in Griffen, province of Carinthia (Kärntnen), Austria.
1944–48	Lives in Berlin.
1948–54	Attends Hauptschule in Griffen.
1954–59	Attends Marianum, a Catholic boys school, in Tanzenberg bei Klagenfurt.
1959–61	Attends Klagenfurter Gymnasium; graduates in 1961.
1961–65	Attends University of Graz, studying law; involved in Forum Stadtpark and the Graz Group.
1964	First publication, a short story entitled "The Flood" ("Die Überschwemmung"), appears in *manuskripte*.
1966	*The Hornets (Die Hornissen), Offending the Audience (Publikumsbeschimpfung), Self-Accusation (Selbstbezichtigung)*, and *Prophecy (Weissagung)* published; *Offending the Audience, Self-Accusation*, and *Prophecy* performed; marries Libgart Schwarz, an actress; leaves Austria for Germany (over the next seven years, lives in Düsseldorf, Berlin, Paris, Cologne, and Kronberg bei Frankfurt); attends Group 47 meeting in Princteon.
1967	*The Peddler (Der Hausierer), Calling for Help (Hilferufe)*, and *Kaspar* published; *Calling for Help* performed; awarded Gerhart Hauptmann Prize.
1968	*Kaspar* performed.
1969	*My Foot My Tutor (Das Mündel will Vormund sein)* published and performed; daughter Amina born in Berlin; with ten other writers, establishes publishing house, Verlag der Autoren.
1970	*Quodlibet, The Ride Across Lake Constance (Der Ritt über den Bodensee)*, and *The Goalie's Anxiety at the Penalty Kick (Die Angst des Tormanns beim Elfmeter)* published; *Quodlibet* performed.
1971	*The Ride Across Lake Constance* performed.
1972	*Short Letter, Long Farewell (Der kurze Brief zum langen Abschied)* and *A Sorrow Beyond Dreams (Wunschloses Unglück)* published; he and wife separate.
1973	*They Are Dying Out (Die Unvernünftigen sterben aus)* published; awarded Georg Büchner Prize; moves to Clamart, a suburb of Paris.
1974	*They Are Dying Out* performed.
1975	*A Moment of True Feeling (Die Stunde der wahren Empfindung)* published.

1976   *The Left-Handed Woman (Die linkshändige Frau)* published.
1977   *The Weight of the World (Das Gewicht der Welt)* published.
1979   *Slow Homecoming (Langsame Heimkehr)* published; awarded (but declines) Austria's Franz Kafka Prize; returns to Austria with daughter to live in Salzburg.

Notes

1. Introduction

1. In "Ach ja, da liest ja einer," *Der Spiegel*, May 6, 1966, Erich Kuby reports the conversation he had with an American professor who asked which modern German writers were *not* associated with Group 47. Aside from Dürrenmatt and Frisch (both Swiss), Nossack, Hans Arp, Arno Schmidt, and Christoph Meckel, Kuby could name no one. Kuby's essay, along with other reactions to the Princeton meeting, is reprinted in part in *Gruppe 47: Eine Dokumentation*, ed. Horst Ziermann (Frankfurt: Wolter Editionen, 1966).

2. For an account of the origin and development of the group, see Siegfried Mandel, *Group 47: The Reflected Intellect* (Carbondale: Southern Illinois University Press, 1973). Other useful books include: Hans Werner Richter, *Almanach der Gruppe 47, 1947–1962* (Reinbek bei Hamburg: Rowohlt, 1964); *Die Gruppe 47: Bericht, Kritik, Polemik: Ein Handbuch*, ed. Reinhard Lettau (Neuwied and Berlin: Luchterhand, 1967); and Friedhelm Kroll, *Die "Gruppe 47": Soziale Lage und gesellschaftliches Bewußtsein literarischer Intelligenz in der Bundesrepublik* (Stuttgart: J. B. Metzler, 1977). In addition to Ziermann's collection, the following offer remarks on the Princeton meeting: "Group 47 at Princeton University," *German-American Review*, Special Supplement, April 1966; Joseph P. Bauke, "Group 47 at Princeton," *New York Times Book Review*, May 15, 1966, pp. 43–45; "Group 47: Nation's Conscience," *Newsweek*, May 16, 1966, pp. 118, 118C, 118D, 118F.

3. "Group 47: Nation's Conscience," p. 118.

4. See, for example, Joachim Kaiser, "Drei Tage und ein Tag," *Süddeutsche Zeitung*, April 30, 1966, reprinted in Ziermann, *Gruppe 47*, p. 16; and Fritz J. Raddatz, "Die Bilanz von Princeton," *Frankfurte Hefte*, July 1966, reprinted in Ziermann, *Gruppe 47*, p. 41.

5. "Für eine neue Literatur," *konkret*, June 1966, reprinted in Ziermann, *Gruppe 47*, pp. 51–56. This essay, in slightly different form, appears as "Zur Tagung der Gruppe 47 in den USA," in *Ich bin ein Bewohner des Elfenbeinturms* (Frankfurt: Suhrkamp, 1972), pp. 29–34, and is reprinted in *Positionen der Erzählens: Analyses und Theorien zur deutschen Gegenwartsliteratur*, ed. Heinz Ludwig Arnold and Theo Beck (Munich: C. H. Beck, 1976), pp. 181–85. The quotation is from *Ich bin ein Bewohner des Elfenbeinturms*, pp. 29–30. Handke's remarks are expanded in an essay written in 1966, "Die Literatur ist romantisch" (Berlin: Oberbaumpresse, 1967), reprinted in *Prosa Gedichte Theaterstücke Hörspiel Aufsätze* (Frankfurt: Suhrkamp, 1969), pp. 273–87, hereafter cited as *Prosa Gedichte*, and *Ich bin ein Bewohner des Elfenbeinturms*, pp. 35–50.

6. Walter Höllerer, "Zur Princeton-Diskussion," in Ziermann, *Gruppe 47*, pp. 103–04; Kuby, ibid., pp. 19–28. Shortly after the Princeton meeting, Handke wrote a letter to *Der Spiegel* which congratulates himself facetiously for having received the attention of that prestigious publication. See "Pantoffeln," *Der Spiegel*, May 23, 1966, pp. 11–12; Nicholas Hern reprints the relevant portion of this letter, in English translation, in *Peter Handke* (New York: Frederick Ungar, 1972), p. 7.

7. Jakov Lind, *"Die Hornissen:* zarte Seelen, trockene Texte," *Der Spiegel,* July 11, 1966, p. 79.

8. "Wenn ich schreibe," *Akzente,* 13, 5 (October 1966), 467.

9. Handke's first publication, "Die Überschwemmung" [1963], is reprinted in *Der Rand der Wörter: Erzählungen Gedichte Stücke* (Stuttgart: Reclam, 1975), pp. 3-6; *Begrüßung des Aufsichtstrats: Prosatexte* (Salzburg: Residenz, 1967), pp. 43-47; and *Prosa Gedichte,* pp. 38-41.

10. For an account of Handke's role in Forum Stadtpark and the Graz Group, see Alfred Holzinger, "Peter Handkes literarische Anfänge in Graz," in *Wie die Grazer auszogen, die Literatur zu erobern: Texte, Porträts, Analysen und Dokumente junger österreichischer Autoren,* ed. Peter Laemmle and Jörg Drews (Munich: Karl M. Lipp, 1975), pp. 183-98.

11. For the manifesto of the Vienna Group, as well as samples of writing by its members, see *Die Wiener Gruppe: Achleitner, Artmann, Bayer, Rühm, Wiener: Texte, Gemeinschaftsarbeiten, Aktionen,* ed. Gerhard Rühm (Reinbek bei Hamburg: Rowohlt, 1967).

12. Robert Pynsent, "Contemporary German Fiction: The Dimensions of Experimentation," in *Surfiction: Fiction Now . . . and Tomorrow,* ed. Raymond Federman (Chicago: Swallow Press, 1975), p. 139.

13. "Begrüßung des Aufsichtsrats" [1964] appears in *Begrüßung des Aufsichtsrats,* pp. 5-11, and *Prosa Gedichte,* pp. 9-14; "Augenzeugenbericht" [1965] appears in *Begrüßung des Aufsichtsrats,* pp. 102-03, and *Prosa Gedichte,* pp. 83-84.

14. *The Innerworld of the Outerworld of the Innerworld,* trans. Michael Roloff (New York: The Seabury Press, 1974), pp. 24-25. The poems in this bilingual edition are selected from *Die Innenwelt der Außenwelt der Innenwelt* (Frankfurt: Suhrkamp, 1969), which has been partially reprinted in *Prosa Gedichte,* pp. 111-52. Some of these and others of Handke's poems also appear in *Der Rand der Wörter,* pp. 32-56, and *Als das Wunschen noch geholfen hat* (Frankfurt: Suhrkamp, 1974), pp. 9-23, 55-69, 103-19. Three of the poems from the latter collection ("Leben ohne Poesie," "Blaues Gedicht," and "Die Sinnlosigkeit und das Glück") appear, along with *Das Ende des Flanierens* (Vienna: Davidpresse, 1976), in *Nonsense and Happiness,* a bilingual edition, trans. Michael Roloff (New York: Urizen Books, 1976). "Die Einzahl und die Mehrzahl" also appears in *Der Rand der Wörter,* pp. 39-41.

15. *The Innerworld of the Outerworld of the Innerworld,* pp. 50-51.

16. Ibid., pp. 112-19.

17. Ibid., pp. 120-25.

18. Ibid., pp. 150-51, 94-99. The latter poem also appears in *Der Rand der Wörter,* pp. 43-45.

19. See Christian Linder, *Schreiben und Leben: Gespräche mit Jürgen Becker, Peter Handke, Walter Kempowski, Wolfgang Koeppen, Günter Wallroff, Dieter Wellershoff* (Cologne: Kiepenheuer und Witsch, 1974), p. 39.

20. "Ich bin ein Bewohner des Elfenbeinturms," in *Prosa Gedichte,* p. 264; and *Ich bin ein Bewohner des Elfenbeinturms,* p. 20.

21. Lev Jakubinskij, "On Sounds in Verse Language" [1916], quoted in Boris M. Èjxenbaum, "The Theory of the Formal Method" [1926], in *Readings in Russian Poetics: Formalist and Structuralist Views,* ed. Ladislav Matejka and Krystyna Pomorska (Cambridge, Mass.: The MIT Press, 1971), p. 9.

22. Viktor Sklovskij, "On the Theory of Prose" [1929], quoted in Robert Scholes, *Structuralism in Literature: An Introduction* (New Haven: Yale University Press, 1974), pp. 83-84.

23. *Die Hornissen* (Frankfurt: Suhrkamp, 1978), p. 244.

24. "Approximations," *Times Literary Supplement,* October 3, 1968, p. 1103.

25. "Über meinen neuen Roman *Der Hausierer,*" *Dichten und Trachten,* 29 (1967), 27–29.

2. The *Sprechstücke*

1. The full title of Weiss's play is *The Persecution and Assassination of Jean Paul Marat as Performed by the Inmates of the Asylum of Charenton Under the Direction of the Marquis de Sade (Die Verfolgung und Ermordung Jean Paul Marats dargestellt durch die Schauspielgruppe des Hospizes zu Charenton unter Anleitung des Herrn de Sade).*

2. See Michael Patterson, *German Theatre Today: Post-war Theatre in West and East Germany, Austria and Northern Switzerland* (London: Pitman Publishing, 1976), pp. 114–17. Patterson lists the most frequently produced plays and playwrights in the countries of his subtitle during the years 1964 through 1974.

3. "Zur *Publikumsbeschimpfung,*" in *Stücke 1* (Frankfurt: Suhrkamp, 1972), p. 203.

4. Ibid.

5. "Bemerkung zu meinen Sprechstücken," in *Stücke 1,* p. 201.

6. "Note on *Offending the Audience* and *Self-Accusation,*" in *Kaspar and Other Plays,* trans. Michael Roloff (New York: Farrar, Straus & Giroux, 1969), p. ix.

7. See Alfred Holzinger, "Peter Handkes literarische Anfänge in Graz," in *Wie die Grazer auszogen, die Literatur zu erobern: Texte, Porträts, Analysen und Dokumente junger österreichischer Autoren,* ed. Peter Laemmle and Jörg Drews (Munich: Karl M. Lipp, 1975), p. 194.

8. See Claus Peymann, "Directing Handke," trans. Claus Brucher-Herpel, *The Drama Review,* 16, 2 (June 1972), 48–49.

9. *Publikumsbeschimpfung,* in *Stücke 1,* pp. 19–20. Subsequent citations in German are from this edition and appear parenthetically in the text.

10. *Offending the Audience,* in *Kaspar and Other Plays,* p. 8. Subsequent citations in English are from this edition and appear parenthetically in the text.

11. Nicholas Hern, *Peter Handke* (New York: Frederick Ungar, 1972), p. 27.

12. These words are not literal translations of the German, which Roloff has rendered freely in order to "create new acoustic patterns in English." See "A Note on the Translation," in *Kaspar and Other Plays,* p. vii.

13. Joachim Neugroschel, "The Theater as Insult," *American German Review,* 33 (1967), 28.

14. Helmut Heißenbüttel, "Peter Handke und seine Dichtung," *Universitas,* 25 (1970), 121–29; reprinted as "Peter Handke" in *Text und Kritik,* 24 (October 1969), 14–20, and 24/24a (July 1971), 1–7, and as "Peter Handkes Ruhm" in Helmut Heißenbüttel, *Zur Tradition der Moderne* (Neuwied and Berlin: H. Luchterhand, 1972), pp. 346–57. The essay appears in English translation as "Peter Handke and his Writings" in *Universitas,* 12, 3 (1970), 243–51.

15. Artur Joseph, *Theater unter vier Augen: Gespräche mit Prominenten* (Cologne: Kiepenheuer und Witsch, 1969), p. 32.

16. Artur Joseph, "Nauseated by Language: From an Interview with Peter Handke," trans. E. B. Ashton, in *The Drama Review,* 15, 1 (Fall 1970), 59.

17. Following its successful run in Frankfurt, *Offending the Audience* opened in Berlin at the Forum Theater, where it was to have the longest run of any contemporary play on a German stage: over five years. According to Patterson, *German Theatre Today,* this play had nine separate productions in West Germany, Austria, and Switzerland during the 1967–68 season.

18. Hern, *Peter Handke*, p. 38.

19. *Weissagung*, in *Stücke 1*, pp. 53, 55, 56. Subsequent citations in German are from this edition and appear parenthetically in the text.

20. *Prophecy*, in *The Ride Across Lake Constance and Other Plays*, trans. Michael Roloff (New York: Farrar, Straus & Giroux, 1976), pp. 3, 7, 7. Subsequent citations in English are from this edition and appear parenthetically in the text.

21. "Theater und Film: Das Elend des Vergleichens," in *Prosa Gedichte Theaterstücke Hörspiel Aufsätze* (Frankfurt: Suhrkamp, 1969), p. 314. Hereafter cited in the text.

22. "Theater and Film: The Misery of Comparison," trans. Donald Nordberg, in *Focus on Film and Theatre*, ed. James Hurt (Englewood Cliffs, N.J.: Prentice-Hall, 1974), p. 165. Hereafter cited in the text.

23. "Über das Stück *Weissagung*," in *Stücke 1*, p. 204.

24. The passage is from "Whoever Finds a Horseshoe," from "Poems, 1921–1925." The poem may be read, in a somewhat different translation, in *Complete Poetry of Osip Mandelstam*, trans. Burton Raffel and Alla Burago, with introduction and notes by Sidney Monas (Albany: State University of New York Press, 1973), pp. 131–33.

25. Joseph, *Theater unter vier Augen*, p. 39.

26. Joseph, "Nauseated by Language," p. 61.

27. Joseph, *Theater unter vier Augen*, p. 28.

28. Joseph, "Nauseated by Language," pp. 57–58.

29. *Selbstbezichtigung*, in *Stücke 1*, pp. 69–72. Subsequent citations in German are from this edition and appear parenthetically in the text.

30. *Self-Accusation*, in *Kaspar and Other Plays*, pp. 37–40. Subsequent citations in English are from this edition and appear parenthetically in the text.

31. "1957," in *Als ich 15 war*, ed. Eckart Kroneberg (Gütersloh o. J., 1968); reprinted in *Ich bin ein Bewohner des Elfenbeinturms* (Frankfurt: Suhrkamp, 1972), pp. 11–16.

32. "Über das Stück *Selbstbezichtigung*, in *Stücke 1*, p. 205.

33. Ludwig Wittgenstein, *Philosophical Investigations*, bilingual edition, trans. G. E. M. Anscombe (New York: Macmillan, 1953), p. 29. See Anthony Kenny, *Wittgenstein* (Harmondsworth: Penguin Books, 1973), which analyzes this concept in detail and identifies *Tractatus* 3.23 and 3.24 and *Prototractatus* 3.20106 as points at which Wittgenstein deals with this argument (p. 80).

34. Joseph, *Theater unter vier Augen*, pp. 28–29.

35. Joseph, "Nauseated by Language," p. 58.

36. Joseph, *Theater unter vier Augen*, p. 38.

37. Joseph, "Nauseated by Language," p. 61.

38. Joseph, *Theater unter vier Augen*, p. 38.

39. Joseph, "Nauseated by Language," p. 61.

40. On Brecht, see "Horváth ist besser," *Theater heute*, 9, 3 (March 1968), 28; reprinted as "Horváth und Brecht," in *Ich bin ein Bewohner des Elfenbeinturms*, pp. 63–64, and *Theater im Umbruch: Eine Dokumentation aus "Theater heute*," ed. Henning Rischbieter (Velber bei Hannover: Friedrich, 1970), pp. 62–63. See also "Noch Einmal über Brecht—und über das Straßentheater der Studenten," *Theater heute*, 9, 4 (April 1968), 6–7; reprinted as "Straßentheater und Theatertheater," in *Prosa Gedichte*, pp. 303–07, and *Ich bin ein Bewohner des Elfenbeinturms*, pp. 51–55, and as "Brecht, Spiel, Theater, Agitation," in Rischbieter, *Theater im Umbruch*, pp. 64–67. The essay also appears in English translation by Nicholas Hern as "Brecht, Play, Theatre, Agitation," in *Theatre Quarterly*, 1, 4 (October–December 1971), 89–90. On a "literature of engagement," see "Die Literatur ist romantisch" (Berlin: Oberbaumpresse, 1967), reprinted in *Prosa Gedichte*, pp. 273–87, and *Ich bin ein Bewohner des Elfenbeinturms*, pp. 35–50.

41. Joseph, *Theater unter vier Augen*, p. 39.

42. Joseph, "Nauseated by Language," p. 61.

43. John Simon, *Uneasy Stages: A Chronicle of the New York Theater, 1963–1973* (New York: Random House, 1975), pp. 366–67.

44. *Hilferufe*, in *Stücke 1*, p. 93. Subsequent citations in German are from this edition and appear parenthetically in the text.

45. *Calling for Help*, in *The Ride Across Lake Constance and Other Plays*, p. 22. Subsequent citations in English are from this edition and appear parenthetically in the text.

46. Joseph, *Theater unter vier Augen*, p. 38.

47. Joseph, "Nauseated by Language," p. 61.

48. Kenny, *Wittgenstein*, p. 45.

3. Kaspar

1. See Joachim Kaiser, "Schauspiel in der Bundesrepublik," *Theater heute*, 11, 10 (October 1970), p. 9. Kaiser records 508 performances, with a total audience of 54,868. His comparisons deal only with "modern, serious" drama.

2. Jack Kroll, "Mind Bending," *Newsweek*, February 26, 1973, p. 91; Clive Barnes, "Theater: Handke's *Kaspar* Is Staged in Brooklyn," *New York Times*, February 16, 1973, p. 26.

3. For an account of the historical and legendary Kaspar Hauser, see A. F. Bance, "The Kaspar Hauser Legend and Its Literary Survival," *German Life & Letters*, n.s., 28, 3 (April 1975), 199–210.

4. Artur Joseph, *Theater unter vier Augen: Gespräche mit Prominenten* (Cologne: Kiepenheuer und Witsch, 1969), p. 35.

5. Artur Joseph, "Nauseated by Language: From an Interview with Peter Handke," trans. E. B. Ashton, in *The Drama Review*, 15, 1 (Fall 1970), 60.

6. Preface to *Kaspar*, in *Kaspar* (Frankfurt: Suhrkamp, 1967), p. 7. Subsequent citations in German are from this edition and appear parenthetically in the text.

7. Preface to *Kaspar*, in *Kaspar and Other Plays*, trans. Michael Roloff (New York: Farrar, Straus & Giroux, 1969), p. 59. Subsequent citations in English are from this edition and appear parenthetically in the text.

8. Linda Hill, "The Struggle Against Language and Behavior Patterns: Handke's *Kaspar*," in *Language As Aggression: Studies in the Postwar Drama* (Bonn: Bouvier, 1976), lists these models as "condition contrary to fact, active/passive, aber, correlative conjunctions (sowohl . . . als auch, nicht nur . . . sondern auch, zwar . . . aber), je . . . desto, selbstverständlich, jeder (adjective)/niemand, kein, condition contrary to fact, unwahr/wahr, dich (direct object and reflexive), schon and noch, du, object and adverbial clauses, and modal verbs" (p. 176).

9. For a speculative treatment of the relationship between *Kaspar* and *Othello*, see June Schlueter, "'Goats and Monkeys' and the 'Idiocy of Language': Handke's *Kaspar* and Shakespeare's *Othello*," *Modern Drama*, 23, 1 (March 1980), pp. 25–32.

10. This ending appears in the play as published in *Theater heute*, 9, 13 (1968 Jahrbuch), 69–88. In *Stücke 1*, the final lines are: "Ich/bin/nur/Ziegen und Affen/ Ziegen und Affen."

11. Joseph, *Theater unter vier Augen*, p. 35.

12. Joseph, "Nauseated by Language," p. 59.

13. Pierre Biner, *The Living Theatre: A History without Myths*, trans. Robert Meister (New York: Avon, 1972), pp. 132–33.

14. Ibid., pp. 133–34.

15. Ibid., p. 136.

16. Christopher Innes, *Modern German Drama: A Study in Form* (Cambridge: Cambridge University Press, 1979), pp. 244–45.

4. *My Foot My Tutor*

1. Hans Bertram Bock, "Alibi für Intendanten: Gespräch mit Peter Handke über seine neuen Projekte," Munich *Abendzeitung*, September 26, 1968.

2. "Über dem ganzen Bild liegt etwas, was man, mit einem Bild, als tiefer Frieden bezeichnen könnte." *Das Mündel will Vormund sein*, in *Stücke 2* (Frankfurt: Suhrkamp, 1973), p. 11.

3. "The picture as a whole exudes something of the quality of what one might call profound peacefulness." *My Foot My Tutor*, in *The Ride Across Lake Constance and Other Plays*, trans. Michael Roloff (New York: Farrar, Straus & Giroux, 1976), p. 31.

4. See Bock "Alibi für Intendanten."

5. Ibid.

6. "Theater und Film: Das Elend des Vergleichens," in *Prosa Gedichte Theaterstücke Hörspiel Aufsätze* (Frankfurt: Suhrkamp, 1969), p. 325.

7. "Theater and Film: The Misery of Comparison," trans. Donald Nordberg, in *Focus on Film and Theater*, ed. James Hurt (Englewood Cliffs, N.J.: Prentice-Hall, 1974), p. 174.

8. Quoted in "Stille Macht: Handke's *Mündel* in Frankfurt," *Der Spiegel*, February 10, 1969, p. 126.

9. Preface, in *Kaspar* (Frankfurt: Suhrkamp, 1967), p. 8.

10. Preface to *Kaspar*, in *Kaspar and Other Plays*, trans. Michael Roloff (New York: Farrar, Straus & Giroux, 1969), p. 60.

11. Dieter Bachmann, et al., "Eine Bewegte Handke-Premiere in Frankfurt," *Theater heute*, 10, 3 (March 1969), 40–43; Nicholas Hern, *Peter Handke* (New York: Frederick Ungar, 1972), pp. 81–82.

12. "Mich faszinierte der Gedanke, optische und akustische Vorgänge auf die Bühne zu bringen." In Bock, "Alibi für Intendanten."

13. Handke comments that he fears that after 15 minutes of the play, the theater would be completely empty. Ibid.

14. Hern points to some similarities to Buster Keaton routines and other scenes from the silent screen, as well as to likenesses to Beckett plays (*Eh Joe, Acts Without Words*) which themselves draw upon this tradition (*Peter Handke*, pp. 83–85).

15. "Ich möchte gewisse Vorgänge—wie Sitzen, Gehen oder Essen—isolieren, aus einer Handlung lösen."

16. "Das Stück ist eine Etüde, die Vorbereitung auf das nächste große Stück." In Bock, "Alibi für Intendanten."

17. Ibid.

5. *Quodlibet*

1. This comment, as well as the reaction of several members of the discussion group, is reported by Peter Hamm in "Handke endeckt sich selbst," in *Über Peter Handke*, ed. Michael Scharang (Frankfurt: Suhrkamp, 1972), p. 162.

2. "Zur Aufführung von *Quodlibet*," in *Stücke 2* (Frankfurt: Suhrkamp, 1973), p. 158. Handke's comments were originally published as "Nachbemerkung zu *Quodlibet*," in *Theater heute*, 11, 4 (April 1970), 47.

3. As Michael Roloff points out in a note to his translation, much of *Quodlibet* cannot be rendered literally in English, since the linguistic associations depend entirely upon sound correspondences in German. Roloff's adaptation, which he considers a model for American performances, admirably preserves the flavor of the original text, literally translating wherever possible the negative word or phrase the audience is supposed to think it hears and supplying English phrases with similar sounds. All the examples given are from Roloff's English version of *Quodlibet*, in *The Ride Across Lake Constance and Other Plays* (New York: Farrar, Straus & Giroux, 1976), pp. 55–56.

4. Rainer Litten, "Theater der Verstörung: Ein Gespräch mit Peter Handke," in Scharang, *Über Peter Handke*, p. 158.

5. "Zur Aufführung von *Quodlibet*," p. 157.

6. Ibid., p. 159.

7. Litten, "Theater der Verstörung," p. 158.

6. *The Ride Across Lake Constance*

1. William L. Lederer, "Handke's Ride," *Chicago Review*, 26, 2 (1974), 175, 171.

2. Interview with Andreas Müller, "Das Schreiben ist unglaublich sinnlich," Munich *Abendzeitung*, July 22, 1971.

3. In the interview with Müller, Handke noted that he had originally intended to have the play produced at the Münchner Kammerspiele, but the project did not materialize.

4. Stanley Kauffmann, "Two Different Talents," *The New Republic*, February 5, 1972, p. 24.

5. Clive Barnes, "The Theater: Peter Handke's *Ride Across Lake Constance*," *New York Times*, January 14, 1972, p. 16.

6. In an advertisement for the English language translation of the play, Handke's U.S. publisher, Farrar, Straus & Giroux, quotes the *Chicago Sun-Times* as having called the play a "landmark in avant-garde theater."

7. Handke's explanatory essay is reprinted in *Stücke 2* (Frankfurt: Suhrkamp, 1973), pp. 57–59; quotation is from p. 57. The notes are reprinted as "Aus den Notizen zu *Der Ritt über den Bodensee*, pp. 161–77.

8. *Der Ritt über den Bodensee*, in *Stücke 2*, p. 63. Subsequent citations in German are from this edition and appear parenthetically in the text.

9. *The Ride Across Lake Constance and Other Plays*, trans. Michael Roloff (New York: Farrar, Straus & Giroux, 1976), p. 72. Subsequent citations in English are from this edition and appear parenthetically in the text.

10. *Kaspar* (Frankfurt: Suhrkamp, 1967), p. 57; *Kaspar*, in *Kaspar and Other Plays*, trans. Michael Roloff (New York: Farrar, Straus & Giroux, 1969), p. 102.

11. Michael Roloff, "Postscript: A Note on Methods," in *The Innerworld of the Outerworld of the Innerworld*, trans. Michael Roloff (New York: The Seabury Press, 1974), p. 165.

12. Explanatory note to *Der Ritt über den Bodensee*, in Schaubühne am Halleschen Ufer program, reprinted in *Stücke 2*, p. 57.

13. T. E. Kalem, "Spengler Redux," *Time*, January 24, 1972, p. 53.

14. The first three lines of the quotation are spoken by Antipholus of Syracuse (Arden Edition, ed. R. A. Foakes, II.ii.212–14); the fourth is spoken, in slightly altered form, by Dromio of Syracuse (II.ii.195).

15. "Ein Kind, wie vor dem Schlafengehen, wird hereingebracht." "Auf den Notizen zu *Der Ritt über den Bodensee*," p. 175.

16. Rainer Nägele and Renate Voris, *Peter Handke* (Munich: C. H. Beck, 1978), p. 88.

See Jacques Lacan, *The Language of the Self: The Function of Language in Psychoanalysis* (Baltimore: The Johns Hopkins University Press, 1968), and "The Insistence of the Letter in the Unconscious," *Yale French Studies*, 1966, reprinted in *Structuralism,* ed. Jacques Ehrmann (Garden City, N.Y.: Doubleday, 1970), pp. 101–37.

17. Nicholas Hern, *Peter Handke* (New York: Frederick Ungar, 1971), p. 94.

18. Botho Strauss, "Versuch, ästhetische und politische Ereignisse zusammenzuden-ken—neues Theater 1967–70," *Theater heute,* 11, 10 (October 1970), 68.

19. Translation in Hern, *Peter Handke,* p. 94. Because it appears to me a contradiction, I have omitted the work "somnambulism" from the quotation.

20. Ira Hauptmann, "Aspects of Handke: A Play," *Partisan Review,* 45, 3 (1978), 427.

21. Richard Gilman, *The Making of Modern Drama: A Study of Büchner, Ibsen, Strindberg, Chekhov, Pirandello, Brecht, Beckett, Handke* (New York: Farrar, Straus & Giroux, 1974), p. 271.

7. The Goalie's Anxiety at the Penalty Kick

1. See, for example, Horst-Dieter Ebert, "Ein Kimble von Kafka," *Der Spiegel,* May 25, 1970; p. 182, and Stanley Kauffmann, "Inside Out," *World,* 1 (July 18, 1972), 62.

2. Anthony Thorlby, "Anti-Mimesis: Kafka and Wittgenstein," *On Kafka: Semi-Centenary Perspective,* ed. Franz Kuna (London: Paul Elek, 1976), p. 59.

3. Susan Sontag, "Against Interpretation" [1964], in *Against Interpretation* (New York: Dell Publishing Co., 1966), p. 8.

4. Thorlby, "Anti-Mimesis," pp. 62–63.

5. Jean-Paul Sartre, *La Nausée* (Paris: Gallimard, 1938), p. 179.

6. Jean-Paul Sartre, *Nausea,* trans. Lloyd Alexander (New York: New Directions, n.d.), pp. 170–71.

7. *Die Angst des Tormanns beim Elfmeter* (Frankfurt: Suhrkamp, 1970), pp. 51–52. Subsequent citations in German are from this edition and appear parenthetically in the text.

8. *The Goalie's Anxiety at the Penalty Kick* (New York: Farrar, Straus & Giroux, 1972), pp. 57–58. Subsequent citations in English are from this edition and appear parenthetically in the text.

9. Artur Joseph, "Nauseated by Language: From an Interview with Peter Handke," trans. E. B. Ashton, in *The Drama Review,* 15, 1 (Fall 1970), 61.

10. "Die Literatur ist romantisch" (Berlin: Oberbaumpresse, 1967), reprinted in *Prosa Gedichte Theaterstücke Hörspiel Aufsätze* (Frankfurt: Suhrkamp, 1969), pp. 273–87, and *Ich bin ein Bewohner des Elfenbeinturms* (Frankfurt: Suhrkamp, 1972), pp. 35–50.

11. For a discussion of semiotics in *The Goalie's Anxiety at the Penalty Kick* and *Short Letter, Long Farewell,* see J. J. White, "Signs of Disturbance: The Semiological Import of Some Recent Fiction by Michel Tournier and Peter Handke," *Journal of European Studies,* 4 (1974), 242–54.

12. "Die Angst des Tormanns beim Elfmeter," *Text und Kritik,* 24/24a (July 1971), 45. The example is from Klaus Conrad, *Die beginnende Schizophrenie: Versuch einer Gestaltanalyse des Wahns* (Stuttgart: Thieme, 1958), p. 12, but the observations about language are Handke's.

13. Handke, in *Text und Kritik,* p. 45.

14. Roland Barthes, *Eléments de Sémiologie,* in *Le Dégreé Zéro de l'Ecriture, suivide Eléments de Sémiologie* (Paris: Gonthier 1964), p. 80.

15. Barthes, *Elements of Semiology,* trans. Annette Lavers and Colin Smith (New York: Hill and Wang, 1967), p. 10.

16. Barthes, *Eléments de Sémiologie,* p. 130.

17. Barthes, *Elements of Semiology,* p. 57.

18. "Ich bin ein Bewohner des Elfenbeinturms," in *Ich bin ein Bewohner des Elfenbeinturms,* p. 20.

8. *Short Letter, Long Farewell*

1. The allusion is to Raymond Chandler's *The Long Goodbye.* In an interview, Hellmuth Karasek asked Handke about the allusion. He called it nothing more than a quotation, adding that for Chandler the long goodbye is a metaphor for death, whereas in his novel it is a metaphor for the separation and isolation of the protagonist and his wife. "Ohne zu verallgemeinern: Ein Gespräch mit Peter Handke," *Die Zeit,* March 31, 1972, reprinted in *Über Peter Handke,* ed. Michael Scharang (Frankfurt: Suhrkamp, 1972), pp. 85–90.

2. Karasek, in Scharang, p. 87.

3. Ibid., p. 86.

4. *Der kurze Brief zum langen Abschied* (Frankfurt: Suhrkamp, 1972), p. 81. Subsequent citations in German are from this edition and appear parenthetically in the text.

5. *Short Letter, Long Farewell,* trans. Ralph Manheim (New York: Farrar, Straus & Giroux, 1974), p. 67. Subsequent citations in English are from this edition and appear parenthetically in the text.

6. Karasek, in Scharang, p. 85.

7. Rainer Nägele explores Handke's treatment of America as fiction and reality in "Die vermittelte Welt: Reflexionen zum Verhältnis von Fiktion und Wirklichkeit in Peter Handkes Roman *Der kurze Brief zum langen Abschied,*" in *Jahrbuch der deutschen Schiller-Gesellschaft,* 19 (1975), 389–418; reprinted as "Amerika als Fiktion und Wirklichkeit in Peter Handkes Roman *Der kurze Brief zum langen Abschied,*" in *Die USA und Deutschland: Wechselseitige Spiegelungen in der Literatur der Gegenwart,* ed. Wolfgang Paulsen (Bern: Francke, 1976), pp. 110–15.

8. Günther Schiwy, *Strukturalismus und Zeichensysteme* (Munich: Beck, 1973), pp. 28–39. Schiwy's argument is summarized, in English, in Robert Detweiler, *Story, Sign and Self* (Philadelphia: Fortress Press, 1978), pp. 148–51.

9. This is mentioned by Manfred Durzak, who interviewed Handke in Kronberg in 1973, on the occasion of Handke's winning the Büchner Prize. The interview appeared as "Vom Büchner-Preis habe ich sogar geträumt" in *Die Welt,* November 1, 1973.

9. *They Are Dying Out*

1. See Claus Peymann, "Directing Handke," *The Drama Review,* 16, 2 (June 1972), 48, 53.

2. Promotional advertisement for the Yale Repertory Theatre's fourteenth season, 1979–80.

3. Rainer Nägele and Renate Voris, *Peter Handke* (Munich: C. H. Beck, 1978), p. 92.

4. Manfred Mixner, *Peter Handke* (Kronberg: Athenäum, 1977), p. 189.

5. *Die Unvernünftigen sterben aus* (Frankfurt: Suhrkamp, 1973), p. 42. Subsequent citations in German are from this edition and appear parenthetically in the text.

6. *They Are Dying Out,* in *The Ride Across Lake Constance and Other Plays,* trans. Michael

Roloff (New York: Farrar, Straus & Giroux, 1976), p. 199. Subsequent citations in English are from this edition and appear parenthetically in the text.

7. Joseph A. Federico, "The Hero as Playwright in Dramas by Frisch, Dürrenmatt, and Handke," *German Life & Letters,* n.s., 32, 2 (January 1979), 171.

8. Christian Schultz-Gerstein, "Das Leiden als Geschäfts-Trick: Gespräch mit Peter Handke über sein Stück," *Die Zeit,* April 26, 1974, p. 18.

9. Georg Lukács, *The Theory of the Novel* [1916], trans. Anna Bostock (Cambridge, Mass.: The MIT Press, 1971), pp. 29–39.

10. Georg Lukács, "Narrate or Describe?" [1936], in *Writer and Critic, and Other Essays,* ed. and trans. Arthur Kahn (London: Merlin Press, 1978), p. 127.

11. George Steiner, "Georg Lukács—A Preface," in Georg Lukács, *Realism in Our Time* (New York: Harper & Row, 1962), p. 12.

12. Mel Gussow, "Two Plays That Challenge as They Entertain," *New York Times,* November 11, 1979, p. 24.

13. Heinz Ludwig Arnold, "Gespräch mit Peter Handke," *Text und Kritik,* 24/24a (September 1976), 16.

14. Bruno Bettelheim, *The Uses of Enchantment: The Meaning and Importance of Fairy Tales* (New York: Alfred A. Knopf, 1975), p. 127.

15. See, in particular, Georg Lukács, "Die Zerstörung der Vernunft" (Berlin: Aufbau-Verlag, 1954).

16. Arnold Blumer, "Peter Handkes romantische Unvernunft," *Acta germanica,* 8 (1973), 123–32.

17. Georg Lukács, "On the Romantic Philosophy of Life: Novalis" [1910, in Hungarian], in *Soul and Form,* trans. Anna Bostock (London: Merlin Press, 1974), pp. 42–54.

18. George Lichtheim, *George Lukács* (New York: Viking, 1970); this point is made by Terry Eagleton, *Marxism and Literary Criticism* (Berkeley and Los Angeles: University of California Press, 1976), pp. 53–54.

10. *A Sorrow Beyond Dreams*

1. "1957," in *Als ich 15 war,* ed. Eckart Kroneberg (Gütersloh o. J., 1968); reprinted in *Ich bin ein Bewohner des Elfenbeinturms* (Frankfurt: Suhrkamp, 1972), pp. 11–16. Characteristics given in the preceding paragraph are paraphrased translations of parts of this essay. (Actually, Handke *had* been in a "foreign land," having lived in Berlin for approximately four years as a young child.)

2. Günther Schiwy, *Strukturalismus und Zeichensysteme* (Munich: Beck, 1973), pp. 28–39.

3. *Wunschloses Unglück* (Frankfurt: Suhrkamp, 1972), p. 20. Subsequent citations in German are from this edition and appear parenthetically in the text.

4. *A Sorrow Beyond Dreams,* trans. Ralph Manheim (New York: Farrar, Straus & Giroux, 1974), p. 12. Subsequent citations in English are from this edition and appear parenthetically in the text.

5. *Der kurze Brief zum langen Abschied* (Frankfurt: Suhrkamp, 1972), p. 150.

6. *Short Letter, Long Farewell,* trans. Ralph Manheim (New York: Farrar, Straus & Giroux, 1974), p. 128.

7. Roman Jakobson, "On Realism in Art" [1921], in *Readings in Russian Poetics: Formalist and Structuralist Views,* ed. Ladislav Matejka and Krystyna Pomorska (Cambridge, Mass.: The MIT Press, 1971), p. 13.

8. Quoted in Boris M. Èjxenbaum, "The Theory of the Formal Method" [1926], in Matejka and Pomorska, *Readings in Russian Poetics*, p. 13.

9. Boris Tomasevskij, "Literature and Biography" [1923], in Matejka and Pomorska, *Readings in Russian Poetics*, p. 51.

10. Georg Lukács, "Narrate or Describe?" [1936], in *Writer and Critic, and Other Essays*, ed. and trans. Arthur Kahn (London: Merlin Press, 1978), pp. 110–48.

11. For an excellent discussion of Lukács's and Jakobson's theories of realism and their application to Handke's novel, see David H. Miles, "Reality and the Two Realisms: Mimesis in Auerbach, Lukács, and Handke," *Monatshefte*, 71, 4 (Winter 1979), 371–78. Miles concludes that "neither 'realism' can stand by itself: each, by implicitly repressing the other, implies the other, and the two are irrevocably bound together in a dialectic both historical (diachronic) and aesthetic (synchronic)" (Abstract, Table of Contents).

12. Roman Jakobson, "Closing Statement: Linguistics and Poetics," in *Style in Language*, ed. Thomas A. Sebeok (Cambridge, Mass.: The MIT Press, 1960), pp. 374–75.

13. David Lodge, *The Modes of Modern Writing: Metaphor, Metonymy, and the Typology of Modern Literature* (Ithaca: Cornell University Press, 1977).

14. James Joyce, *Ulysses* [1922] (Bodley Head edn., 1954), p. 34; quoted in Lodge, *Modes of Modern Writing*, pp. 140–41.

15. Lodge, *Modes of Modern Writing*, p. 141.

16. Joyce, *Ulysses*, p. 52; quoted in Lodge, *Modes of Modern Writing*, p. 141.

17. Lodge, *Modes of Modern Writing*, p. 141.

18. Samuel Beckett, *Murphy* [1963], p. 5; quoted in Lodge, *Modes of Modern Writing*, p. 224.

19. Raymond Federman, *Double or Nothing* [1971], p. 85; quoted in Lodge, *Modes of Modern Writing*, p. 232.

20. Leonard Michaels, *I Would Have Saved Them If I Could* [1975], pp. 59–60; quoted in Lodge, *Modes of Modern Writing*, pp. 233–34.

21. See Georg Lukács, "Appearance and Essence" [1961], trans. Eva LeRoy, in *Preserve and Create: Essays in Marxist Literary Criticism*, ed. Gaylord C. LeRoy and Ursula Beitz (New York: Humanities Press, 1973), pp. 17–22.

22. S. Petrov, "Realism—the Generally Human" [1964], trans. Mark Yaron, in LeRoy and Beitz, *Preserve and Create*, p. 23.

11. *A Moment of True Feeling*

1. *Die Stunde der wahren Empfindung* (Frankfurt: Suhrkamp, 1975), p. 13. Subsequent citations in German are from this edition and appear parenthetically in the text.

2. *A Moment of True Feeling*, trans. Ralph Manheim (New York: Farrar, Straus & Giroux, 1977), p. 8. Subsequent citations in English are from this edition and appear parenthetically in the text.

3. Bruno Bettelheim, *The Uses of Enchantment: The Meaning and Importance of Fairy Tales* (New York: Alfred A. Knopf, 1975), p. 219.

4. "Peter Handke Filme *La Femme Gauchère:* Entrer par une porte mythique où les lois ont disparu," as told to Yvonne Baby, in *Le Monde*, May 18, 1978, p. 17.

5. Olaf Hansen, "Exorcising Reality," *New Boston Review*, 4, 1 (Summer 1978), 5.

6. Umberto Eco, *The Role of the Reader* (Bloomington: Indiana University Press, 1979), p. 61.

12. The Left-Handed Woman

1. See Peter Handke, *"Die linkshändige Frau,"* in *Scene Kassel* [Kassel, West Germany], Nr. 8 (November 1978), pp. 2-3. The essay was originally written as part of the German press materials for the film.

2. *Die linkshändige Frau* (Frankfurt: Suhrkamp, 1976), p. 22. Subsequent citations in German are from this edition and appear parenthetically in the text.

3. *The Left-Handed Woman*, trans. Ralph Manheim (New York: Farrar, Straus & Giroux, 1978), p. 13. Subsequent citations in English are from this edition and appear parenthetically in the text.

4. *Die Stunde der waren Empfindung* (Frankfurt: Suhrkamp, 1975), p. 7.

5. *A Moment of True Feeling*, trans. Ralph Manheim (New York: Farrar, Straus & Giroux, 1975), p. 3.

6. "Peter Handke Filme *La Femme Gauchère:* Entrer par une porte mythique où les lois ont disparu," as told to Yvonne Baby, in *Le Monde*, May 18, 1978, p. 17.

7. Marielouise Janssen-Jurreit, "Ein Buch für traurige Tage," *Der Spiegel*, October 11, 1976, p. 241.

8. "Peter Handke Filme *La Femme Gauchère*," p. 17.

9. Ibid.

10. Ibid.

11. Siegfried Schoker, "'Es soll mythisch sein, mythisch!'" *Der Spiegel*, May 2, 1977, p. 180.

12. "Die linkshändige Frau," in *Scene Kassel*, p. 3.

13. "Peter Handke Filme *La Femme Gauchère*," p. 17.

14. "Ich bin ein Bewohner des Elfenbeinturms," in *Prosa Gedichte Theaterstücke Hörspiel Aufsätze* (Frankfurt: Suhrkamp, 1969), p. 268, and in *Ich bin ein Bewohner des Elfenbeinturms* (Frankfurt: Suhrkamp, 1972), p. 24.

13. The Forthcoming Handke

1. Handke's speech on receiving the Gerhart Hauptmann Prize was a protest regarding a local political incident. The speech, originally appearing in the *Frankfurter Allgemeine Zeitung* on December 8, 1967, appears as "Rede anläßich der Verleihung des Gerhart-Hauptmann-Preises"; it is reprinted as "Peter Handkes Rede zum Verleihung des Gerhart-Hauptmann Preises" in *Theater heute*, 9, 1 (January 1968), 35, and as "Bemerkung zu einem Gerichtsurteil," in *Ich bin ein Bewohner des Elfenbeinturms* (Frankfurt: Suhrkamp, 1972), pp. 161-62. His acceptance speech for the Georg Büchner Prize originally appeared in *Süddeutsche Zeitung*, October 27-28, 1973, as "Die Geborgenheit unter der Schädeldecke." It is reprinted in *Theater heute*, 14, 2 (December 12, 1973), 1-2, and in *Als das Wunschen noch geholfen hat* (Frankfurt: Suhrkamp, 1974), pp. 71-80. Along with a companion piece by Rolf Michaelis entitled "Die Katze vor dem Spiegel oder: Peter Handkes Traum von der 'Anderen Zeit': Rede auf den Preisträger," it appears in *Deutsche Akademie für Sprache und Dichtung Jahrbuch*, 1973, pp. 55-70; and as "Wie wird man ein poetischer Mensch—oder Der Ekel vor der Macht: Rede des Büchner-Preisträgers vor der Deutschen Akademie für Sprache und Dichtung," in *Der Literat*, 15 (1973), 253-54. Saying that money meant very little to him, Handke passed the Kafka award on to two newer writers, Gerhard Mayer (from Switzerland) and Franz Weinzettl (from Austria). See Wolfgang Kraus, "Laudatio auf Peter Handke: Zur

Verleihung des Kafka-Preises 10. Oktober 1979, *Literatur und Kritik*, 140 (1979), 577-78.

2. See Heinz Ludwig Arnold, "Gespräch mit Peter Handke," *Text und Kritik*, 24/24a (1976), 19.

3. *Das Gewicht der Welt: Ein Journal, November 1975–März 1977* (Salzburg: Residenz, 1977; Frankfurt: Suhrkamp, 1979); citations in German are from this edition and appear parenthetically in the text. *Langsame Heimkehr* (Frankfurt: Suhrkamp, 1979). English translations by Ralph Manheim are forthcoming from Farrar, Straus & Giroux. As this book went to press, an additional prose work by Handke, *Die Lehre der Sainte-Victoire* (Frankfurt: Suhrkamp, 1980), was published.

Bibliography

Works by Peter Handke

Collections of Plays or Novels in German

Publikumsbeschimpfung und andere Sprechstücke. Frankfurt: Suhrkamp, 1966. [*Publikumsbeschimpfung, Weissagung, Selbstbezichtigung*]

Prosa Gedichte Theaterstücke Hörspiel Aufsätze. Frankfurt: Suhrkamp, 1969 (hereafter cited as *Prosa Gedichte*). [short stories, poems, *Publikumsbeschimpfung, Das Mündel will Vormund sein*, a radio play, essays]

Stücke 1. Frankfurt: Suhrkamp, 1972. [*Publikumsbeschimpfung, Weissagung, Selbstbezichtigung, Hilferufe, Kaspar*]

Stücke 2. Frankfurt: Suhrkamp, 1973. [*Das Mündel will Vormund sein, Quodlibet, Der Ritt über den Bodensee*]

Der Rand der Wörter: Erzählungen Gedichte Stücke. Ed. Heinz F. Schafroth. Stuttgart: Philipp Reclam, 1975. [short stories, poems, *Weissagung, Hilferufe, Quodlibet*]

Collections of Plays or Novels in English

Kaspar and Other Plays. Trans. Michael Roloff. New York: Farrar, Straus & Giroux, 1969. [*Offending the Audience, Self-Accusation, Kaspar*]

Offending the Audience and Self-Accusation. Trans. Michael Roloff. London: Methuen, 1971. [*Offending the Audience, Self-Accusation*]

The Ride Across Lake Constance and Other Plays. Trans. Michael Roloff. New York: Farrar, Straus & Giroux, 1976. [*Prophecy, Calling for Help, My Foot My Tutor, Quodlibet, The Ride Across Lake Constance, They Are Dying Out*]

Three by Peter Handke. Trans. Michael Roloff and Ralph Manheim. New York: Farrar, Straus & Giroux, 1977. [*The Goalie's Anxiety at the Penalty Kick, Short Letter, Long Farewell, A Sorrow Beyond Dreams*]

Two Novels by Peter Handke. Trans. Ralph Manheim. New York: Farrar, Straus & Giroux, 1979. [*A Moment of True Feeling, The Left-Handed Woman*]

Plays

Note: Individual plays may also appear in anthologies other than those cited here.

Offending the Audience (written in 1965; first performed on June 8, 1966, at Theater am Turm, Frankfurt, under the direction of Claus Peymann)

   German publication as *Publikumsbeschimpfung:*
       in *Publikumsbeschimpfung und andere Sprechstücke*, pp. 5–48;
       in *Spectaculum*, 10 (1967), 63–84;
       in *Prosa Gedichte*, pp. 180–211;
       in *Stücke 1*, pp. 9–47.

195

196 : Bibliography

English publication:

as *Tongue-Lashing*, trans. A. Leslie Willson, in *Dimension*, 1, 1 (1968), 118–67;

in *Kaspar and Other Plays*, pp. 1–32;

in *Offending the Audience and Self-Accusation*, pp. 9–39.

Prophecy (written in 1964; first performed in a double bill with *Self-Accusation* on October 22, 1966, at Städtische Bühne, Oberhausen, under the direction of Günther Büch)

German publication as *Weissagung*:

in *Publikumsbeschimpfung und andere Sprechstücke*, pp. 49–65;

in *Stücke 1*, pp. 49–63;

in *Der Rand der Wörter*, pp. 57–68.

English publication:

in *The Ride Across Lake Constance and Other Plays*, pp. 3–17.

Self-Accusation (written in 1965; first performed in a double bill with *Prophecy* on October 22, 1966, at Städtische Bühne, Oberhausen, under the direction of Günther Büch)

German publication as *Selbstbezichtigung*:

in *Publikumsbeschimpfung und andere Sprechstücke*, pp. 67–93;

in *Stücke 1*, pp. 65–88.

English publication:

in *Kaspar and Other Plays*, pp. 33–51;

in *The New Theatre of Europe*, vol. 4. Ed. Martin Esslin. New York: Dell Publishing, 1970, pp. 289–305;

in *Offending the Audience and Self-Accusation*, pp. 41–57.

Calling for Help (written in 1967; first performed on September 12, 1967, in Stockholm by actors from Städtische Bühne, Oberhausen, under the direction of Günther Büch)

German publication as *Hilferufe*:

in *Deutsches Theater der Gegenwart, 2*. Ed. Karlheinz Braun. Frankfurt: Suhrkamp, 1967, pp. 201–09;

in *Stücke 1*, pp. 89–97;

in *Der Rand der Wörter*, pp. 68–73.

English publication:

trans. Michael Roloff, in *American German Review*, 35 (April–May 1969), 14–15;

trans. Michael Roloff, in *The Drama Review*, 15, 1 (Fall 1970), 84–87;

trans. Michael Roloff, in *Postwar German Culture: An Anthology*. Ed. Charles E. McClelland and Steven P. Scher. New York: E. P. Dutton, 1974, pp. 265–69;

in *The Ride Across Lake Constance and Other Plays*, pp. 21–26.

Kaspar (written ca. 1967–68; first performed on May 11, 1968, at Theater am Turm, Frankfurt, under the direction of Claus Peymann, and at Städtische Bühne, Oberhausen, under the direction of Günther Büch)

German publication as *Kaspar*:

Kaspar. Frankfurt: Suhrkamp, 1967;

in *Theater heute*, 9, 13 (1968 Jahrbuch), 69–88;

in *Spectaculum*, 12 (1969), 113–81;

in *Stücke 1*, pp. 99–198.

A radio play version appears as *Kaspar in Tonbandreihe: Das Hörspiel*. Bonn: Inter Nationes, Kultureller Tonbanddienst, 1971.

English publication:

Kaspar. Trans. Michael Roloff. London: Methuen, 1972;

in *Kaspar and Other Plays*, pp. 53–140.

My Foot My Tutor (written ca. 1968; first performed on January 31, 1969, at Theater am
Turm, Frankfurt, under the direction of Claus Peymann)
  German publication as *Das Mündel will Vormund sein*:
    in *Theater heute*, 10, 2 (February 1969), 52–56;
    in *Stücke 2*, pp. 7–38;
    in *Prosa Gedichte*, pp. 157–79.
  English publication:
    trans. Michael Roloff, in *The Drama Review*, 15, 1 (Fall 1970), 62–83;
    in *The Ride Across Lake Constance and Other Plays*, pp. 29–52;
    in *Bauer, Fassbinder, Handke, Kroetz, Shakespeare the Sadist and Others*. London:
      Methuen, 1977, pp. 55–73.
Quodlibet (written in 1969; first performed on January 24, 1970, at the Basler Theater,
Basel, under the direction of Hans Hollmann)
  German publication as *Quodlibet*:
    in *Theater heute*, 11, 3 (March 1970), 41–44;
    in *Spectaculum*, 13 (1970), 183–90;
    Quodlibet. Frankfurt: Verlag der Autoren, 1970;
    in *Neues deutsches Theater*. Ed. Karlheinz Braun and Peter Iden. Zürich: Diogenes,
      1971, pp. 46–54;
    in *Stücke 2*, pp. 39–54;
    in *Der Rand der Wörter*, pp. 74–83.
  English publication:
    in *The Ride Across Lake Constance and Other Plays*, pp. 55–66.
The Ride Across Lake Constance (written in 1970; first performed on January 23, 1971, at
Schaubühne am Halleschen Ufer, Berlin, under the direction of Claus Peymann and
Wolfgang Wiens)
  German publication as *Der Ritt über den Bodensee*:
    Der Ritt über den Bodensee. Frankfurt: Verlag der Autoren, 1970;
    in *Theater heute*, 11, 10 (October 1970), 69–84;
    in *Spectaculum*, 14 (1971), 211–58;
    Der Ritt über den Bodensee. Frankfurt: Suhrkamp, 1971;
    in *Stücke 2*, pp. 55–154.
  English publication:
    trans. Michael Roloff, in *The Contemporary German Theater*. Ed. Michael Roloff. New
      York: Avon Books, 1972, pp. 295–379;
    trans. Michael Roloff. *The Ride Across Lake Constance*. London: Methuen, 1973;
    in *The Ride Across Lake Constance and Other Plays*, pp. 69–159.

Novels

The Hornets
  Die Hornissen. Frankfurt: Suhrkamp, 1966; Reinbek bei Hamburg: Rowohlt, 1968. A
    slightly shortened version appears as a Suhrkamp Taschenbuch (1978).
The Peddler
  Der Hausierer. Frankfurt: Suhrkamp, 1967; Frankfurt: Fischer, 1970.
The Goalie's Anxiety at the Penalty Kick
  Die Angst des Tormanns beim Elfmeter. Frankfurt: Suhrkamp, 1970;
  The Goalie's Anxiety at the Penalty Kick. Trans. Michael Roloff. New York: Farrar, Straus
    & Giroux, 1972; London: Methuen, 1977;

in *Three by Peter Handke*, pp. 1-97.
Handke and Wim Wenders collaborated on a film version of this novel.
Short Letter, Long Farewell
  Der kurze Brief zum langen Abschied. Frankfurt: Suhrkamp, 1972;
  Short Letter, Long Farewell. Trans. Ralph Manheim. New York: Farrar, Straus & Giroux,
    1974; London: Methuen, 1977;
  in *Three by Peter Handke*, pp. 99-238.
There is also a film version of this novel, by Herbert Vesely.
A Sorrow Beyond Dreams
  Wunschloses Unglück. Salzburg: Residenz, 1972; Frankfurt: Suhrkamp, 1974;
  A Sorrow Beyond Dreams. Trans. Ralph Manheim. New York: Farrar, Straus & Giroux,
    1975; London: Condor Books, Souvenir Press, 1976;
  in *Three by Peter Handke*, pp. 239-98.
A Moment of True Feeling
  Die Stunde der wahren Empfindung. Frankfurt: Suhrkamp, 1975;
  A Moment of True Feeling. Trans. Ralph Manheim. New York: Farrar, Straus & Giroux,
    1977;
  in *Two Novels by Peter Handke*, pp. 7-102.
The Left-Handed Woman
  Die linkshändige Frau. Frankfurt: Suhrkamp, 1976;
  trans. Ralph Manheim, in *The New Yorker*, 53 (November 7, 1977), 50-100;
  The Left-Handed Woman. Trans. Ralph Manheim. New York: Farrar, Straus & Giroux,
    1978; London: Methuen, 1980;
  in *Two Novels by Peter Handke*, pp. 103-60.
Handke also produced a film version of this novel.
The Weight of the World
  Das Gewicht der Welt: Ein Journal (November 1975-März 1977). Salzburg: Residenz,
    1977; Frankfurt: Suhrkamp, 1979.
A translation is forthcoming from Farrar, Straus & Giroux.
Slow Homecoming
  Langsame Heimkehr. Frankfurt: Suhrkamp, 1979.
A translation is forthcoming from Farrar, Straus & Giroux.

Other

Begrüßung des Aufsichtsrats: Prosatexte. Salzburg: Residenz, 1967; Munich: Deutscher
  Taschenbuch, 1970; reprinted in *Prosa Gedichte*. [short stories]
Deutsche Gedichte. Frankfurt: Euphorion, 1969. [poems, miscellaneous]
(ed.) *Der gewöhnliche Schrecken: Neue Horrorgeschichten*. Salzburg: Residenz, 1969;
  Munich: Deutscher Taschenbuch, 1971. [includes story by Handke: "Das Umfallen
  der Kegel von einer Bäuerlichen Kegelbahn," pp. 120-30]
Die Innenwelt der Außenwelt der Innenwelt. Frankfurt: Suhrkamp, 1969. [poems]
Chronik der laufenden Ereignisse. Frankfurt: Verlag der Autoren, 1970; Frankfurt:
  Suhrkamp, 1971. [television script]
Horspiel Nr. 2, 3 und 4. Frankfurt: Verlag der Autoren, 1970. [radio plays]
Wind und Meer: Vier Hörspiele. Frankfurt: Suhrkamp, 1970. [radio plays]
Ich bin ein Bewohner des Elfenbeinturms. Frankfurt: Suhrkamp, 1972. [essays]
Als das Wünschen noch geholfen hat. Frankfurt: Suhrkamp, 1974. [poems, essays, photo-
  graphs]

The Innerworld of the Outerworld of the Innerworld. Trans. Michael Roloff. New York: The Seabury Press, 1974. [bilingual edition of poems]

Petrikat, Didi. *Wiener Läden,* mit Sätzen von Peter Handke. Munich and Vienna: Hanser, 1974.

Falsche Bewegung. Frankfurt: Suhrkamp, 1975. [screenplay]

(ed.) *Franz Nabl: Charakter, Der Schwur des Martin Krist, Dokument: Frühe Erzählung.* Salzburg: Residenz, 1975. [includes essay by Handke: "Franz Nabls Größe und Kleinlichkeit," pp. 5–24]

Das Ende des Flanierens. Vienna: Davidpress, 1976; reprinted in *Nonsense and Happiness* (see below). [poem]

Nonsense and Happiness. Trans. Michael Roloff. New York: Urizen Books, 1976. [bilingual edition of poems]

A Selection of Works About Peter Handke

Bibliographies

Müller, Harald. "Auswahlbibliographie zu Peter Handke." *Text und Kritik,* 24 (October 1969), 66–76; 24/24a (July 1971), 69–79; 24/24a (September 1976), 97–112; reprinted in *Über Peter Handke,* ed. Michael Scharang (Frankfurt: Suhrkamp, 1972), pp. 358–93.

Schlueter, June, and Ellis Finger. *Peter Handke: An Annotated Bibliography.* New York: Garland Publishing, forthcoming, 1982.

Also see bibliographies in books below.

Books

Durzak, Manfred. *Peter Handke.* Stuttgart: Kohlhammer, forthcoming.

Falkenstein, Henning. *Peter Handke.* Berlin: Colloquium, 1974.

Heintz, Günter. *Peter Handke.* Stuttgart: Ernst Klett, 1971; Munich: R. Oldenbourg, 1974.

Hern, Nicholas. *Peter Handke.* New York: Frederick Ungar, 1972. (British edition: *Peter Handke: Theatre and Anti-theatre.* London: Oswald Wolff, 1971.) [drama]

König, Hartmut. *Peter Handke: Sprachkritik und Sprachverwendung: Anmerkungen zu ausgesuchten Texten.* Hollfeld: Joachim Beyer, 1978.

Mixner, Manfred. *Peter Handke.* Kronberg: Athenäum, 1977.

Nägele, Rainer, and Renate Voris. *Peter Handke.* Munich: C. H. Beck, 1978.

Schultz, Uwe. *Peter Handke.* Velber bei Hannover: Friedrich, 1973. [drama]

Sergooris, Gunther. *Peter Handke und die Sprache.* Bonn: Bouvier, 1979.

Thuswalder, Werner. *Sprach- und Gattungsexperiment bei Peter Handke: Praxis und Theorie.* Salzburg: Alfred Winter, 1976.

Wellershoff, Irene. *Innen und Außen: Wahrnehmung und Vorstellung bei Alain Robbe-Grillet und Peter Handke.* Munich: Wilhelm Fink, 1980.

Collections of Essays

Note: Essays appearing in these collections are not listed separately.

Jurgensen, Manfred, ed. *Handke: Ansätze Analysen Anmerkungen.* Bern and Munich: Francke, 1979.

Scharang, Michael, ed. *Über Peter Handke.* Frankfurt: Suhrkamp, 1972.

Text und Kritik, 24 (October 1969), 24/24a (July 1971), 24/24a (September 1976).

Interviews

Arnold, Heinz Ludwig. "'Ich will über das schreiben, was die Leute verdrängen': Ein Gespräch zwischen Peter Handke und Heinz Ludwig Arnold." *Die Zeit,* March 5, 1976· reprinted in *Text und Kritik,* 24/24a (September 1976), 15–37, and as "'Nicht Literatur machen, sondern als Schriftsteller leben': Gespräch mit Peter Handke," in *Als Schriftsteller leben: Gespräche mit Peter Handke, Franz Xaver Kroetz, Gerhard Zwerenz, Walter Jens, Peter Rühmkorf, Günter Grass,* ed. Heinz Ludwig Arnold. Reinbek bei Hamburg: Rowohlt, 1979, pp. 7–34.

Baby, Yvonne. "Peter Handke Filme *La Femme Gauchère:* Entrer par une porte mythique où les lois ont disparu." *Le Monde,* May 18, 1978, p. 17.

Bloch, Peter André, and Alexander Jon Schneller. "Peter Handke," in *Der Schriftsteller und sein Verhältnis zur Sprache, dargestellt am Problem der Tempuswahl: Eine Dokumentation zu Sprache und Literatur der Gegenwart,* ed. Peter André Bloch. Bern and Munich: Francke, 1971, pp. 170–78.

Bock, Hans Bertram. "Alibi für Intendanten: Gespräch mit Peter Handke über seine neuen Projekte." Munich *Abendzeitung,* September 26, 1968. [*My Foot My Tutor*]

Borski, A. "Politisch reden ist doch nur Geschwätz." *Berliner Zeitung,* May 16, 1969.

Durzak, Manfred. "'Für mich ist Literatur auch eine Lebenshaltung': Gespräch mit Peter Handke," in *Gespräche über den Roman,* ed. Manfred Durzak. Frankfurt: Suhrkamp, 1976, pp. 314–43.

——. "Vom Büchner-Preis habe ich sogar geträumt." *Die Welt,* November 1, 1973, p. 6.

Hohler, Franz. *Fragen an andere: Interviews mit Wolf Biermann, Peter Handke, Ernst Jandl, Mani Matte, Hannes Wader.* Bern: Zytglogge, 1973, pp. 18–39.

Joseph, Artur. *Theater unter vier Augen: Gespräche mit Prominenten.* Cologne: Kiepenheuer und Witsch, 1969, pp. 27–39; reprinted, in part, in English translation by E. B. Ashton, as "Nauseated by Language: From an Interview with Artur Joseph." *The Drama Review,* 15, 1 (Fall 1970), 56–61. [especially *Kaspar*]

Kurz, Paul Konrad. "Eine Flucht?—Nein, eine Reise." *Bücherkommentare,* 2 (1972), p. 11. [*Short Letter, Long Farewell*]

Linder, Christian. *Schreiben und Leben: Gespräche mit Jürgen Becker, Peter Handke, Walter Kempowski, Wolfgang Koeppen, Gunter Wallroff, Dieter Wellershoff.* Cologne: Kiepenheuer und Witsch, 1974, pp. 32–45.

[Lottman, H. R.] "Two Authors, Two Points of View: Peter Handke, Hans Hellmut Kirst." *Publishers Weekly,* 212, 11 (September 12, 1977), 54–56.

Müller, Andreas. "Das Schreiben ist unglaublich sinnlich." *Abendzeitung* (Munich), July 22, 1971, p. 13. [especially *The Ride Across Lake Constance*]

Nenning, Günther Karl. "Peter Handke: Gespräch mit Günther Nenning" (5 parts). *Neue Freie Presse,* 4 (1973), p. 7; 5 (1973), p. 7; 6 (1973), p. 6; 7 (1974), p. 41; 8 (1974), p. 7.

Ossowski, Rudolf, ed. *Jugend fragt—Prominente antworten.* Berlin: Colloquium, 1975, pp. 149–61.

Petit, Chris. "Voyages Into Inner Space." *Time Out* (London), June 8–14, 1979, pp. 20–22. [*The Left-Handed Woman*]

Schlueter, June. "An Interview with Peter Handke [July 23, 1979]." *Studies in Twentieth Century Literature,* 4, 1 (Fall 1979), 63–73.

Schultz-Gerstein, Christian. "Das Leiden als Geschäfts-Trick: Gespräch mit Peter Handke über sein Stück." *Die Zeit,* April 26, 1974, pp. 17–18.

Simon, Karl Günter. "Porträt eines Schimpfers." *Der Monat,* 217 (October 1966), 92–94. [especially *Offending the Audience*]

Springer, Michael. "Besuch bei Peter Handke: Aus Anlaß des neuen Romans *Der kurze Brief zum langen Abschied.*" *Neues Forum,* 219 (March 1972), 55–57.

Zipes, Jack. "Contrary Position: An Interview with Peter Handke." Trans. Mark Goldberg. *Performance,* 1, 4 (1972), 63–65, 68.

Essays: General

Batt, Kurt. "Leben im Zitat: Notizen zu Peter Handke." *Sinn und Form,* 26 (1974), 603–23; reprinted in *Revolte intern: Betrachtungen zur Literatur in der Bundesrepublik Deutschland.* Munich: C. H. Beck, 1975, pp. 208–28.

Blöcker, Günter. "Peter Handkes Entdeckungen." *Merkur,* 21, 236 (1967), 1090–94.

Bondy, François. "'Zu echt, um wahr zu sein'." *Schweizer Monatshefte,* 53 (1973), 189–97.

Buselmeier, Michael. "Das Image des Peter Handke." *Frankfurter Hefte,* 25, 4 (April 1970), 281–88.

[Ebert, Horst-Dieter]. "Handke: Unerschrocken naiv." *Der Spiegel,* May 25, 1970, pp. 174–76, 180, 183–84, 187–90.

Gugelberger, Georg M. "Endlessly DESCRIBING novel experiences: Peter Handke Translations in/and America." *Dimension,* 8, 1-2 (1975), 180–90.

Holzinger, Alfred. "Peter Handkes literarische Anfänge in Graz," in *Wie die Grazer auszogen, die Literatur zu erobern: Texte, Porträts, Analysen und Dokumente junger österreichischer Autoren,* ed. Peter Laemmle and Jörg Drews. Munich: Karl M. Lipp, 1975, pp. 183–98.

Kermode, Frank. "The Model of a Modern Modernist." *New York Review of Books,* May 1, 1975, pp. 20–23.

Kraus, Wolfgang. "Laudatio auf Peter Handke: Zur Verleihung des Kafka-Preises 10. Oktober 1979." *Literatur und Kritik,* 140 (1979), 577–78.

Kurz, Paul K. "Peter Handke: Sprach-Exerzitien als Gegenspiel." *Über moderne Literatur IV.* Frankfurt: Knecht, 1973, pp. 9–52.

Laemmle, Peter. "Von der Außenwelt zur Innenwelt: Das Ende der deutschen Nachkriegsliteratur: Peter Handke und die Folgen," in *Positionen im deutschen Roman der sechziger Jahre,* ed. Heinz Ludwig Arnold and Theo Buck. Munich: Richard Boorberg, 1974, pp. 147–70.

Nef, Ernst. "Peter Handke: Identifikation und Sprache." *Universitas,* 26 (1971), 603–10.

——— . "Peter Handkes neue Schriften und seine Entwicklung." *Universitas,* 31 (1976), 1141–45.

Ries, Klaus. "Peter Handke: Autor einer deutschen Nachmoderne?" *Boletín de Estudios Germánicos,* 9 (1972), 155–70.

Ritter, Roman. "Die 'Neue Innerlichkeit'—von innen und außen betrachtet (Karin Struck, Peter Handke, Rolf Dieter Brinkmann)," in *Kontext 1: Literatur und Wirklichkeit,* ed. Uwe Timm and Gerd Fuchs. Munich: C. Bertelsmann, 1976, pp. 238–57.

Rorrison, Hugh. "The 'Grazer Gruppe,' Peter Handke and Wolfgang Bauer." *Modern Austrian Writing: Literature and Society After 1945,* ed. Alan Best and Hans Wolfschütz. London: Oswald Wolff, 1980, pp. 252–66.

Timm, Uwe. "Peter Handke oder sicher in die 70er Jahre." *Kürbiskern,* 4 (1970), 611–21.

Wegener, Adolph. "Fussnoten zu den Welten Peter Handkes," in *Views and Reviews of Modern German Literature: Festschrift for Adolf D. Klarmann,* ed. Karl S. Weimar. Munich: Delp, 1974, pp. 240–50.

Essays About Handke's Plays

Angermeyer, Hans Christoph. *Zuschauer im Drama: Brecht, Dürrenmatt, Handke.* Frankfurt: Athenäum, 1971, pp. 40–46, 106–17.

Blumer, Arnold. "Peter Handkes romantische Unvernunft." *Acta germanica,* 8 (1973), 123–32. [*They Are Dying Out*]

Bly, Mark. "Theater in New Haven: Weber on Handke." *Theater,* 11, 2 (Spring 1980), 83–87. [*They Are Dying Out*]

Buddecke, Wolfram, and Jörg Hienger. "Jemand lernt sprechen: Sprachkritik bei Peter Handke." *Neue Sammlung,* 11, (1971), 553–65. [*Kaspar*]

Dixon, Christa K. "Peter Handkes *Kaspar:* Ein Modellfall." *The German Quarterly,* 46, 1 (January 1973), 31–46.

Federico, Joseph A. "The Hero as Playwright in Dramas by Frisch, Dürrenmatt, and Handke." *German Life & Letters,* n.s., 32, 2 (January 1979), 166–76. [*They Are Dying Out*]

Finger, Ellis. "Kaspar Hauser Doubly Portrayed: Peter Handke's *Kaspar* and Werner Herzog's *Every Man for Himself and God Against All.*" *Literature/Film Quarterly,* 7, 3 (1979), 235–43.

Franke, Hans-Peter. "*Kaspar* von Peter Handke: Versuch einer literatursoziologischen Interpretation." *Der Deutschunterricht,* 23, 5 (October 1971), 15–23.

Geißler, Rolf. "Peter Handke: *Kaspar,*" in Rolf Geißler and Gertrud Valiaparampil, *Sprachversuchungen: Einsichten in eine zeitgenössische literarische Tendenz: Interpretationen zu Texten von Bichsel, Cummings, Handke, Heißenbüttel, Ionesco, und Jonke.* Frankfurt: Diesterweg, 1971, pp. 106–22.

Gilbert, W. Stephen. "*The Ride Across Lake Constance.*" *Plays and Players,* January 1974, pp. 48–49.

Gilman, Richard. "Peter Handke." *American Review* (New York), 17 (May 1973), 206–28; reprinted in *The Making of Modern Drama: A Study of Büchner, Ibsen, Strindberg, Chekhov, Pirandello, Brecht, Beckett, Handke.* New York: Farrar, Straus & Giroux, 1974, pp. 267–88.

Hauptmann, Ira. "Aspects of Handke: A Play." *Partisan Review,* 45, 3 (1978), 425–30. [*The Ride Across Lake Constance*]

Hayman, Ronald. *Theatre and Anti-theatre: New Movements Since Beckett.* London: Secker and Warburg; New York: Oxford University Press, 1979, pp. 95–123.

Hays, Michael. "Peter Handke and the End of the 'Modern'." *Modern Drama,* 23, 4 (January 1981), 346–66.

Herbrandt, Lilo. "Peter Handkes *Kaspar:* ein Modell der Inhaltsbezogenen Grammatik." *Diskussion Deutsch,* 6 (December 1975), 529–45.

Hill, Linda. *Language as Aggression: Studies in the Postwar Drama.* Bonn: Bouvier, 1976, pp. 164–94. [*Kaspar*]

——. "Obscurantism and Verbal Resistance in Handke's *Kaspar.*" *The Germanic Review,* 52, 4 (1977), 304–15.

Honsza, Norbert. "Peter Handke und seine Theaterstücke." *Universitas,* 28 (1973), 387–92; "Peter Handke as a Dramatist." *Universitas,* 15 (1973), 261–66.

Horn, Peter. "Vergewaltigung durch die Sprache: Peter Handkes *Kaspar.*" *Literatur und Kritik,* 51 (1971), 30–40.

Hübler, Alex. *Drama in der Vermittlung von Handlung, Sprache und Szene.* Bonn: Bouvier, 1973, pp. 273–315. [*Kaspar*]

Innes, Christopher. *Modern German Drama: A Study in Form.* Cambridge: Cambridge University Press, 1979, pp. 235–55.

Jäger, Gerg. "Erinnerung an das Weltgefühl des Herrn Quitt." *Theater heute*, 15, 7 (July 1974), 25–34. [*They Are Dying Out*]

Karasek, Hellmuth, and Peter Iden. "Ratlosigkeit über Handke's Bodensee-Ritt?" *Theater heute*, 12, 3 (March 1971), 18–25.

Kesting, Marianne. *Panorama des zeitgenössischen Theaters: 58 literarische Porträts*. 2d rev. ed. Munich: R. Piper & Co., 1969, pp. 341–46; "The Social World as Platitude," trans. George Schultz-Behrend. *Dimension*, 2 (1969), 177–81. [*Kaspar*]

Klein, Wolfgang. "Über Peter Handkes *Kaspar* und Einige Fragen der poetischen Kommunikation," in *Moderne Dramentheorie*, ed. Aloysius van Kesteren and Herta Schmid. Kronberg: Scriptor, 1975, pp. 300–17.

Kuchenbäcker, Karin. "Das Theater des Peter Handke." *Der Deutschunterricht*, 23, 5 (October 1971), 5–14.

Lederer, Otto. "Über Peter Handkes Sprachspiele." *Literatur und Kritik*, 58 (1971), 478–82.

Lederer, William L. "Handke's Ride." *Chicago Review*, 26, 2 (1974), 171–76.

McAuley, Gay. "The Problem of Identity: Theme, Form and Theatrical Method in *Les Negres, Kaspar* and *Old Times*." *Southern Review: An Australian Journal of Literary Studies*, 8 (1975), 51–65.

Marranca, Bonnie. "Peter Handke's *My Foot My Tutor*: Aspects of Modernism." *Michigan Quarterly Review*, 16 (Summer 1977), 272–79.

——. "The *Sprechstücke*: Peter Handke's Universe of Words." *Performing Arts Journal*, 1 (Fall 1976), 52–62.

Meier, Elisabeth. "Abgründe dort sehen zu lehren, wo Gemeinplätze sind": Zur Sprachkritik von Ödön von Horváth und Peter Handke," in *Sprachnot und Wirklichkeitsverfall: Dargestellt an Beispielen neuerer Literatur*, ed. Elisabeth Meier. Düsseldorf: Patmos, 1972, pp. 19–61.

Mennemeier, F. N. *Modernes deutsches Drama 2*. Munich: Wilhelm Fink, 1975, pp. 263–74. [*They Are Dying Out*]

Nägele, Rainer. "Peter Handke: The Staging of Language." *Modern Drama*, 23, 4 (January 1981), 327–38.

——. "Unbehagen in der Sprache: Zu Peter Handkes *Kaspar*." *Basis: Jahrbuch für deutsche Gegenwartsliteratur*, 6 (1976), 78–96.

Neugroschel, Joachim. "The Theater as Insult." *American German Review*, 33 (1967), 27–30.

Peymann, Claus. "Directing Handke," trans. Claus Brucher-Herpel. *The Drama Review*, 16, 2 (June 1972), 48–54.

Preller, Arno G. "Handke's *Publikumsbeschimpfung*: A New Concept of Language and the Theatre," in *Proceedings: Pacific Northwest Conference on Foreign Languages: Twenty-third Annual Meeting*. Corvallis: Oregon State University, 1972, pp. 165–67.

Roloff, Michael. "Comments on Peter Handke's Speak-ins and a Note on *Kaspar*." *American German Review*, 35 (April–May 1969), 12–13.

Schlueter, June. " 'Goats and Monkeys' and the 'Idiocy of Language': Handke's *Kaspar* and Shakespeare's *Othello*." *Modern Drama*, 23, 1 (March 1980), 25–32.

——. "Peter Handke's *The Ride Across Lake Constance*: The Illusion of Self-Sufficiency." *Comparative Drama*, 11, 2 (Summer 1977), 113–26; reprinted in *Metafictional Characters in Modern Drama*. New York: Columbia University Press, 1979, pp. 105–19.

——. "Politics and Poetry: Peter Handke's *They Are Dying Out*." *Modern Drama*, 23, 4 (January 1981), 339–45.

Sebald, W. G. "Fremdheit, Integration und Krise: Über Peter Handkes Stück *Kaspar*." *Literatur und Kritik*, 93 (1975), 152–58.

Strauss, Botho. "Versuch, ästhetische und politische Ereignisse zusammenzudenken — neues Theater 1967–70." *Theater heute*, 11, 10 (October 1970), 61–68. [especially *The Ride Across Lake Constance*]

Taëni, Rainer. "Chaos versus Order: The Grotesque in *Kaspar* and *Marat/Sade*. *Dimension*, 2, 3 (1969), 592–603.

———. "Handke und das politische Theater." *Neue Rundschau*, 81, 1 (1970), 158–69.

———. "On Thin Ice: Peter Handke's Studies in Alienation." *Meanjin*, 36 (October 1977), 315–25.

Vanderath, Johannes. "Peter Handkes *Publikumsbeschimpfung*: Ende des Aristotelischen Theaters?" *The German Quarterly*, 43, 2 (March 1970), 317–26.

Weber, Carl. "Handke's Stage is a Laboratory." *The Drama Review*, 16, 2 (June 1972), 55–62. [*The Ride Across Lake Constance*]

Wendt, Ernst. *Moderne Dramaturgie: Bond und Genet, Beckett und Heiner Müller, Ionesco und Handke, Pinter und Kroetz, Weiss und Gatti*. Frankfurt: Suhrkamp, 1974, pp. 65–90. [*Kaspar*]

Willson, A. Leslie. "Peter Handke: The Critic On-Stage," in *Saga og Språk: Studies in Language and Literature*, ed. John M. Weinstock. Austin, Tex.: Pemberton Press, 1972, pp. 301–19.

Essays About Handke's Novels

Bialik, Wlodzimierz. "Peter Handkes 'Anti-Kriminalgeschichten'." *Studia Germanica Posnaniensia*, 3 (1974), 21–27. [*The Peddler, The Goalie's Anxiety at the Penalty Kick*]

Bohn, Volker. " 'Später werde ich über das alles Genaueres schreiben': Peter Handkes Erzählung *Wunschloses Unglück* aus literaturtheoretischer Sicht." *Germanisch-romanische Monatsschrift*, n.s., 26, 3/4 (1976), 356–79.

Bohnen, Klaus. "Kommunikationsproblematik und vermittlungsmethode in Handkes *Die Angst des Tormanns beim Elfmeter*." *Wirkendes Wort*, 26, 5 (September–October 1976), 387–400.

Buch, Hans Christoph. *Das Hervortreten des Ichs aus den Wörtern: Aufsätze zur Literatur*. Munich and Vienna: Carl Hanser, 1978, pp. 155–58. [*The Weight of the World*]

Dienstmann, Dichters. "Handkes *Tormann* — Welt ist voller Käuze," in *Schauplätze österreichischer Dichtung: Ein literarische Reiseführer*, ed. Dietmar Grieser. Munich and Vienna: Langen Müller, 1974, pp. 185–91.

Dixon, Christa K. "Peter Handke: *Die Angst des Tormanns beim Elfmeter*: Ein Beitrag zur Interpretation." *Sprachkunst*, 3, 1/2 (1972), 75–97.

Durzak, Manfred. "Erzählmodelle: Peter Handkes Romanversuche." *Studi Germanica*, n.s., 9 (1971), 187–207; *Der deutsche Roman der Gegenwart*. Stuttgart: Kohlhammer, 1971, pp. 313–39. [novel in general, *The Hornets, The Goalie's Anxiety at the Penalty Kick*]

Elm, Theo. "Die Fiktion eines Entwicklungsromans: Zur Erzählstrategie in Peter Handkes Roman *Der kurze Brief zum langen Abschied*." *Poetica*, 6 (1974), 353–77.

Eschbach, Achim, and Wendelin Rader. "Ist die 'linkshändige Frau' trivial? Überlegungen zur literarischen Wertung." *Zeitschrift für Literaturwissenschaft und Linguistik*, 7, 27/28 (1977), 104–16.

Handke, Peter. "Die linkshändige Frau." *Scene Kassel* (Kassel, West Germany), Nr. 8 (November 1978), pp. 2–3.

———. "Über meinen neuen Roman *Der Hausierer*." *Dichten und Trachten*, 29 (1967), 27–29.

Hansen, Olaf. "Exorcising Reality." *New Boston Review*, 4, 1 (Summer 1978), 5-6. [*A Moment of True Feeling*]

Hartung, Rudolf. "Peter Handke: *Der kurze Brief zum langen Abschied*." *Neue Rundschau*, 83, 2 (1972), 336-42.

——. "Traumhafte Wandlung: zu Peter Handkes *Die Stunde der wahren Empfindung*." *Neue Rundschau*, 86, 3 (1975), 521-24.

Hillebrand, Bruno. "Auf der Suche nach der verlorenen Identität: Peter Handke—*Der kurze Brief zum langen Abschied*," in *Der deutsche Roman im 20. Jahrhundert, II: Analysen und Materialien zur Theorie und Soziologie des Romans*, ed. Manfred Brauneck. Bamberg: C. C. Buchners, 1976, pp. 97-117.

Janssen-Jurreit, Marielouise. "Ein Buch für traurige Tage." *Der Spiegel*, October 11, 1976, pp. 241-43. [*The Left-Handed Woman*]

Kircher, Hartmut. "Schema und Anspruch: Zur Destruktion des Kriminalromans bei Dürrenmatt, Robbe-Grillet und Handke." *Germanisch-Romanische Monatsschrift*, n.s., 28 (1978), 195-215. [*The Peddler*]

Klinkowitz, Jerome. "Aspects of Handke: The Fiction." *Partisan Review*, 45, 3 (1978), 416-25.

Konstantinović, Zoran. "Sprache und Welterkenntnis: Drei Modellfälle aus der deutschen Gegenwartsliteratur." *Kwartalnik Neofilologiczny*, 24, 2-3 (1977), 311-15. [*The Left-Handed Woman*]

Kraus, Christine. "Literarische Vorbilder in Peter Handkes Roman *Der kurze Brief zum langen Abschied*." *Österreich in Geschichte und Literatur*, 22, 3 (May-June 1978), 174-80.

Kreis, Rudolf. *Ästhetische Kommunikation als Wunschproduktion: Goethe, Kafka, Handke: Literaturanalyse am "Leitfaden des Leibes."* Bonn: Bouvier, 1978, pp. 163-88. [*A Moment of True Feeling*]

Kruntorad, Paul. "Literaturverweigerung: Gedanken anläßlich Peter Handkes neuem Buch *Wunschloses Unglück*." *Merkur*, 26, 12 (1972), 1263-65.

Lenzen, Arnulf. "Gesellschaft und Umgebung in Handke: *Die Angst des Tormanns beim Elfmeter*." *Wirkendes Wort*, 26, 5 (September-October 1976), 401-06.

Lind, Jakov. "*Die Hornissen*—zarte Seelen, trockene Texte." *Der Spiegel*, July 11, 1966, p. 79.

Maloof, Katharina. "Peter Handkes programmierter Tormann," in *Proceedings of the Pacific Northwest Conference on Foreign Languages: Twenty-sixth Annual Meeting*. Corvallis: Oregon State University, 1975, pp. 116-19.

Matt-Albrecht, Beatrice von. "Journal des Augenblicks: Peter Handkes neue Aufzeichnungen *Das Gewicht der Welt*, 1975-1977." *Universitas*, 32 (1977), 1157-64.

——. "Peter Handke: *Die Stunde der wahren Empfindung*." *Universitas*, 30 (1975), 919-22; "Peter Handke's *The Moment of True Feeling*." *Universitas*, 17, 4 (1975), 337-40.

Michel, Willy. *Die Aktualität des Interpretierens*. Heidelberg: Quelle and Meyer, 1978, pp. 162-75. [*Short Letter, Long Farewell*]

Miles, David H. "Reality and the Two Realisms: Mimesis in Auerbach, Lukács and Handke." *Monatshefte*, 71, 4 (Winter 1979), 371-78. [*A Sorrow Beyond Dreams*]

Mog, Paul. "Kälte und Selbsterfahrung: Anmerkungen zu einem Text von Alexander Kluge und Peter Handkes *Das Gewicht der Welt*." *Neue Sammlung*, 18 (1978), 359-79.

Mommsen, Katharina. "Peter Handke: *Das Gewicht der Welt*: Tagebuch als literarische Form." *Modern Austrian Literature*, 13, 1 (1980), 35-46.

Mount, Ferdinand. "Peter Handke, and 'Alienation-Fiction': The Sorrows of Young Outsiders." *Encounter*, 50, 3 (March 1978), 33-37.

Müller, Joachim. "Auf der Suche nach der wahren Existenz—Peter Handke und seine Erzählungen." *Universitas,* 33 (1978), 683–92.

Nägele, Rainer. "Die vermittelte Welt: Reflexionen zum Verhältnis von Fiktion und Wirklichkeit in Peter Handkes Roman *Der kurze Brief zum langen Abschied.*" *Jahrbuch der deutschen Schiller-Gesellschaft,* 19 (1975), 389–418; reprinted as "Amerika als Fiktion und Wirklichkeit in Peter Handkes Roman *Der kurze Brief zum langen Abschied,*" in *Die USA und Deutschland: Wechselseitige Spiegelungen in der Literatur der Gegenwart,* ed. Wolfgang Paulsen. Bern: Francke, 1976, pp. 110–15.

Pütz, Peter. "Peter Handke: *Die Angst des Tormanns beim Elfmeter,*" in *Deutsche Bestseller-Deutsche Ideologie: Ansätze zu einer Verbraucherpoetik,* ed. Heinz Ludwig Arnold. Stuttgart: Ernst Klett, 1975, pp. 145–56.

Reich-Ranicki, Marcel. "Die Angst des Peter Handkes beim Erzählen: Peter Handke's *Wunschloses Unglück.*" *Die Zeit,* September 15, 1972; *Entgegnung: Zur deutschen Literatur der siebziger Jahre.* Munich: Deutsche Verlags-Anstalt, 1979, pp. 315–22.

——. "Wer ist hier infantil?" *Entgegnung: Zur deutschen Literatur der siebziger Jahre.* Munich: Deutsche Verlags-Anstalt, 1979, pp. 322–29.

Rey, William. H. "Provokation durch den Tod: Peter Handkes Erzählung *Wunschloses Unglück* als Modell stilistischer Integration." *German Studies Review,* 1 (1978), 285–301.

Rossbacher, Karlheinz. "Detail und Geschichte: Wandlungen des Erzählens bei Peter Handke, am Vergleich von *Die Angst des Tormanns beim Elfmeter* und *Der kurze Brief zum langen Abschied.*" *Sprachkunst,* 6, 1 (1975), 87–103.

Schiwy, Günther. *Strukturalismus und Zeichensysteme.* Munich: C. H. Beck, 1973, pp. 28–39. [*Short Letter, Long Farewell*]

Schlueter, June. "Handke's 'Kafkaesque' Novel: Semiotic Processes in *Die Angst des Tormanns beim Elfmeter.*" *Studies in Twentieth Century Literature,* 4, 1 (Fall 1979), 75–88.

Schober, Siegfried. "Es soll mythisch sein, mythisch!" *Der Spiegel,* May 2, 1977, pp. 177, 180, 182. [*The Left-Handed Woman*]

Summerfield, Ellen. "Die Kamera als literarisches Mittel: Zu Peter Handkes *Die Angst des Tormanns beim Elfmeter.*" *Modern Austrian Literature,* 12, 1 (1979), 95–112.

Wagner, Karl. "Peter Handkes Rückzug in den geschichtslosen Augenblick." *Literatur und Kritik,* 134 (1979), 227–40. [*A Moment of True Feeling, The Left-Handed Woman*]

Wapnewski, Peter. "*Das Gewicht der Welt* und sein Eichmeister: Zu Peter Handkes 'Journal'." *Neue Rundschau,* 89 (1978), 268–75.

Weiss, Walter. "Peter Handke: *Wunschloses Unglück* oder Formalismus und Realismus in der Literatur der Gegenwart," in *Austriaca: Beitrage zur österreichischen Literatur: Festschrift für Heinz Politzer zum 65. Geburtstag,* ed. Winfried Kudszus. Tübingen: Max Niemeyer, 1975, pp. 442–59.

White J. J. "Signs of Disturbance: The Semiological Import of Some Recent Fiction by Michel Tournier and Peter Handke." *Journal of European Studies,* 4 (1974), 233–54. [*The Goalie's Anxiety at the Penalty Kick, Short Letter, Long Farewell*]

Zeller, Rosmarie. "Die Infragestellung der Geschichte und der neue Realismus in Handkes Erzählungen." *Sprachkunst,* 9 (1978), 115–40.

Reviews Cited

"Approximations." *Times Literary Supplement,* October 3, 1968, p. 1103. [*The Peddler*]

Barnes, Clive. "Theater: Handke's *Kaspar* Is Staged in Brooklyn." *New York Times,* February 16, 1973, p. 26.

——— . "The Theater: Peter Handke's *Ride Across Lake Constance*." *New York Times,* January 14, 1972, p. 16.

Ebert, Horst-Dieter. "Ein Kimble von Kafka." *Der Spiegel,* May 25, 1970, p. 182. [*The Goalie's Anxiety at the Penalty Kick*]

Gussow, Mel. "Two Plays That Challenge As They Entertain." *New York Times,* November 11, 1979, pp. 3, 24.

Kaiser, Joachim. "Schauspiel in der Bundesrepublik." *Theater heute,* 11, 10 (October 1970), p. 9.

Kalem, T. E. "Spengler Redux." *Time,* January 24, 1972, p. 53. [*The Ride Across Lake Constance*]

Kauffmann, Stanley. "Inside Out." *World,* 1, (July 18, 1972), 62, 64–65.

——— . "Two Different Talents." *The New Republic,* February 5, 1972, pp. 24, 32–33. [*The Ride Across Lake Constance*]

Kroll, Jack. "Mind Bending." *Newsweek,* February 26, 1973, p. 91. [*Kaspar*]

Simon, John. *Uneasy Stages: A Chronicle of the New York Theater, 1963–1973.* New York: Random House, 1975, pp. 366–67. [*The Ride Across Lake Constance*]

"Stille Macht: Handkes Mündel in Frankfurt." *Der Spiegel,* February 10, 1969, pp. 126–27.

Other Works Cited

Arnold, Heinz Ludwig, and Theo Beck, eds. *Positionen der Erzählens: Analyses und Theorien zur deutschen gegenswartsliteratur.* Munich: C. H. Beck, 1976, pp. 181–85.

Bance, A. F. "The Kaspar Hauser Legend and Its Literary Survival." *German Life and Letters,* n.s., 28, 3 (April 1975), 199–210.

Barthes, Roland. *Eléménts de Sémiologie, in Le Dégreé Zéro de l'Ecriture, suivide Eléments de Sémiologie.* Paris: Gonthier, 1964; *Elements of Semiology,* trans. Annette Lavers and Colin Smith. New York: Hill and Wang, 1967.

Bauke, Joseph P. "Group 47 at Princeton." *New York Times Book Review,* May 15, 1966, pp. 43–45.

Bettelheim, Bruno. *The Uses of Enchantment: The Meaning and Importance of Fairy Tales.* New York: Alfred A. Knopf, 1975.

Biner, Pierre. *The Living Theatre: A History Without Myths,* trans. Robert Meister. New York: Avon, 1972.

Conrad, Klaus. *Die beginnende Schizophrenie: Versuch einer Gestaltanalyse des Wahns.* Stuttgart: Thieme, 1958.

Detweiler, Robert. *Story, Sign and Self.* Philadelphia: Fortress Press, 1978.

Eagleton, Terry. *Marxism and Literary Criticism.* Berkeley and Los Angeles: University of California Press, 1976.

Eco, Umberto. *The Role of the Reader.* Bloomington: Indiana University Press, 1979.

Ehrmann, Jacques, ed. *Structuralism.* Garden City, N.Y.: Doubleday, 1970, pp. 101–37.

Federman, Raymond, ed. *Surfiction: Fiction Now . . . and Tomorrow.* Chicago: Swallow Press, 1975.

"Group 47 at Princeton University." *German-American Review,* Special Supplement, April 1966.

"Group 47: Nation's Conscience." *Newsweek,* May 16, 1966, pp. 118, 118C, 118D, 118F.

Heißenbüttel, Helmut. *Zur Tradition der Moderne.* Neuwied and Berlin: Luchterhand, 1972.

208 : Bibliography

Kenny, Anthony. *Wittgenstein.* Harmondsworth: Penguin Books, 1973.

Kroll, Friedhelm. *Die "Gruppe 47": Soziale Lage und gesellschaftliches Bewußtsein literarischer Intelligenz in der Bundesrepublik.* Stuttgart: J. B. Metzler, 1977.

Kuby, Erich. "Ach ja, da liest ja einer." *Der Spiegel,* May 6, 1966.

Kuna, Franz, ed. *On Kafka: Semi-Centenary Perspectives.* London: Paul Elek, 1976.

Lacan, Jacques. *The Language of the Self: The Function of Language in Psychoanalysis.* Baltimore: The Johns Hopkins University Press, 1968.

LeRoy, Gaylord C., and Ursula Beitz, eds. *Preserve and Create: Essays in Marxist Literary Criticism.* New York: Humanities Press, 1973.

Lettau, Reinhard, ed. *Gruppe 47: Bericht, Kritik, Polemik: Ein Handbuch.* Neuwied and Berlin: Luchterhand, 1967.

Lichtheim, George. *George Lukács.* New York: Viking, 1970.

Lodge, David. *The Modes of Modern Writing: Metaphor, Metonymy, and the Typology of Modern Literature.* Ithaca: Cornell University Press, 1977.

Lukács, Georg. *Realism in Our Time.* New York: Harper & Row, 1962.

———. *Soul and Form,* trans. Anna Bostock. London: Merlin Press, 1974.

———. *The Theory of the Novel,* trans. Anna Bostock. Cambridge, Mass.: The MIT Press, 1971.

———. *Writer and Critic, and Other Essays,* ed. and trans. Arthur Kahn. London: Merlin Press, 1978.

———. "Die Zerstörung der Vernunft." Berlin: Aufbau-Verlag, 1954.

Mandel, Siegfried. *Group 47: The Reflected Intellect.* Carbondale: Southern Illinois University Press, 1973.

Mandelstam, Osip. *Complete Poetry of Osip Mandelstam,* trans. Burton Raffel and Alla Burago, with introduction and notes by Sidney Monas. Albany: State University of New York Press, 1973.

Matejka, Ladislav, and Krystyna Pomorska, eds. *Readings in Russian Poetics: Formalist and Structuralist Views.* Cambridge, Mass.: The MIT Press, 1971.

Patterson, Michael. *German Theatre Today: Post-war Theatre in West and East Germany, Austria and Northern Switzerland.* London: Pitman Publishing, 1976.

Richter, Hans Werner. *Almanach der Gruppe 47, 1947–1962.* Reinbek bei Hamburg: Rowohlt, 1964.

Rischbieter, Henning. *Theater in Umbruch: Eine Dokumentation aus "Theater heute."* Velber bei Hannover: Friedrich, 1970.

Rühm, Gerhard. *Die Wiener Gruppe: Achleitner, Artmann, Bayer, Rühm, Wiener: Texte, Gemeinschaftsarbeiten, Aktionen.* Reinbek bei Hamburg: Rowohlt, 1967.

Sartre, Jean-Paul. *La Nausée.* Paris: Gallimard, 1938; *Nausea,* trans. Lloyd Alexander. New York: New Directions, n.d. [1949].

Scholes, Robert. *Structuralism in Literature: An Introduction.* New Haven: Yale University Press, 1974.

Sebeok, Thomas A., ed. *Style in Language.* Cambridge, Mass.: The MIT Press, 1960.

Sontag, Susan. *Against Interpretation.* New York: Dell Publishing Co., 1966.

Wittgenstein, Ludwig. *Philosophical Investigations,* bilingual edition, trans. G. E. M. Anscombe. New York: Macmillan, 1953.

Ziermann, Horst, ed. *Gruppe 47: Eine Dokumentation.* Frankfurt: Wolter Editionen, 1966.

Index